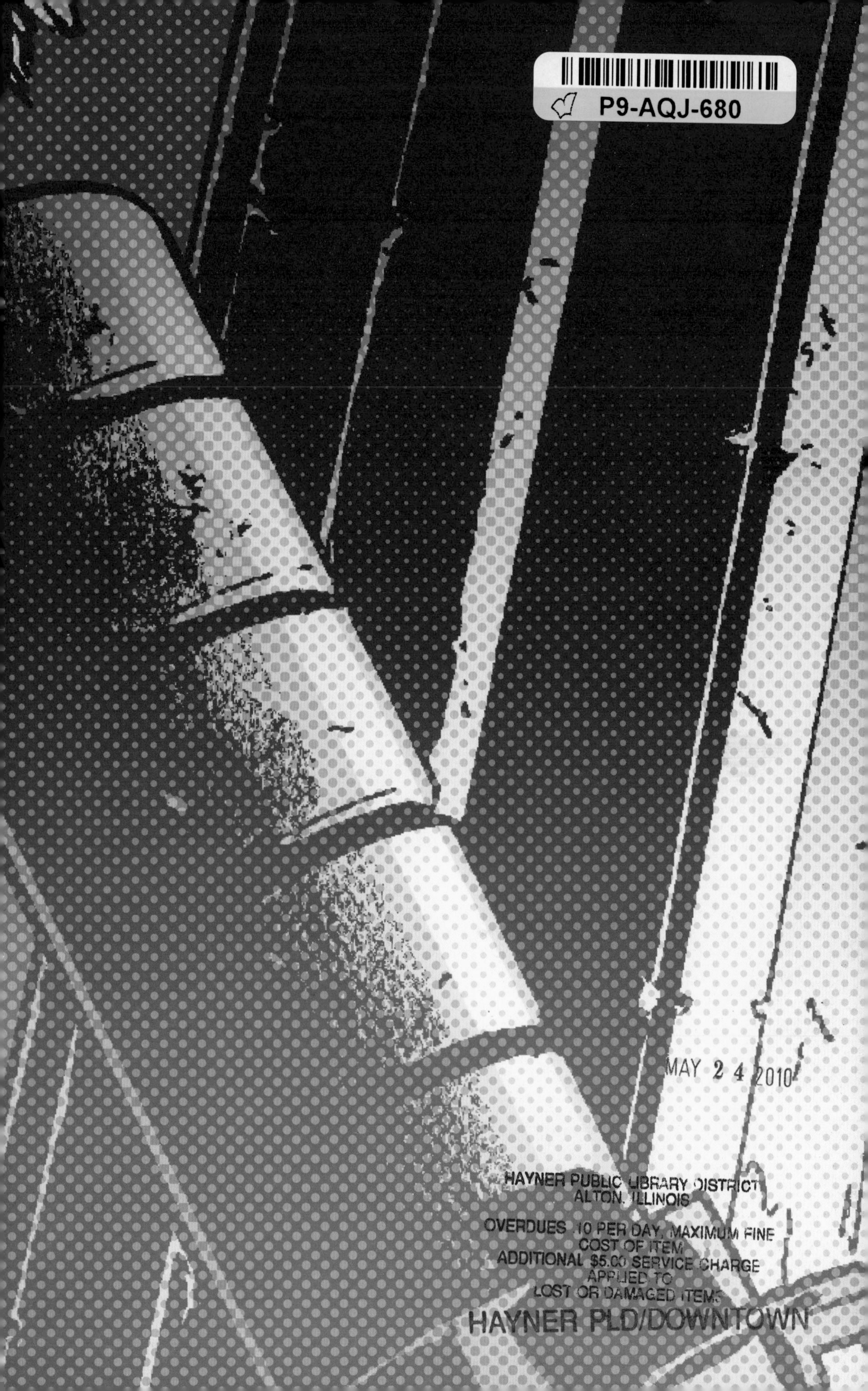

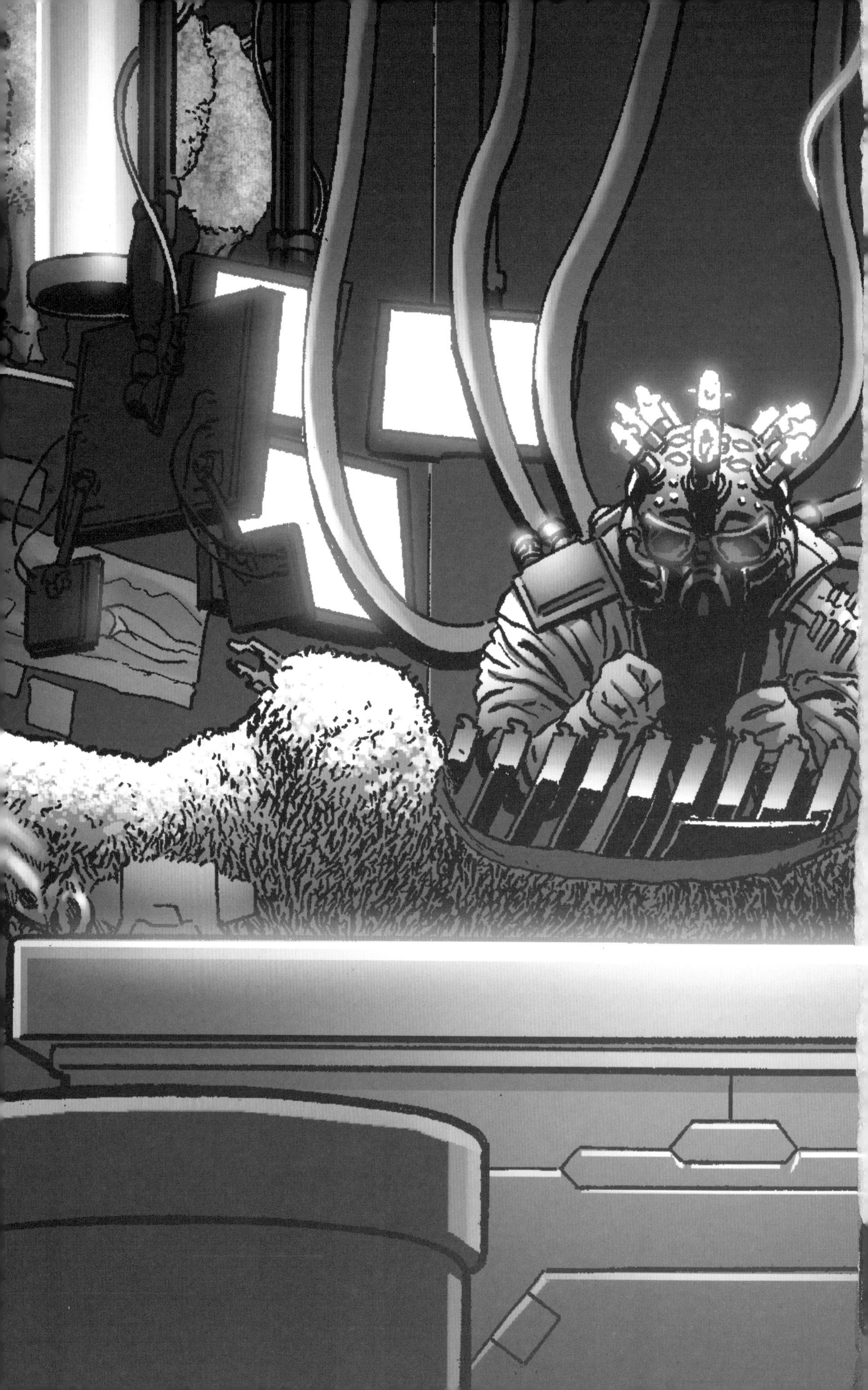

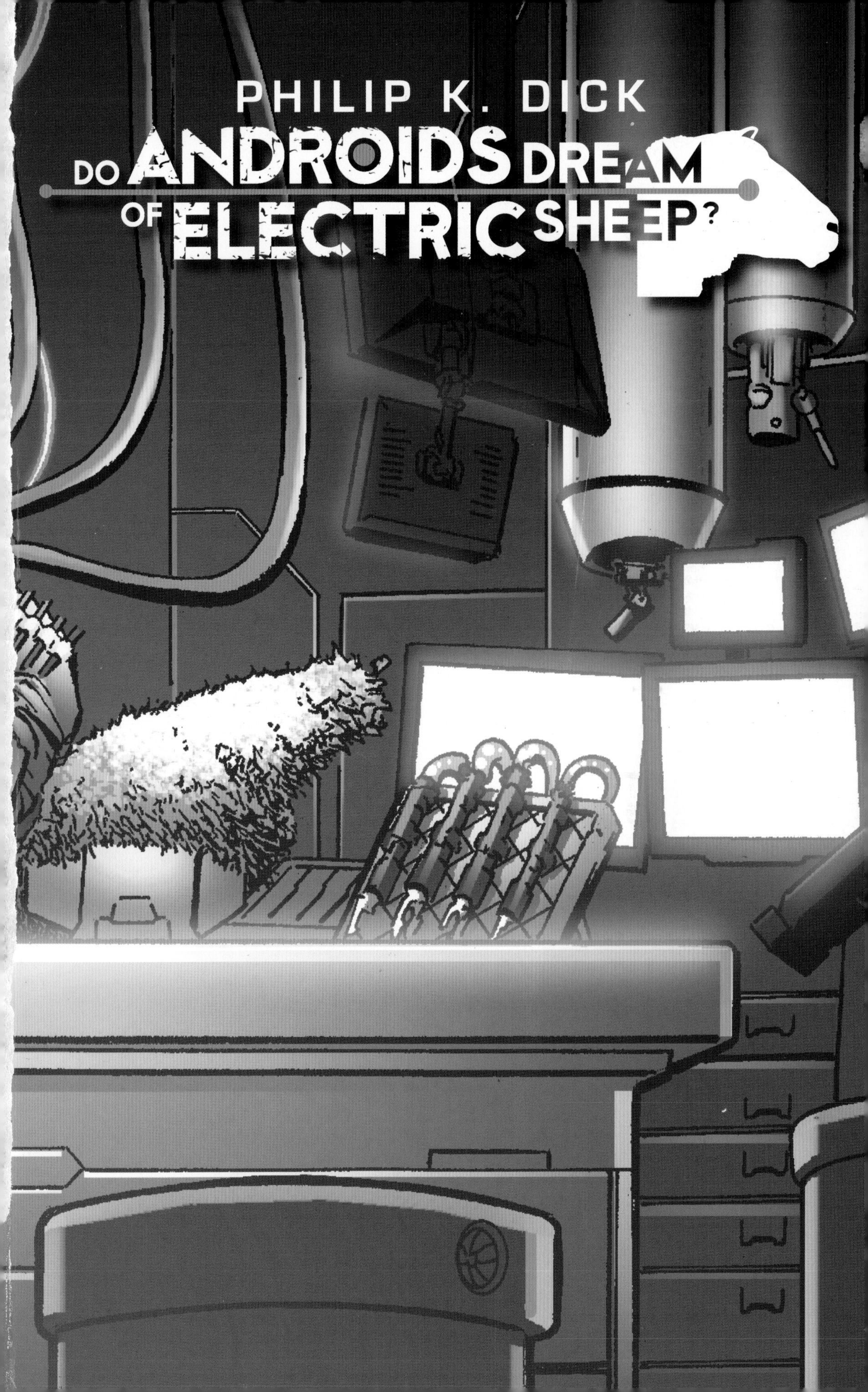
PHILIP K. DICK
DO ANDROIDS DREAM
OF ELECTRIC SHEEP?

"A new type of android
handle but me."

that apparently
nobody can

-- Rick Deckard

BOOM!
STUDIOS

ROSS RICHIE
chief executive officer

MARK WAID
editor-in-chief

ADAM FORTIER
vice president,
publishing

CHIP MOSHER
marketing director

MATT GAGNON
managing editor

JENNY CHRISTOPHER
sales director

Office of publication: 6310 San Vicente Blvd Ste 404, Los Angeles, CA 90048-5457.

FIRST EDITION: FEBRUARY 2010
10 9 8 7 6 5 4 3 2 1

PRINTED IN KOREA

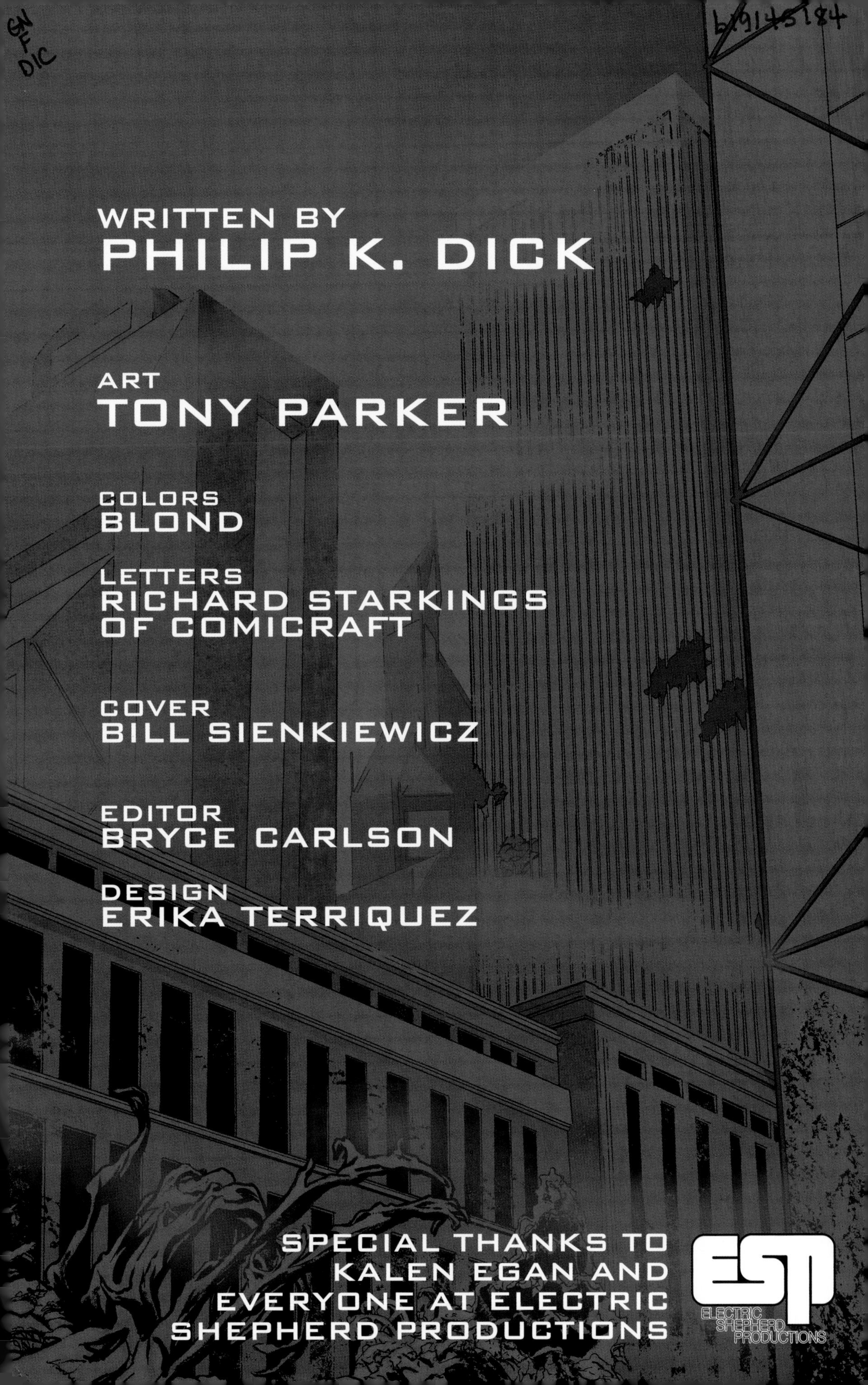

WRITTEN BY
PHILIP K. DICK

ART
TONY PARKER

COLORS
BLOND

LETTERS
RICHARD STARKINGS
OF COMICRAFT

COVER
BILL SIENKIEWICZ

EDITOR
BRYCE CARLSON

DESIGN
ERIKA TERRIQUEZ

SPECIAL THANKS TO
KALEN EGAN AND
EVERYONE AT ELECTRIC
SHEPHERD PRODUCTIONS

ESP
ELECTRIC
SHEPHERD
PRODUCTIONS

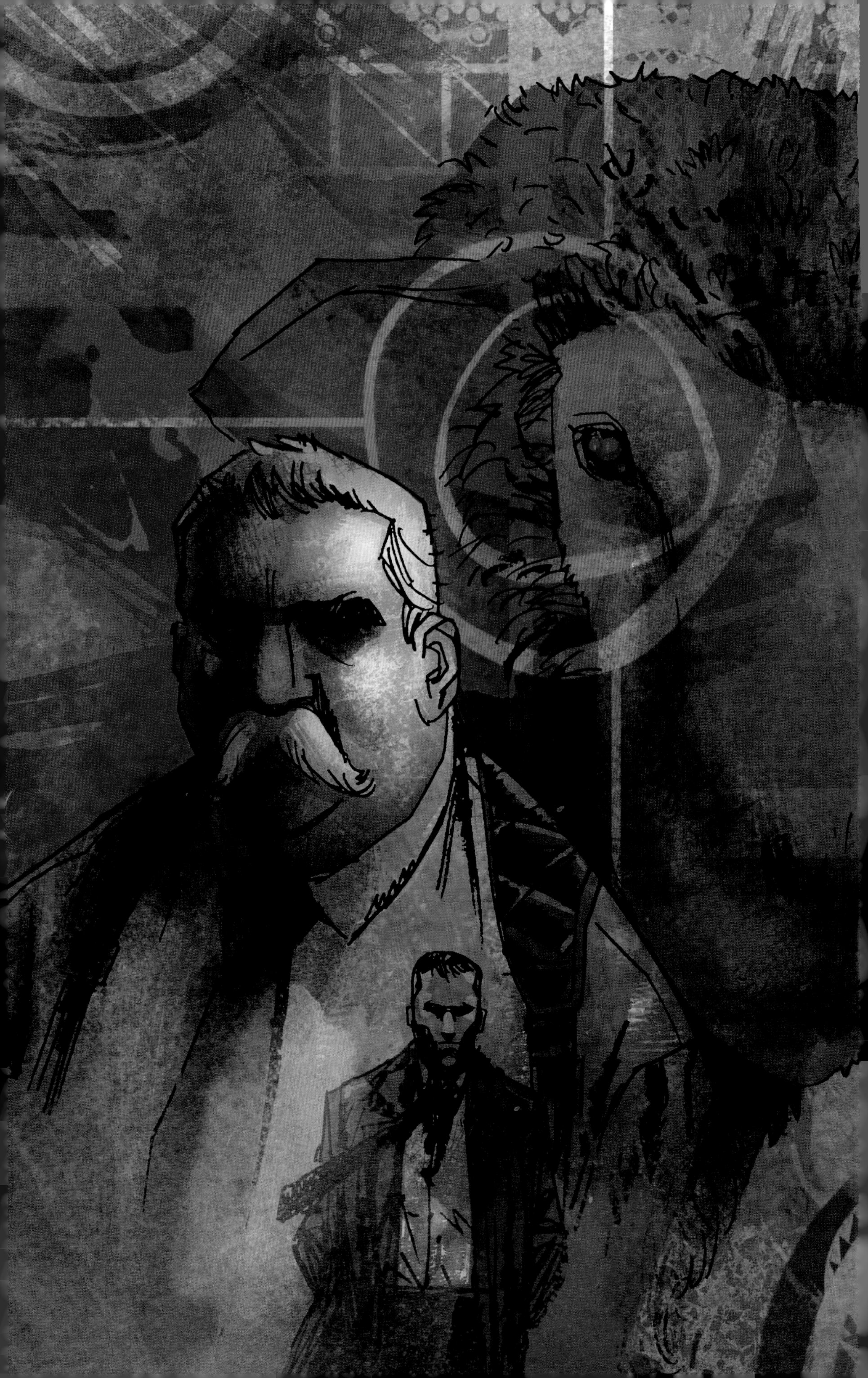

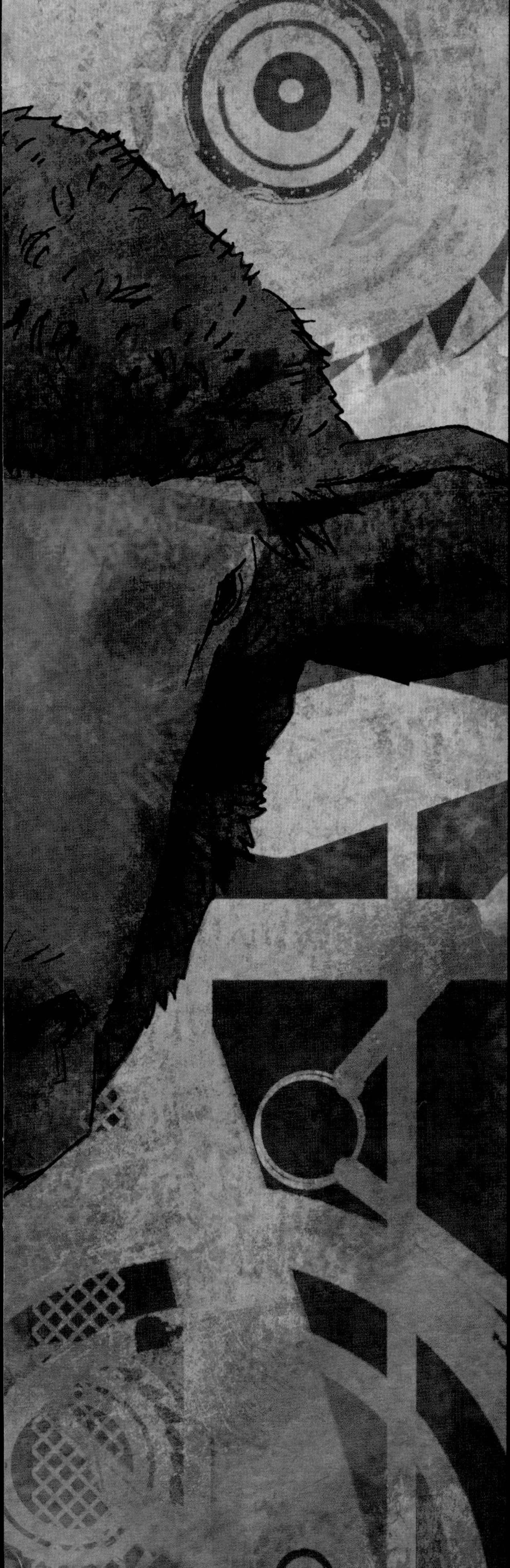

BOOK FIVE

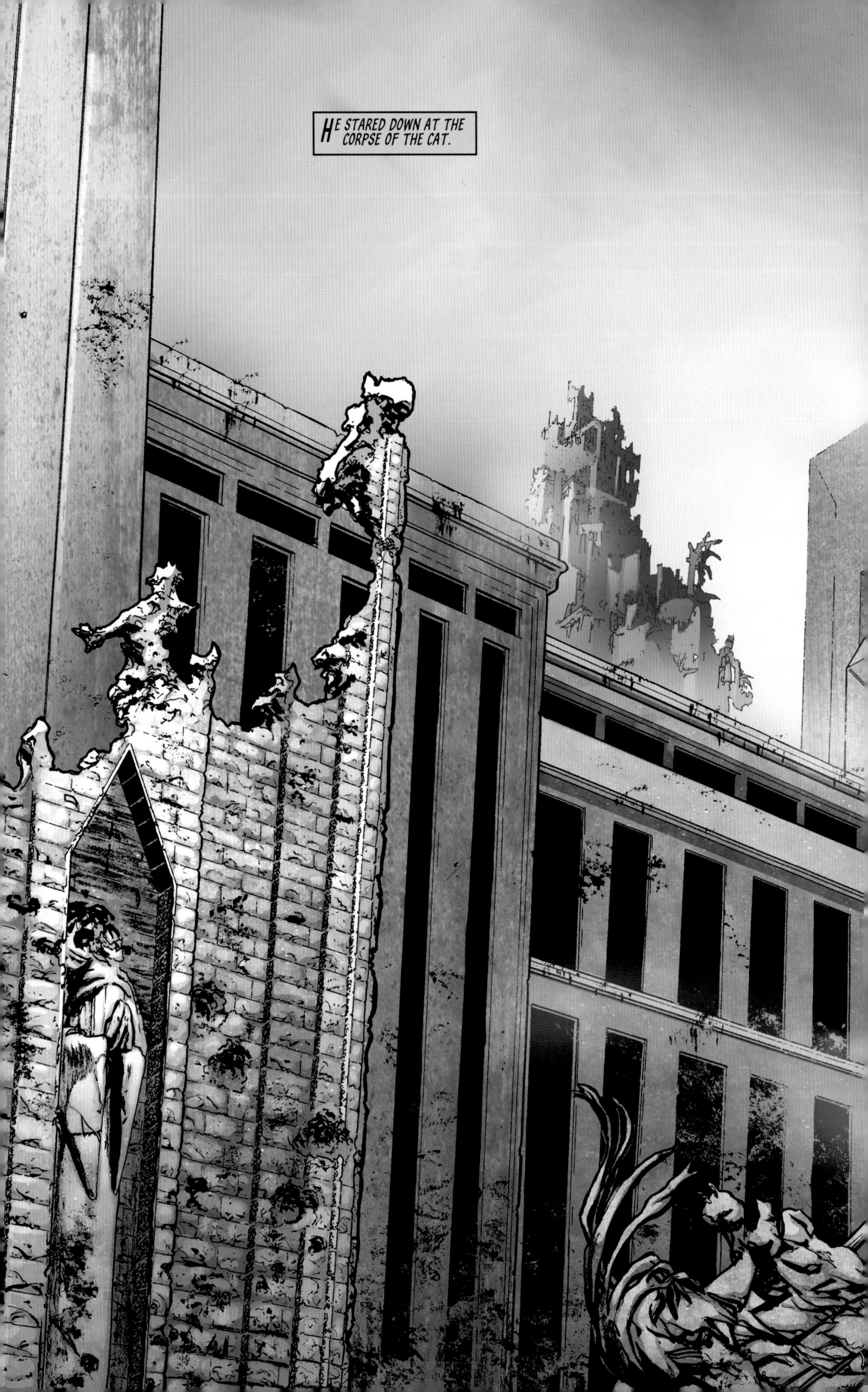
HE STARED DOWN AT THE CORPSE OF THE CAT.

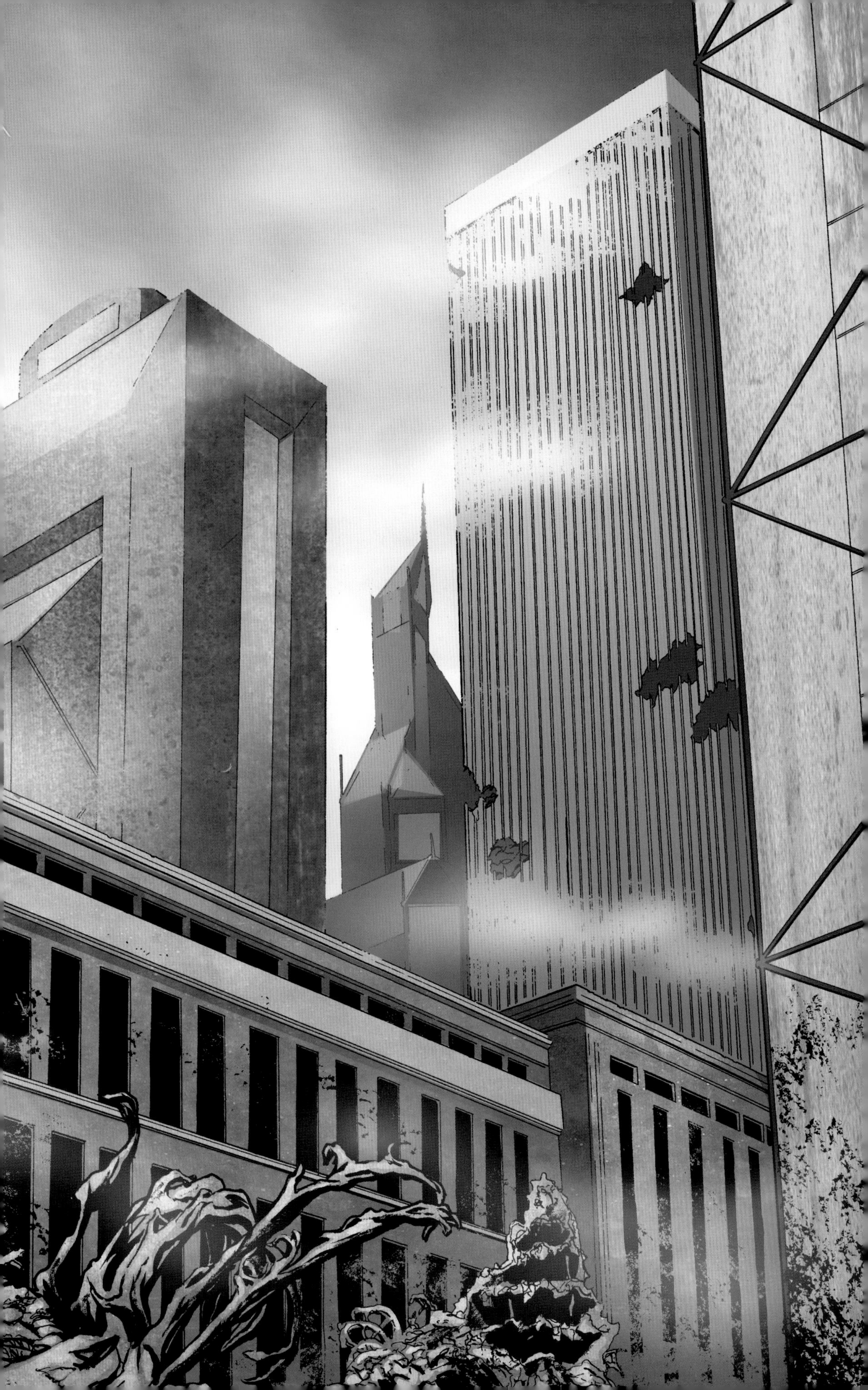

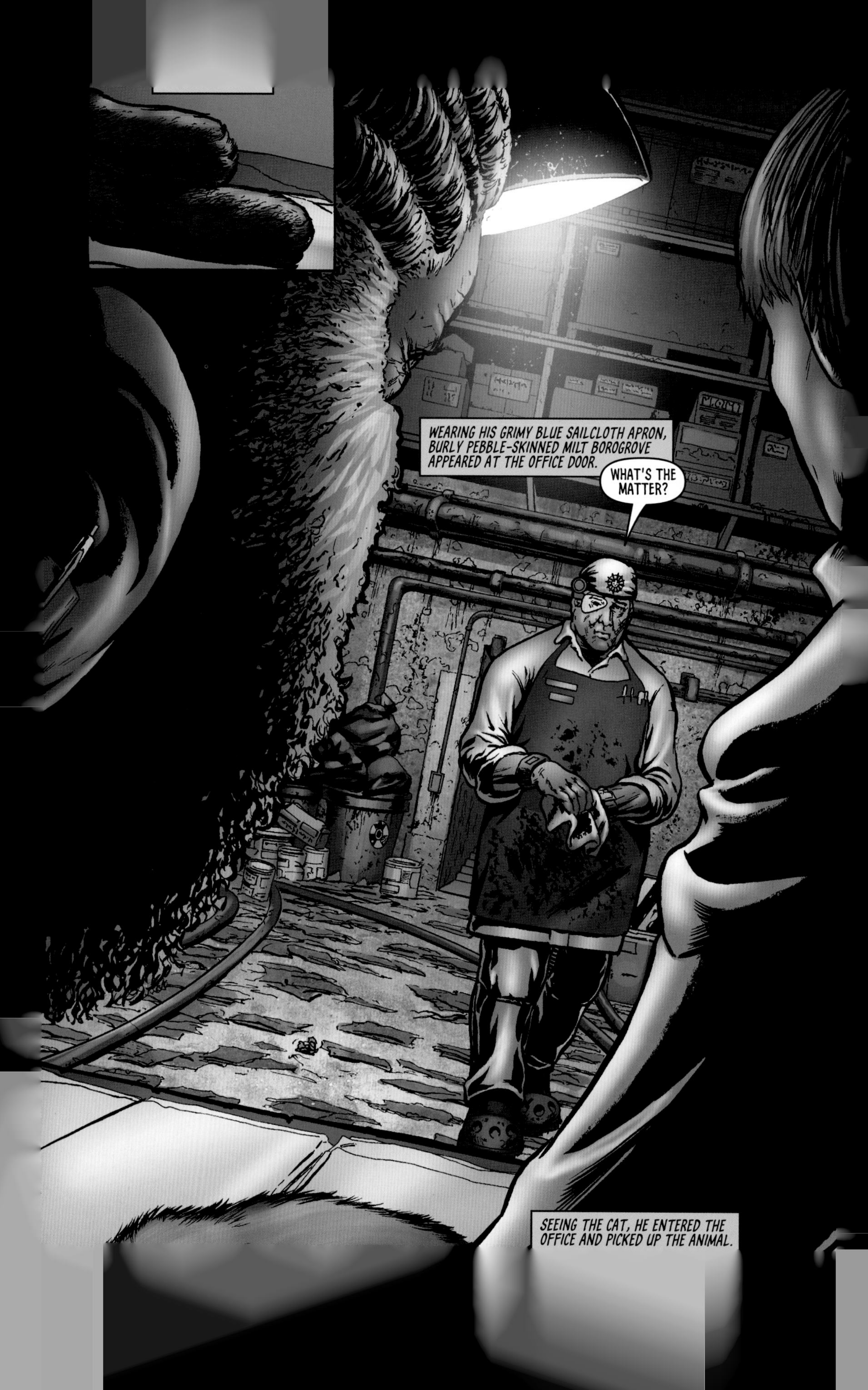
WEARING HIS GRIMY BLUE SAILCLOTH APRON, BURLY PEBBLE-SKINNED MILT BOROGROVE APPEARED AT THE OFFICE DOOR.
WHAT'S THE MATTER?
SEEING THE CAT, HE ENTERED THE OFFICE AND PICKED UP THE ANIMAL.

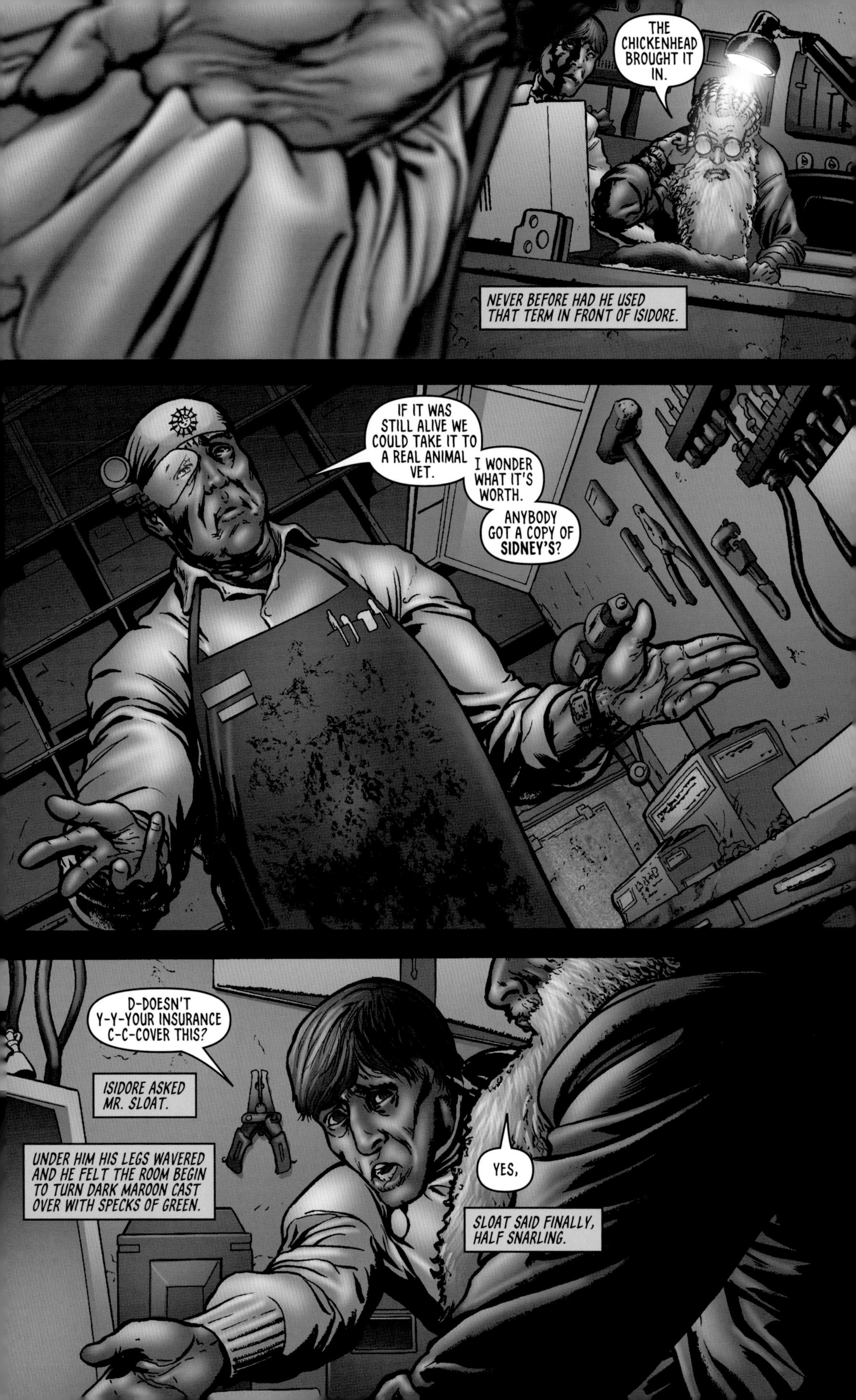
THE CHICKENHEAD BROUGHT IT IN.
NEVER BEFORE HAD HE USED THAT TERM IN FRONT OF ISIDORE.
IF IT WAS STILL ALIVE WE COULD TAKE IT TO A REAL ANIMAL VET.
I WONDER WHAT IT'S WORTH.
ANYBODY GOT A COPY OF SIDNEY'S?
D-DOESN'T Y-Y-YOUR INSURANCE C-C-COVER THIS?
ISIDORE ASKED MR. SLOAT.
UNDER HIM HIS LEGS WAVERED AND HE FELT THE ROOM BEGIN TO TURN DARK MAROON CAST OVER WITH SPECKS OF GREEN.
YES,
SLOAT SAID FINALLY, HALF SNARLING.

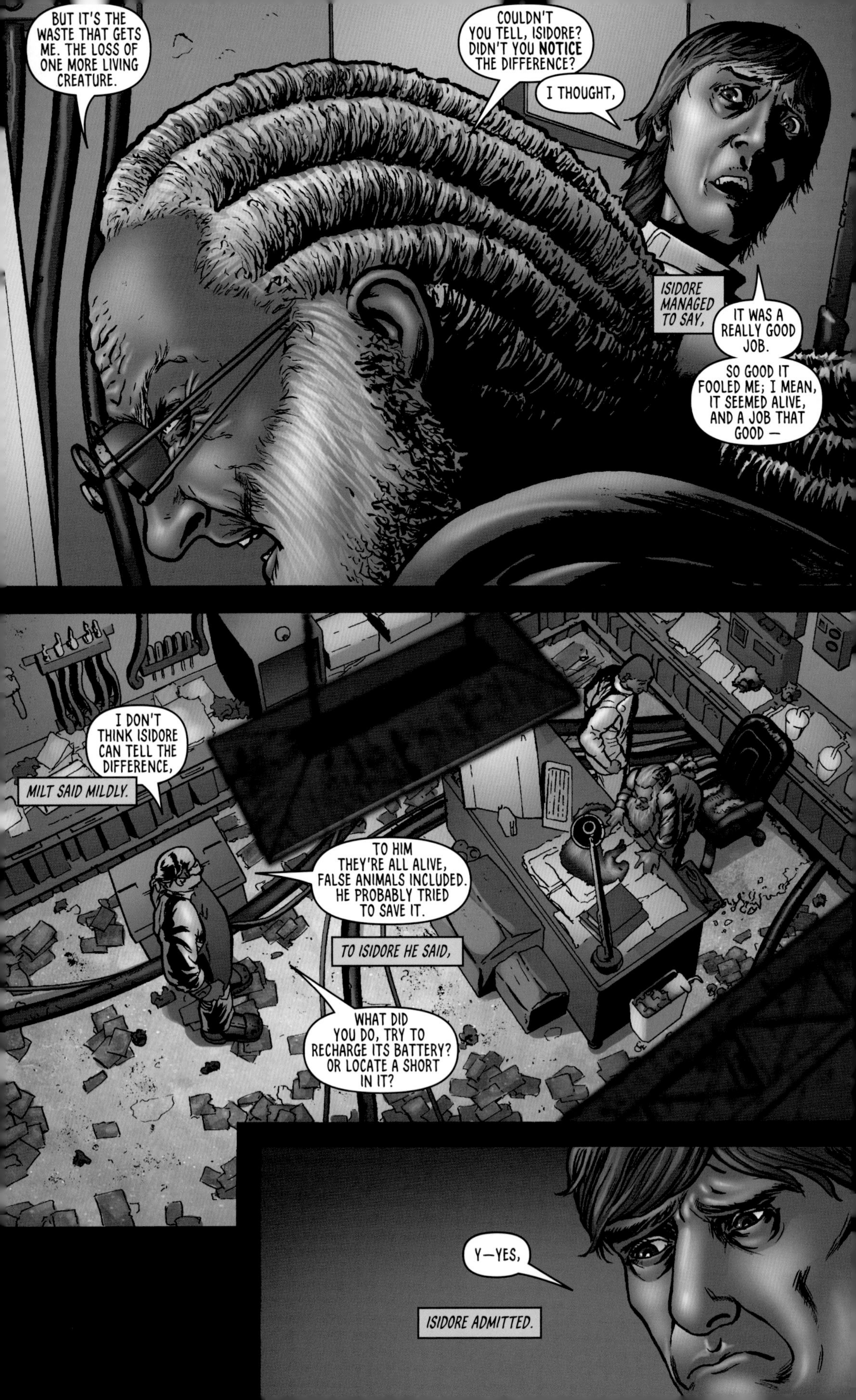
BUT IT'S THE WASTE THAT GETS ME. THE LOSS OF ONE MORE LIVING CREATURE.
COULDN'T YOU TELL, ISIDORE? DIDN'T YOU NOTICE THE DIFFERENCE?
I THOUGHT,
ISIDORE MANAGED TO SAY,
IT WAS A REALLY GOOD JOB.
SO GOOD IT FOOLED ME; I MEAN, IT SEEMED ALIVE, AND A JOB THAT GOOD —
I DON'T THINK ISIDORE CAN TELL THE DIFFERENCE,
MILT SAID MILDLY.
TO HIM THEY'RE ALL ALIVE, FALSE ANIMALS INCLUDED. HE PROBABLY TRIED TO SAVE IT.
TO ISIDORE HE SAID,
WHAT DID YOU DO, TRY TO RECHARGE ITS BATTERY? OR LOCATE A SHORT IN IT?
Y—YES,
ISIDORE ADMITTED.

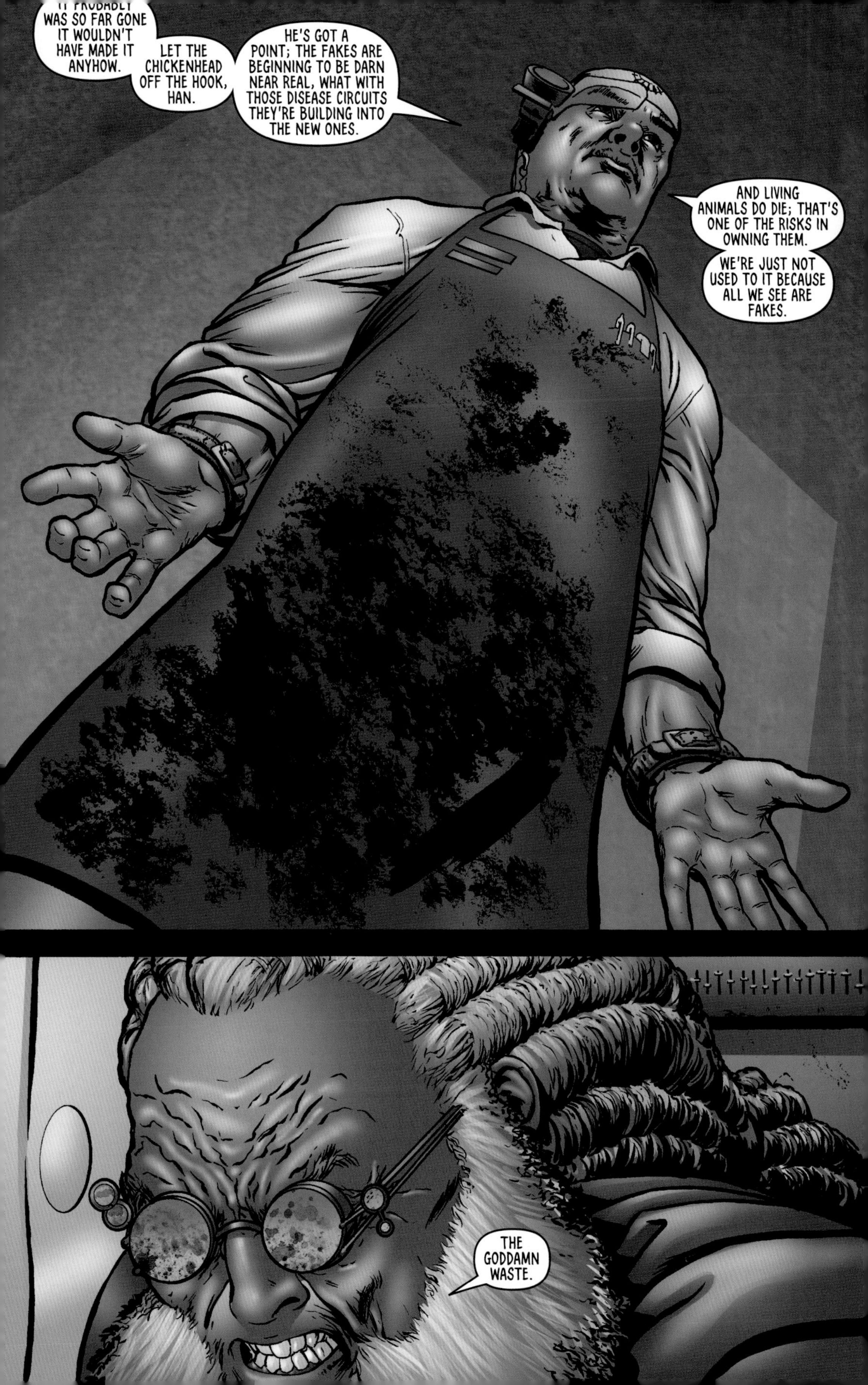
IT PROBABLY WAS SO FAR GONE IT WOULDN'T HAVE MADE IT ANYHOW.
LET THE CHICKENHEAD OFF THE HOOK, HAN.
HE'S GOT A POINT; THE FAKES ARE BEGINNING TO BE DARN NEAR REAL, WHAT WITH THOSE DISEASE CIRCUITS THEY'RE BUILDING INTO THE NEW ONES.
AND LIVING ANIMALS DO DIE; THAT'S ONE OF THE RISKS IN OWNING THEM.
WE'RE JUST NOT USED TO IT BECAUSE ALL WE SEE ARE FAKES.
THE GODDAMN WASTE.

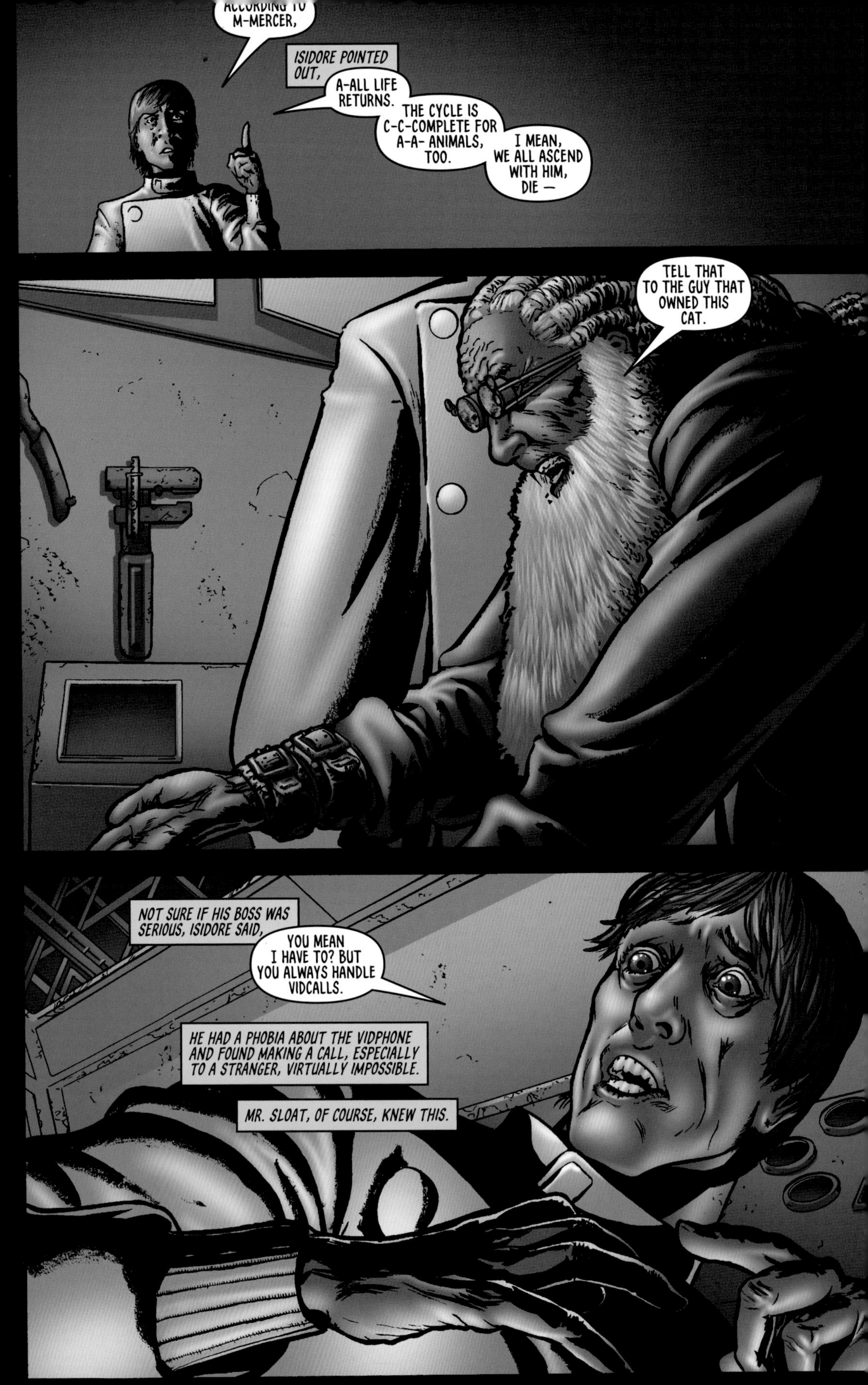
ACCORDING TO M-MERCER,
ISIDORE POINTED OUT,
A-ALL LIFE RETURNS.
THE CYCLE IS C-C-COMPLETE FOR A-A- ANIMALS, TOO.
I MEAN, WE ALL ASCEND WITH HIM, DIE —
TELL THAT TO THE GUY THAT OWNED THIS CAT.
NOT SURE IF HIS BOSS WAS SERIOUS, ISIDORE SAID,
YOU MEAN I HAVE TO? BUT YOU ALWAYS HANDLE VIDCALLS.
HE HAD A PHOBIA ABOUT THE VIDPHONE AND FOUND MAKING A CALL, ESPECIALLY TO A STRANGER, VIRTUALLY IMPOSSIBLE.
MR. SLOAT, OF COURSE, KNEW THIS.

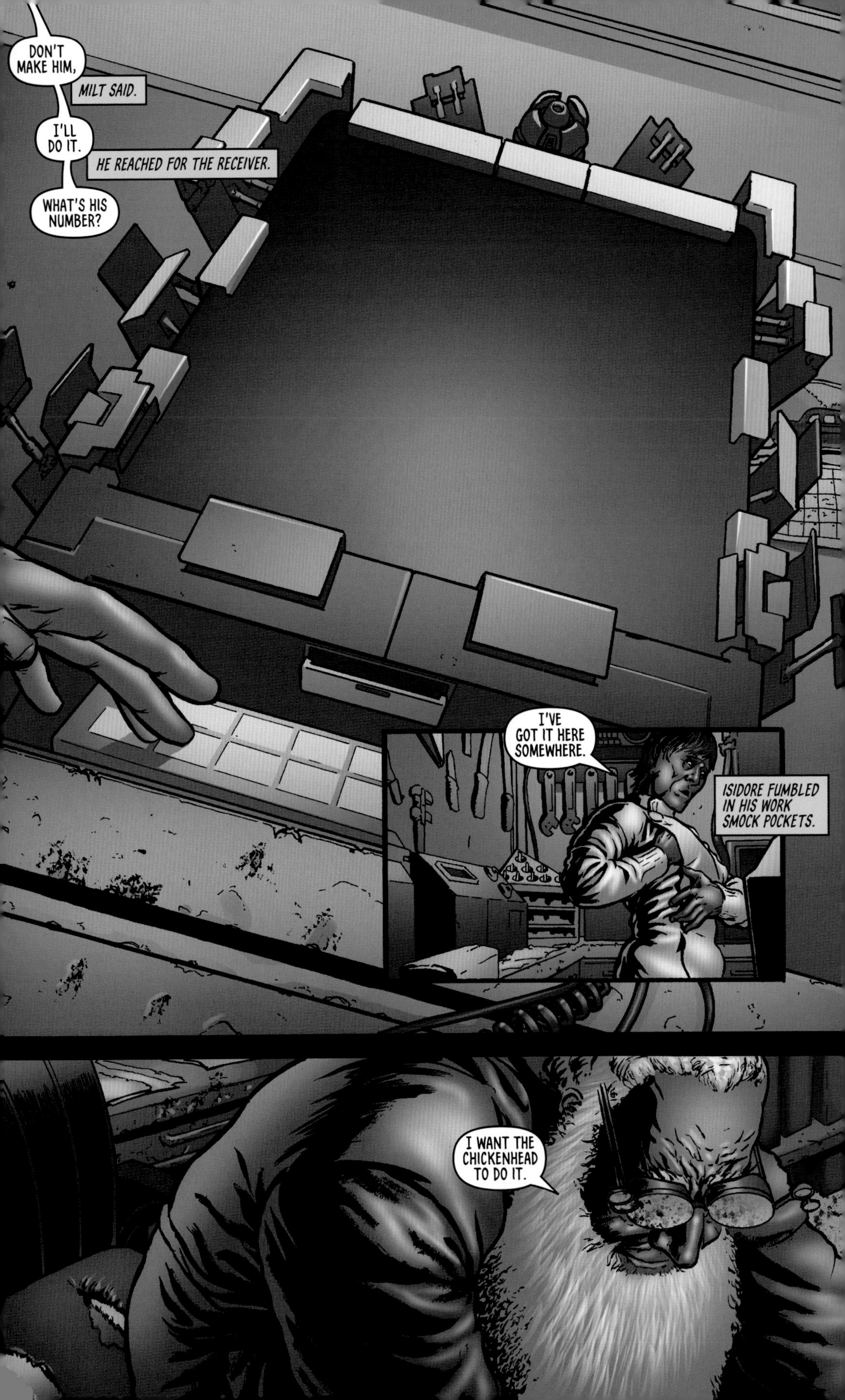
DON'T MAKE HIM,
MILT SAID.
I'LL DO IT.
HE REACHED FOR THE RECEIVER.
WHAT'S HIS NUMBER?
I'VE GOT IT HERE SOMEWHERE.
ISIDORE FUMBLED IN HIS WORK SMOCK POCKETS.
I WANT THE CHICKENHEAD TO DO IT.

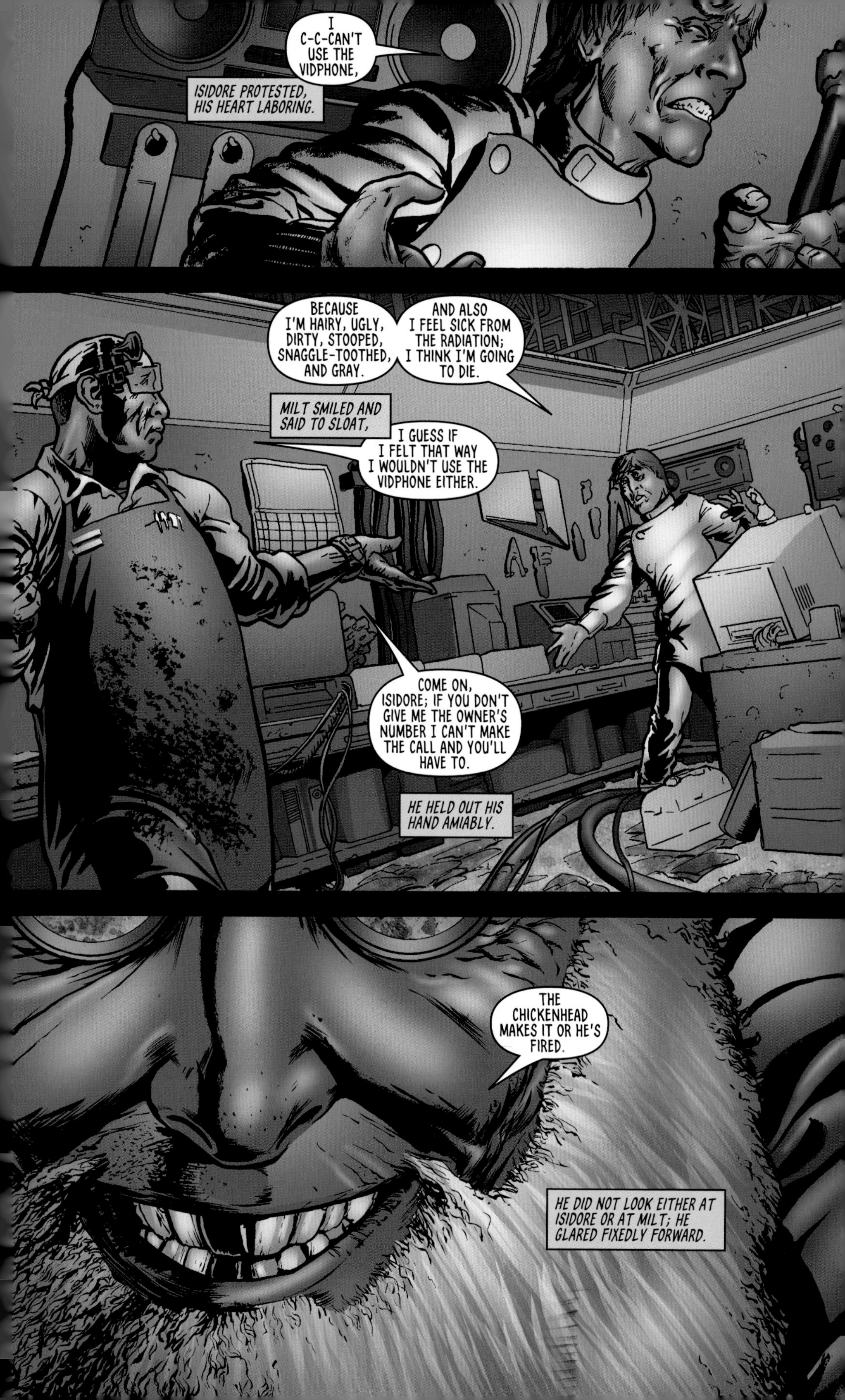
I C-C-CAN'T USE THE VIDPHONE,
ISIDORE PROTESTED, HIS HEART LABORING.
BECAUSE I'M HAIRY, UGLY, DIRTY, STOOPED, SNAGGLE-TOOTHED, AND GRAY.
AND ALSO I FEEL SICK FROM THE RADIATION; I THINK I'M GOING TO DIE.
MILT SMILED AND SAID TO SLOAT,
I GUESS IF I FELT THAT WAY I WOULDN'T USE THE VIDPHONE EITHER.
COME ON, ISIDORE; IF YOU DON'T GIVE ME THE OWNER'S NUMBER I CAN'T MAKE THE CALL AND YOU'LL HAVE TO.
HE HELD OUT HIS HAND AMIABLY.
THE CHICKENHEAD MAKES IT OR HE'S FIRED.
HE DID NOT LOOK EITHER AT ISIDORE OR AT MILT; HE GLARED FIXEDLY FORWARD.

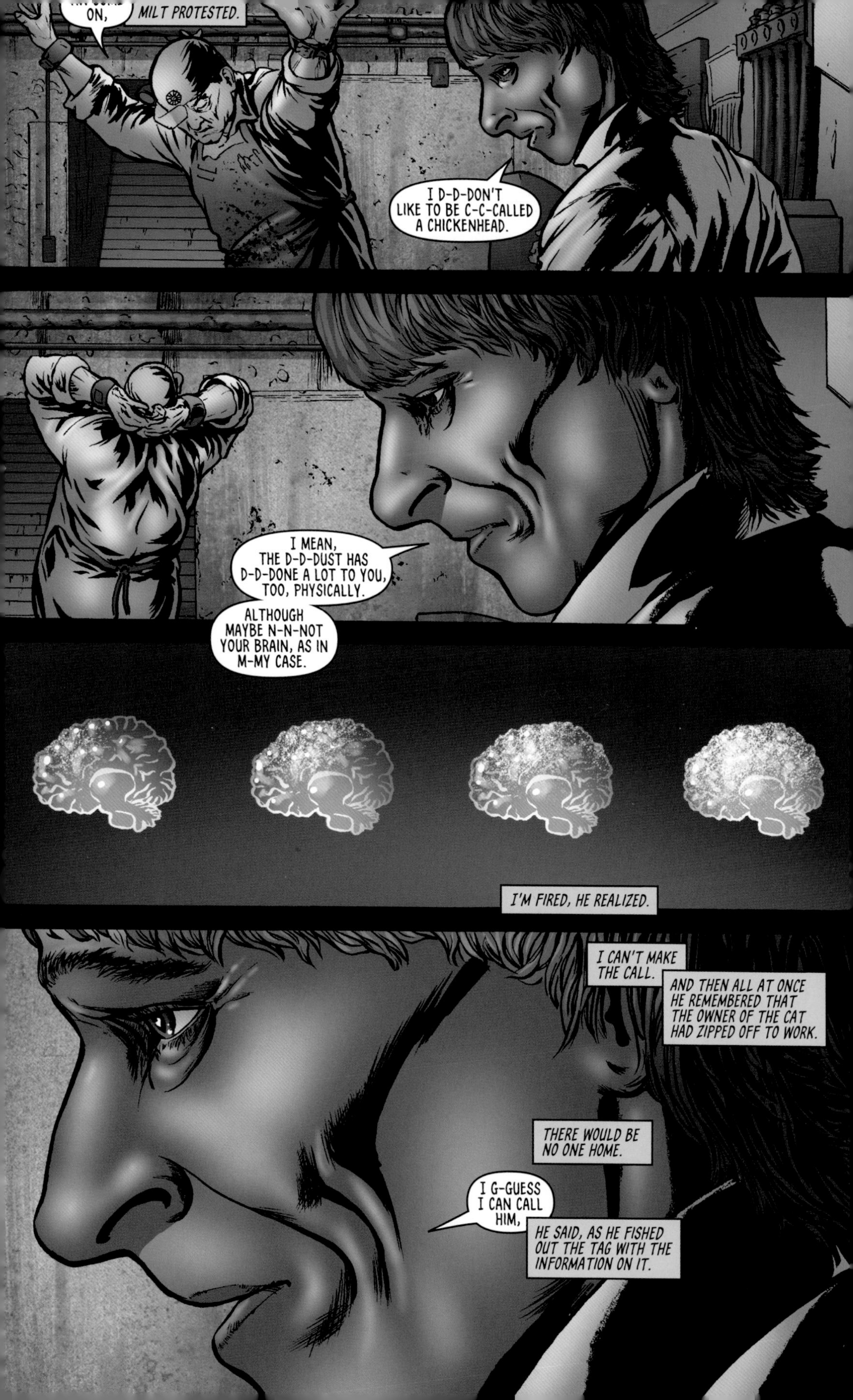
ON,
MILT PROTESTED.
I D-D-DON'T LIKE TO BE C-C-CALLED A CHICKENHEAD.
I MEAN, THE D-D-DUST HAS D-D-DONE A LOT TO YOU, TOO, PHYSICALLY.
ALTHOUGH MAYBE N-N-NOT YOUR BRAIN, AS IN M-MY CASE.
I'M FIRED, HE REALIZED.
I CAN'T MAKE THE CALL.
AND THEN ALL AT ONCE HE REMEMBERED THAT THE OWNER OF THE CAT HAD ZIPPED OFF TO WORK.
THERE WOULD BE NO ONE HOME.
I G-GUESS I CAN CALL HIM,
HE SAID, AS HE FISHED OUT THE TAG WITH THE INFORMATION ON IT.

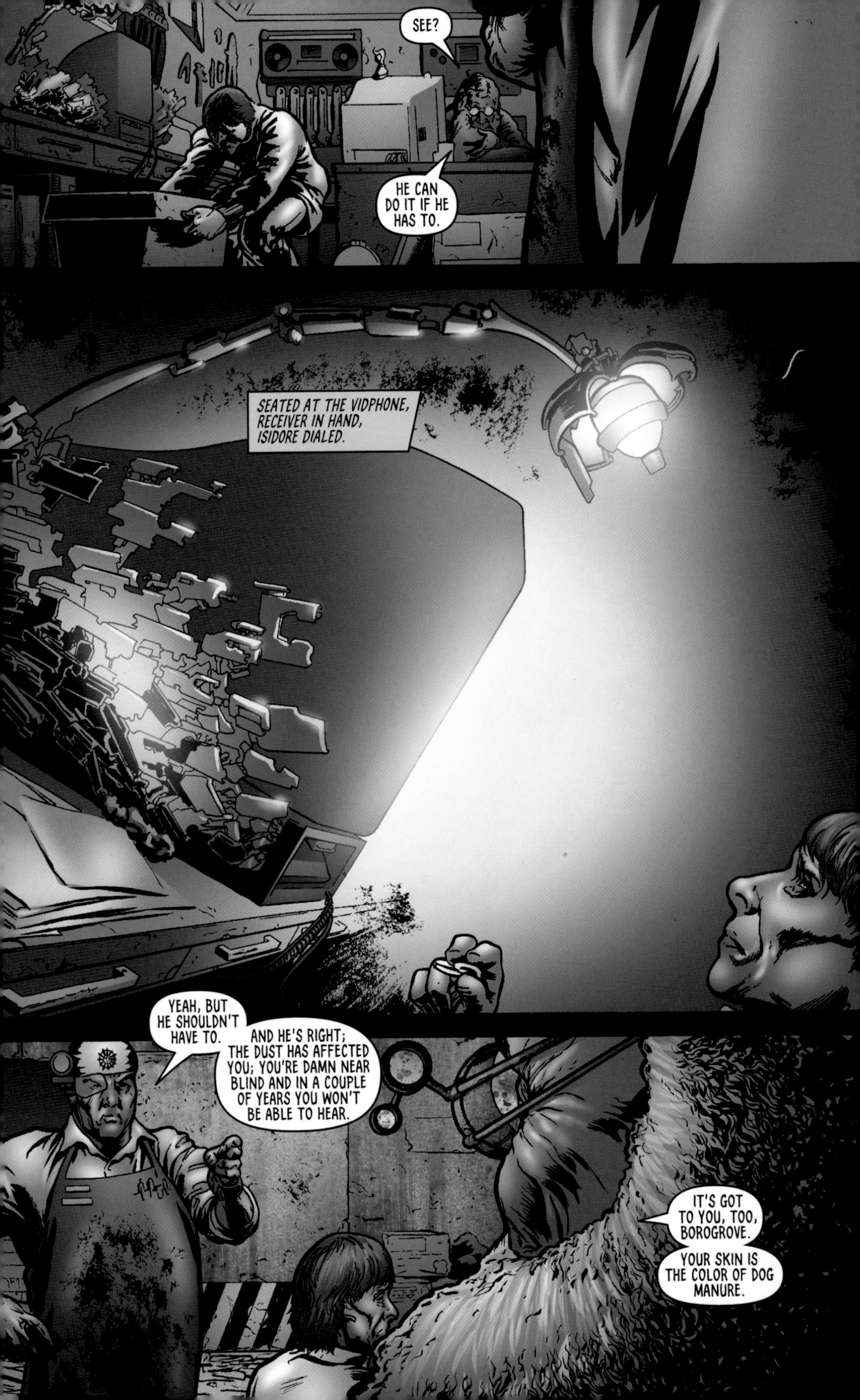

SEE?
HE CAN DO IT IF HE HAS TO.
SEATED AT THE VIDPHONE, RECEIVER IN HAND, ISIDORE DIALED.
YEAH, BUT HE SHOULDN'T HAVE TO.
AND HE'S RIGHT; THE DUST HAS AFFECTED YOU; YOU'RE DAMN NEAR BLIND AND IN A COUPLE OF YEARS YOU WON'T BE ABLE TO HEAR.
IT'S GOT TO YOU, TOO, BOROGROVE.
YOUR SKIN IS THE COLOR OF DOG MANURE.

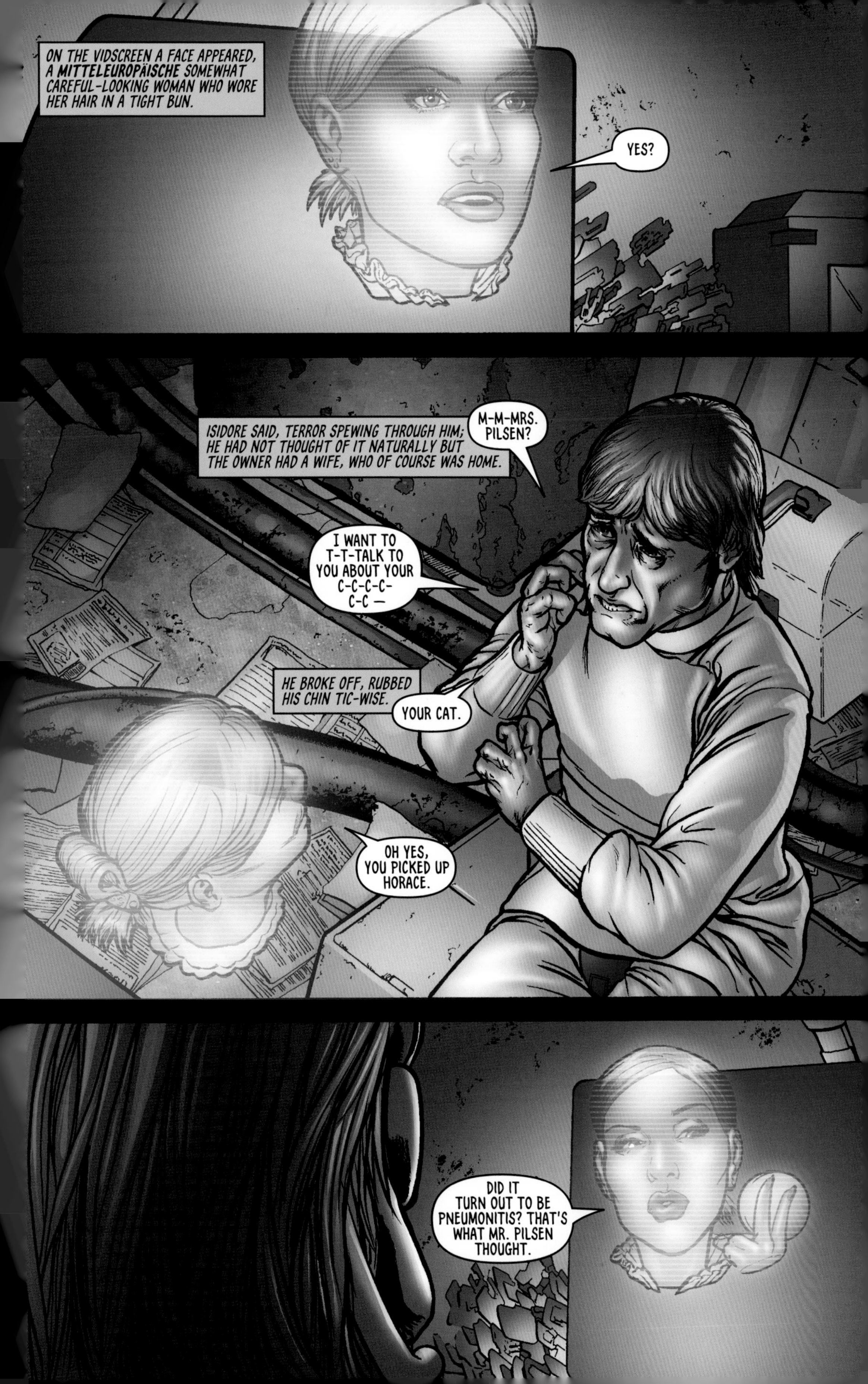

ON THE VIDSCREEN A FACE APPEARED, A **MITTELEUROPÄISCHE** SOMEWHAT CAREFUL-LOOKING WOMAN WHO WORE HER HAIR IN A TIGHT BUN.
YES?
M-M-MRS. PILSEN?
ISIDORE SAID, TERROR SPEWING THROUGH HIM; HE HAD NOT THOUGHT OF IT NATURALLY BUT THE OWNER HAD A WIFE, WHO OF COURSE WAS HOME.
I WANT TO T-T-TALK TO YOU ABOUT YOUR C-C-C-C-C-C —
HE BROKE OFF, RUBBED HIS CHIN TIC-WISE.
YOUR CAT.
OH YES, YOU PICKED UP HORACE.
DID IT TURN OUT TO BE PNEUMONITIS? THAT'S WHAT MR. PILSEN THOUGHT.

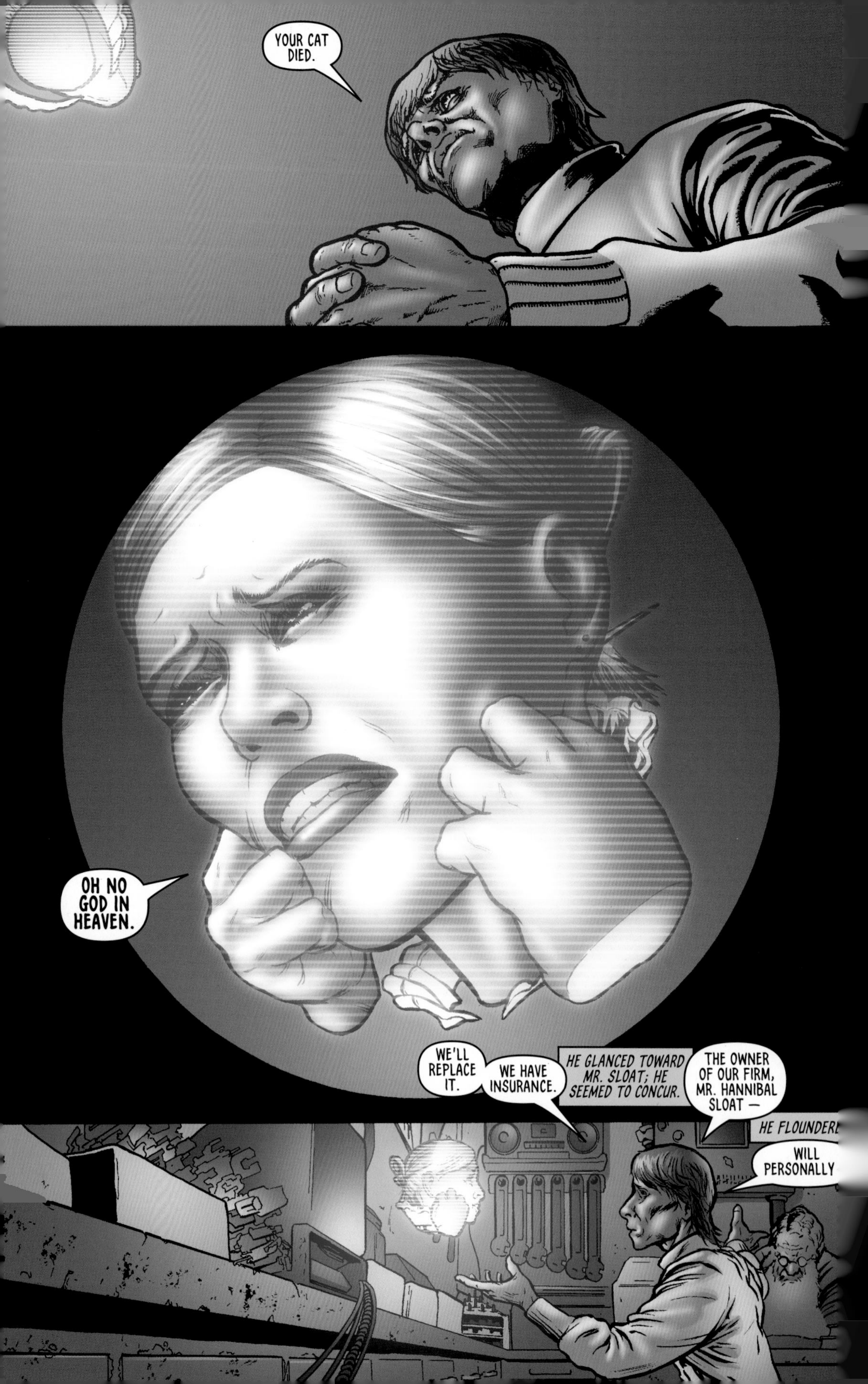
YOUR CAT DIED.
OH NO GOD IN HEAVEN.
WE'LL REPLACE IT.
WE HAVE INSURANCE.
HE GLANCED TOWARD MR. SLOAT; HE SEEMED TO CONCUR.
THE OWNER OF OUR FIRM, MR. HANNIBAL SLOAT —
WILL PERSONALLY

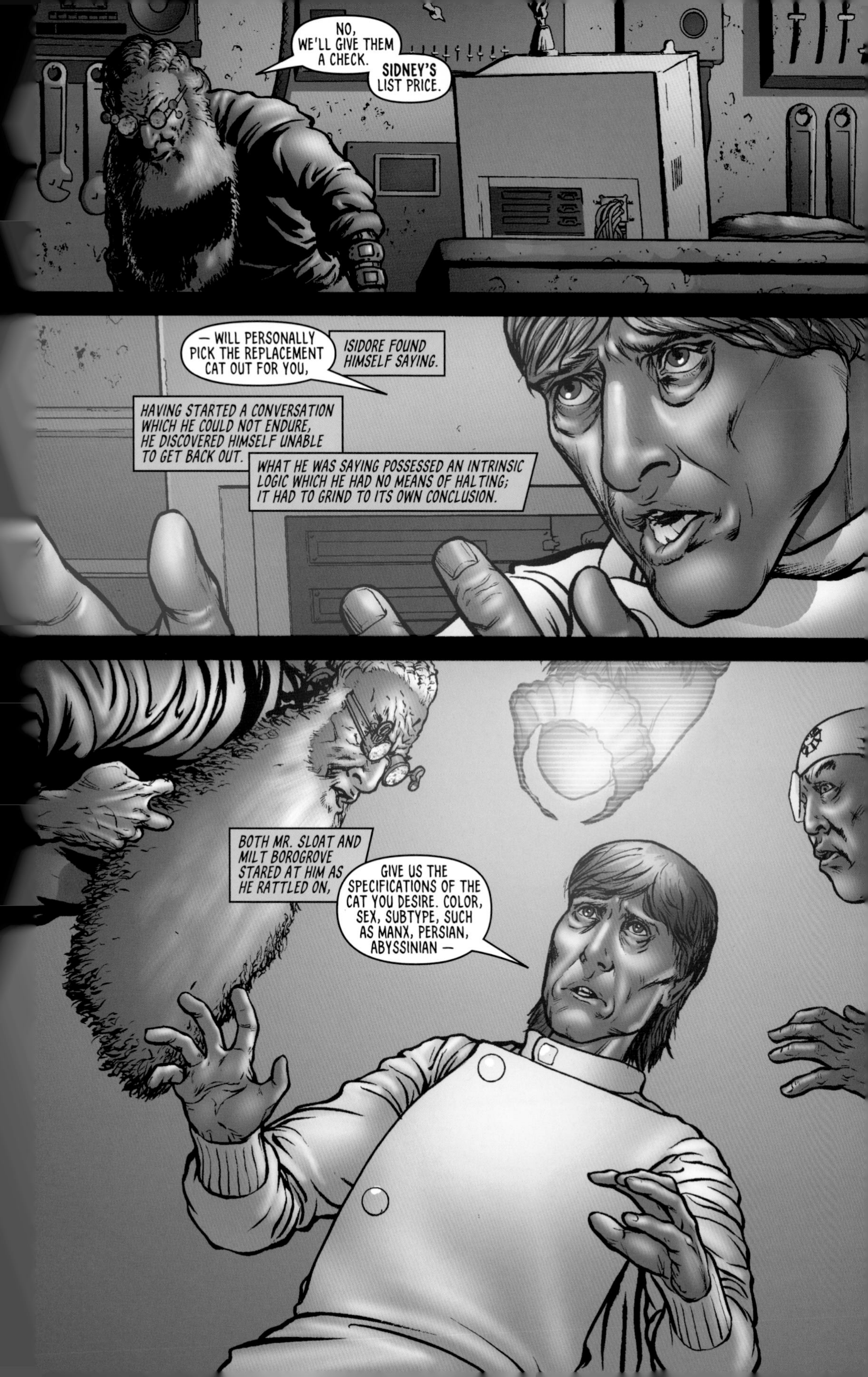
NO, WE'LL GIVE THEM A CHECK.
SIDNEY'S LIST PRICE.
— WILL PERSONALLY PICK THE REPLACEMENT CAT OUT FOR YOU,
ISIDORE FOUND HIMSELF SAYING.
HAVING STARTED A CONVERSATION WHICH HE COULD NOT ENDURE, HE DISCOVERED HIMSELF UNABLE TO GET BACK OUT.
WHAT HE WAS SAYING POSSESSED AN INTRINSIC LOGIC WHICH HE HAD NO MEANS OF HALTING; IT HAD TO GRIND TO ITS OWN CONCLUSION.
BOTH MR. SLOAT AND MILT BOROGROVE STARED AT HIM AS HE RATTLED ON,
GIVE US THE SPECIFICATIONS OF THE CAT YOU DESIRE. COLOR, SEX, SUBTYPE, SUCH AS MANX, PERSIAN, ABYSSINIAN —

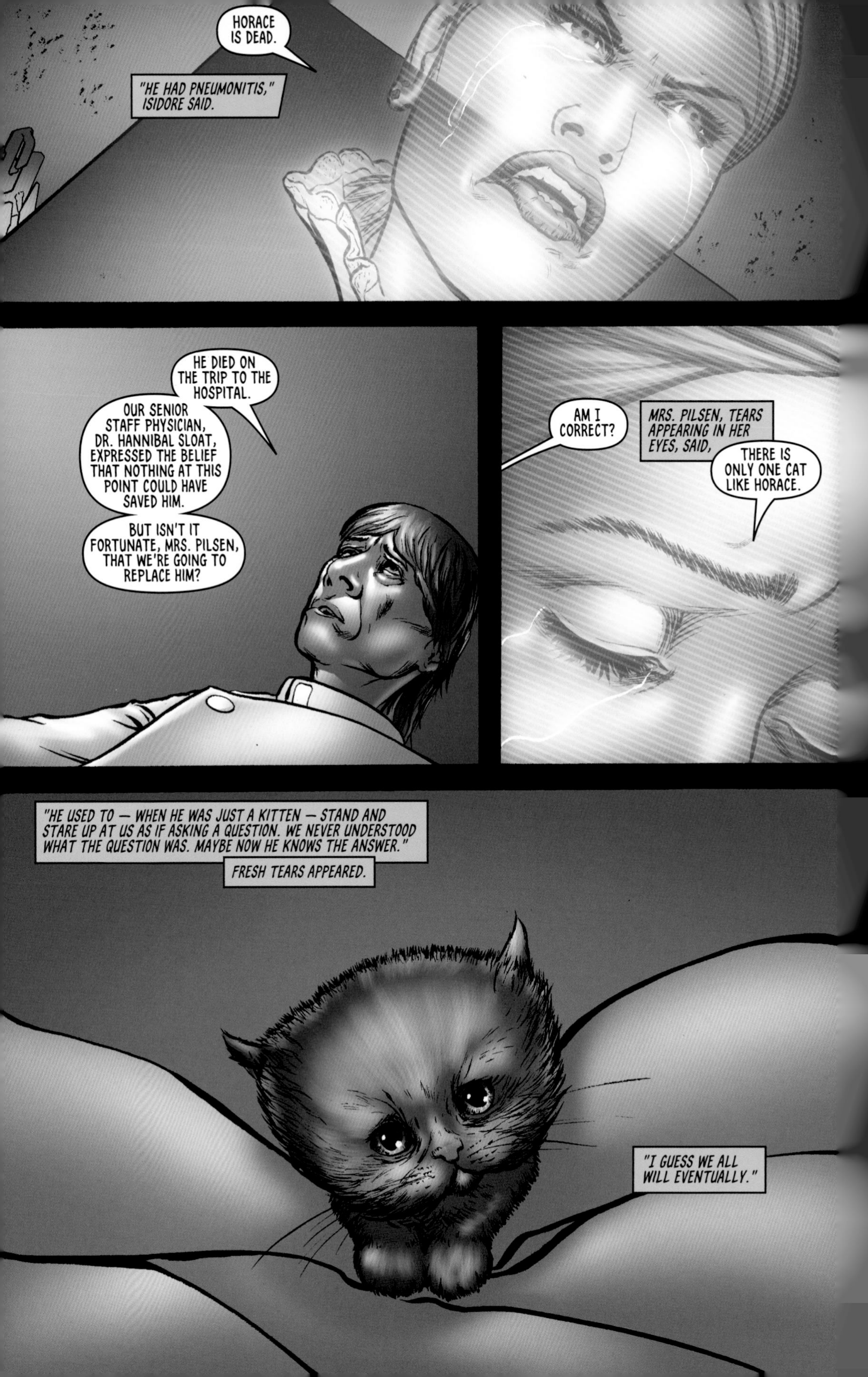
HORACE IS DEAD.
"HE HAD PNEUMONITIS," ISIDORE SAID.
HE DIED ON THE TRIP TO THE HOSPITAL.
OUR SENIOR STAFF PHYSICIAN, DR. HANNIBAL SLOAT, EXPRESSED THE BELIEF THAT NOTHING AT THIS POINT COULD HAVE SAVED HIM.
BUT ISN'T IT FORTUNATE, MRS. PILSEN, THAT WE'RE GOING TO REPLACE HIM?
AM I CORRECT?
MRS. PILSEN, TEARS APPEARING IN HER EYES, SAID,
THERE IS ONLY ONE CAT LIKE HORACE.
"HE USED TO — WHEN HE WAS JUST A KITTEN — STAND AND STARE UP AT US AS IF ASKING A QUESTION. WE NEVER UNDERSTOOD WHAT THE QUESTION WAS. MAYBE NOW HE KNOWS THE ANSWER."
FRESH TEARS APPEARED.
"I GUESS WE ALL WILL EVENTUALLY."

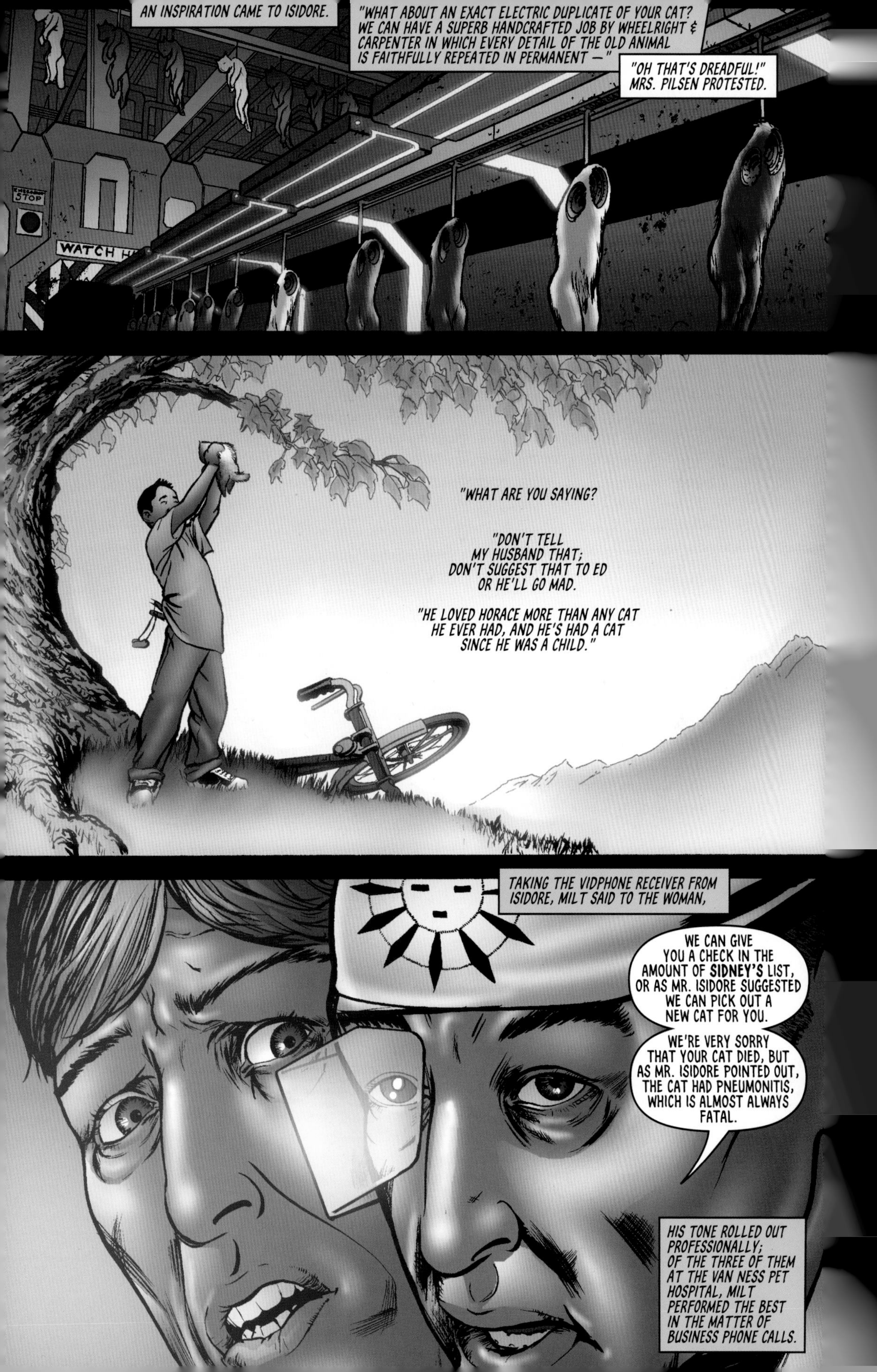
AN INSPIRATION CAME TO ISIDORE.
"WHAT ABOUT AN EXACT ELECTRIC DUPLICATE OF YOUR CAT? WE CAN HAVE A SUPERB HANDCRAFTED JOB BY WHEELRIGHT & CARPENTER IN WHICH EVERY DETAIL OF THE OLD ANIMAL IS FAITHFULLY REPEATED IN PERMANENT —"
"OH THAT'S DREADFUL!" MRS. PILSEN PROTESTED.
STOP
WATCH H
"WHAT ARE YOU SAYING?
"DON'T TELL MY HUSBAND THAT; DON'T SUGGEST THAT TO ED OR HE'LL GO MAD.
"HE LOVED HORACE MORE THAN ANY CAT HE EVER HAD, AND HE'S HAD A CAT SINCE HE WAS A CHILD."
TAKING THE VIDPHONE RECEIVER FROM ISIDORE, MILT SAID TO THE WOMAN,
WE CAN GIVE YOU A CHECK IN THE AMOUNT OF **SIDNEY'S** LIST, OR AS MR. ISIDORE SUGGESTED WE CAN PICK OUT A NEW CAT FOR YOU.
WE'RE VERY SORRY THAT YOUR CAT DIED, BUT AS MR. ISIDORE POINTED OUT, THE CAT HAD PNEUMONITIS, WHICH IS ALMOST ALWAYS FATAL.
HIS TONE ROLLED OUT PROFESSIONALLY; OF THE THREE OF THEM AT THE VAN NESS PET HOSPITAL, MILT PERFORMED THE BEST IN THE MATTER OF BUSINESS PHONE CALLS.

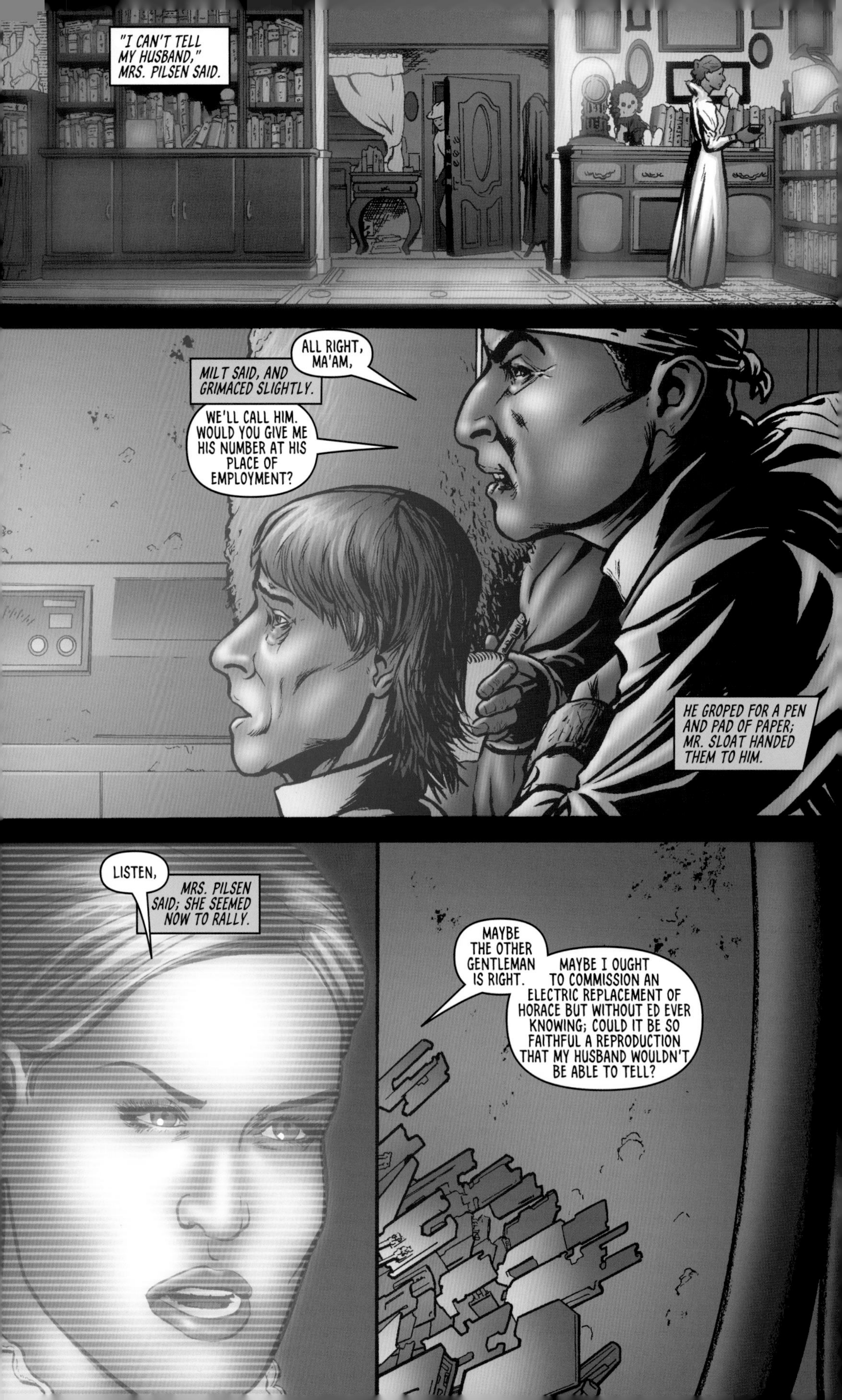
"I CAN'T TELL MY HUSBAND," MRS. PILSEN SAID.
ALL RIGHT, MA'AM,
MILT SAID, AND GRIMACED SLIGHTLY.
WE'LL CALL HIM. WOULD YOU GIVE ME HIS NUMBER AT HIS PLACE OF EMPLOYMENT?
HE GROPED FOR A PEN AND PAD OF PAPER; MR. SLOAT HANDED THEM TO HIM.
LISTEN,
MRS. PILSEN SAID; SHE SEEMED NOW TO RALLY.
MAYBE THE OTHER GENTLEMAN IS RIGHT.
MAYBE I OUGHT TO COMMISSION AN ELECTRIC REPLACEMENT OF HORACE BUT WITHOUT ED EVER KNOWING; COULD IT BE SO FAITHFUL A REPRODUCTION THAT MY HUSBAND WOULDN'T BE ABLE TO TELL?

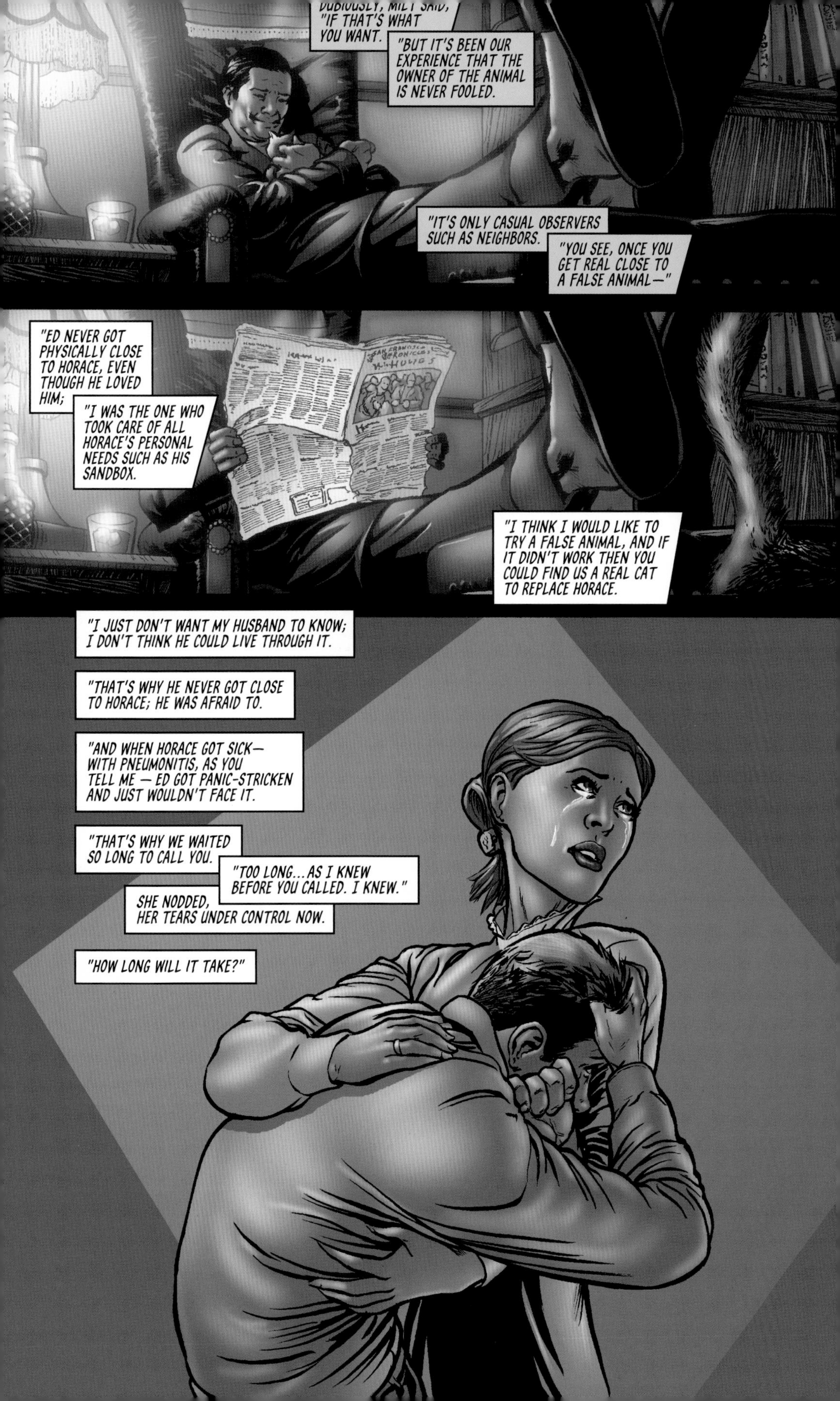
DUBIOUSLY, MILT SAID, "IF THAT'S WHAT YOU WANT.
"BUT IT'S BEEN OUR EXPERIENCE THAT THE OWNER OF THE ANIMAL IS NEVER FOOLED.
"IT'S ONLY CASUAL OBSERVERS SUCH AS NEIGHBORS.
"YOU SEE, ONCE YOU GET REAL CLOSE TO A FALSE ANIMAL—"
"ED NEVER GOT PHYSICALLY CLOSE TO HORACE, EVEN THOUGH HE LOVED HIM;
"I WAS THE ONE WHO TOOK CARE OF ALL HORACE'S PERSONAL NEEDS SUCH AS HIS SANDBOX.
"I THINK I WOULD LIKE TO TRY A FALSE ANIMAL, AND IF IT DIDN'T WORK THEN YOU COULD FIND US A REAL CAT TO REPLACE HORACE.
"I JUST DON'T WANT MY HUSBAND TO KNOW; I DON'T THINK HE COULD LIVE THROUGH IT.
"THAT'S WHY HE NEVER GOT CLOSE TO HORACE; HE WAS AFRAID TO.
"AND WHEN HORACE GOT SICK— WITH PNEUMONITIS, AS YOU TELL ME — ED GOT PANIC-STRICKEN AND JUST WOULDN'T FACE IT.
"THAT'S WHY WE WAITED SO LONG TO CALL YOU.
"TOO LONG...AS I KNEW BEFORE YOU CALLED. I KNEW."
SHE NODDED, HER TEARS UNDER CONTROL NOW.
"HOW LONG WILL IT TAKE?"

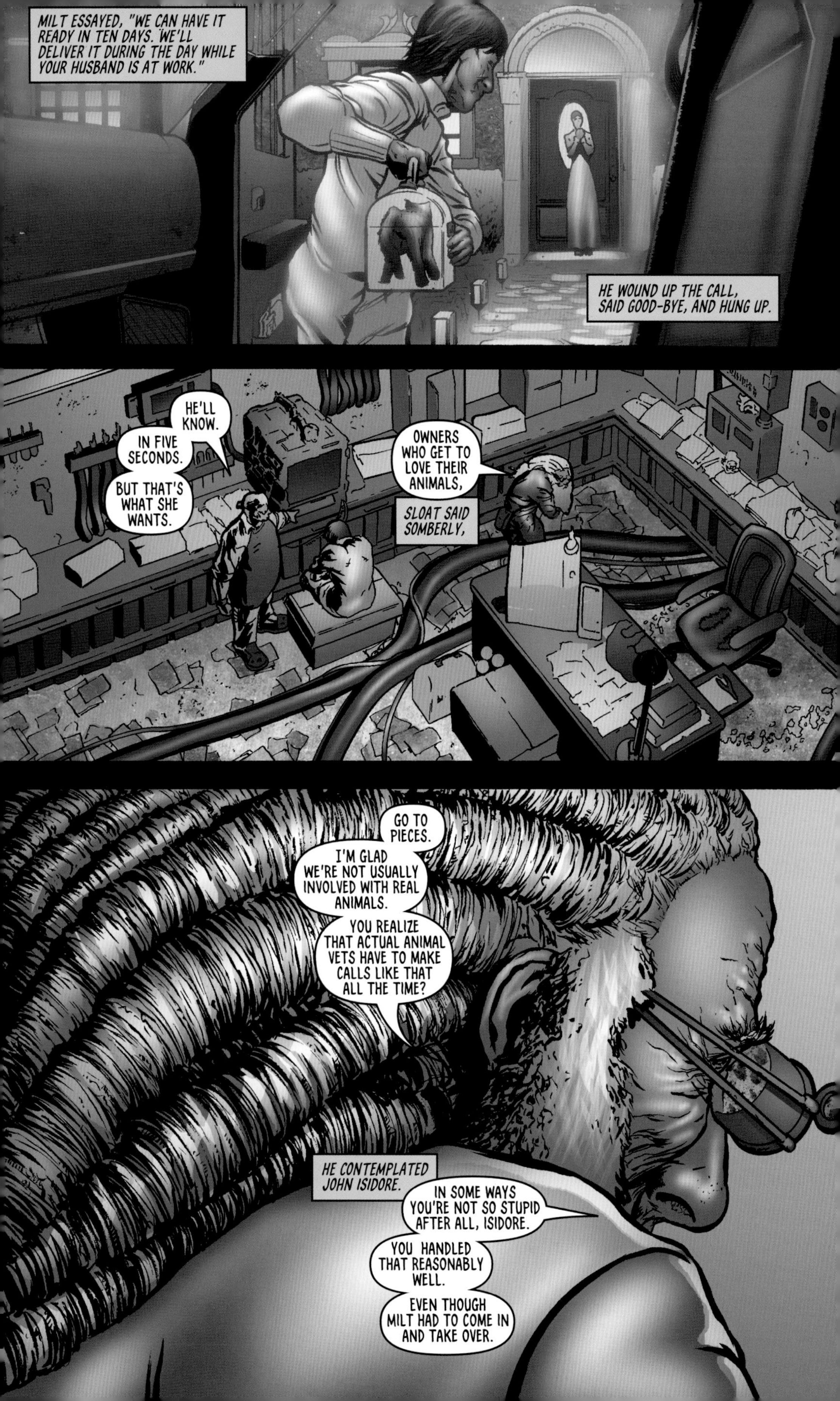

MILT ESSAYED, "WE CAN HAVE IT READY IN TEN DAYS. WE'LL DELIVER IT DURING THE DAY WHILE YOUR HUSBAND IS AT WORK."
HE WOUND UP THE CALL, SAID GOOD-BYE, AND HUNG UP.
HE'LL KNOW.
IN FIVE SECONDS.
BUT THAT'S WHAT SHE WANTS.
OWNERS WHO GET TO LOVE THEIR ANIMALS,
SLOAT SAID SOMBERLY,
GO TO PIECES.
I'M GLAD WE'RE NOT USUALLY INVOLVED WITH REAL ANIMALS.
YOU REALIZE THAT ACTUAL ANIMAL VETS HAVE TO MAKE CALLS LIKE THAT ALL THE TIME?
HE CONTEMPLATED JOHN ISIDORE.
IN SOME WAYS YOU'RE NOT SO STUPID AFTER ALL, ISIDORE.
YOU HANDLED THAT REASONABLY WELL.
EVEN THOUGH MILT HAD TO COME IN AND TAKE OVER.

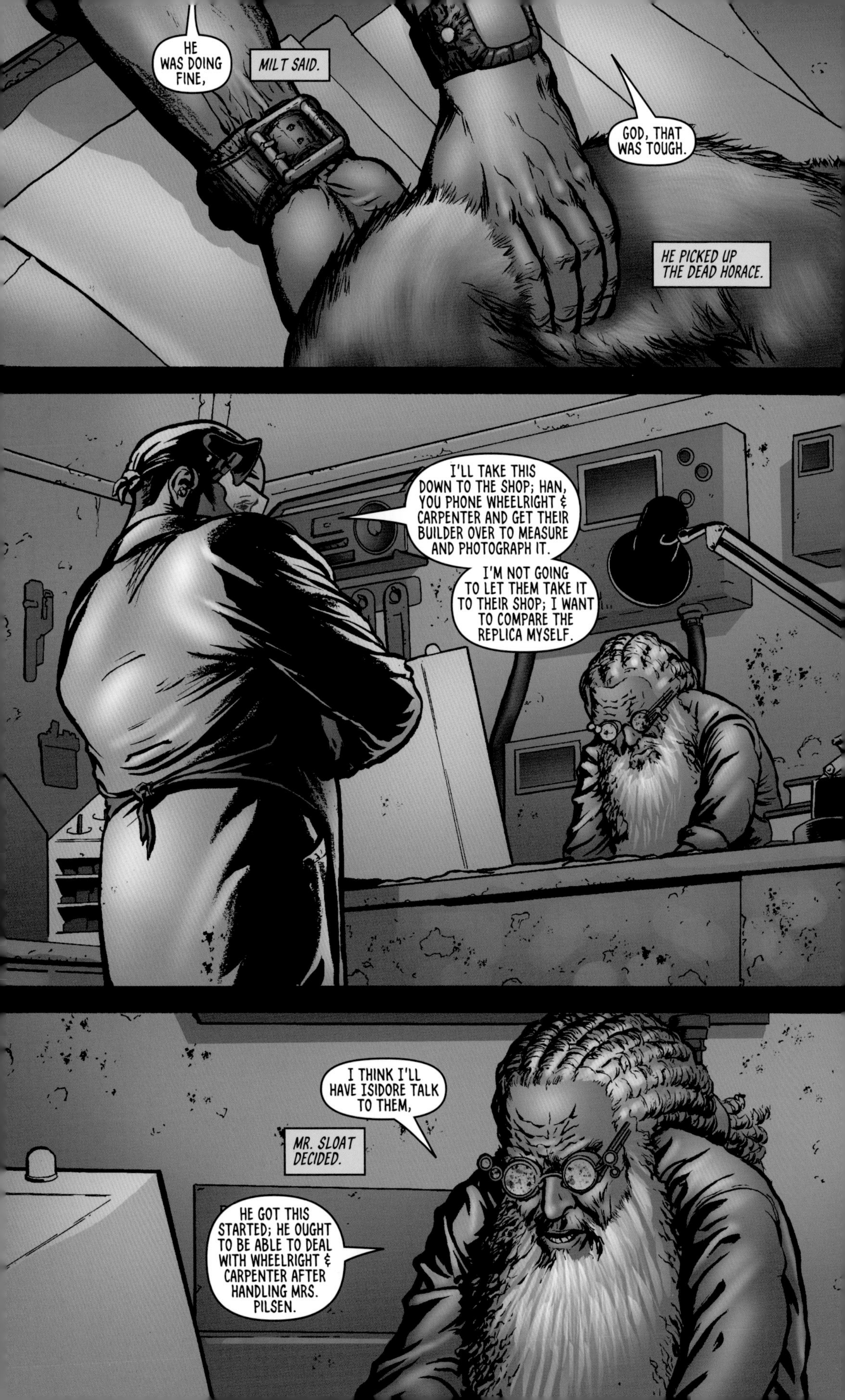
HE WAS DOING FINE,
MILT SAID.
GOD, THAT WAS TOUGH.
HE PICKED UP THE DEAD HORACE.
I'LL TAKE THIS DOWN TO THE SHOP; HAN, YOU PHONE WHEELRIGHT & CARPENTER AND GET THEIR BUILDER OVER TO MEASURE AND PHOTOGRAPH IT.
I'M NOT GOING TO LET THEM TAKE IT TO THEIR SHOP; I WANT TO COMPARE THE REPLICA MYSELF.
I THINK I'LL HAVE ISIDORE TALK TO THEM,
MR. SLOAT DECIDED.
HE GOT THIS STARTED; HE OUGHT TO BE ABLE TO DEAL WITH WHEELRIGHT & CARPENTER AFTER HANDLING MRS. PILSEN.

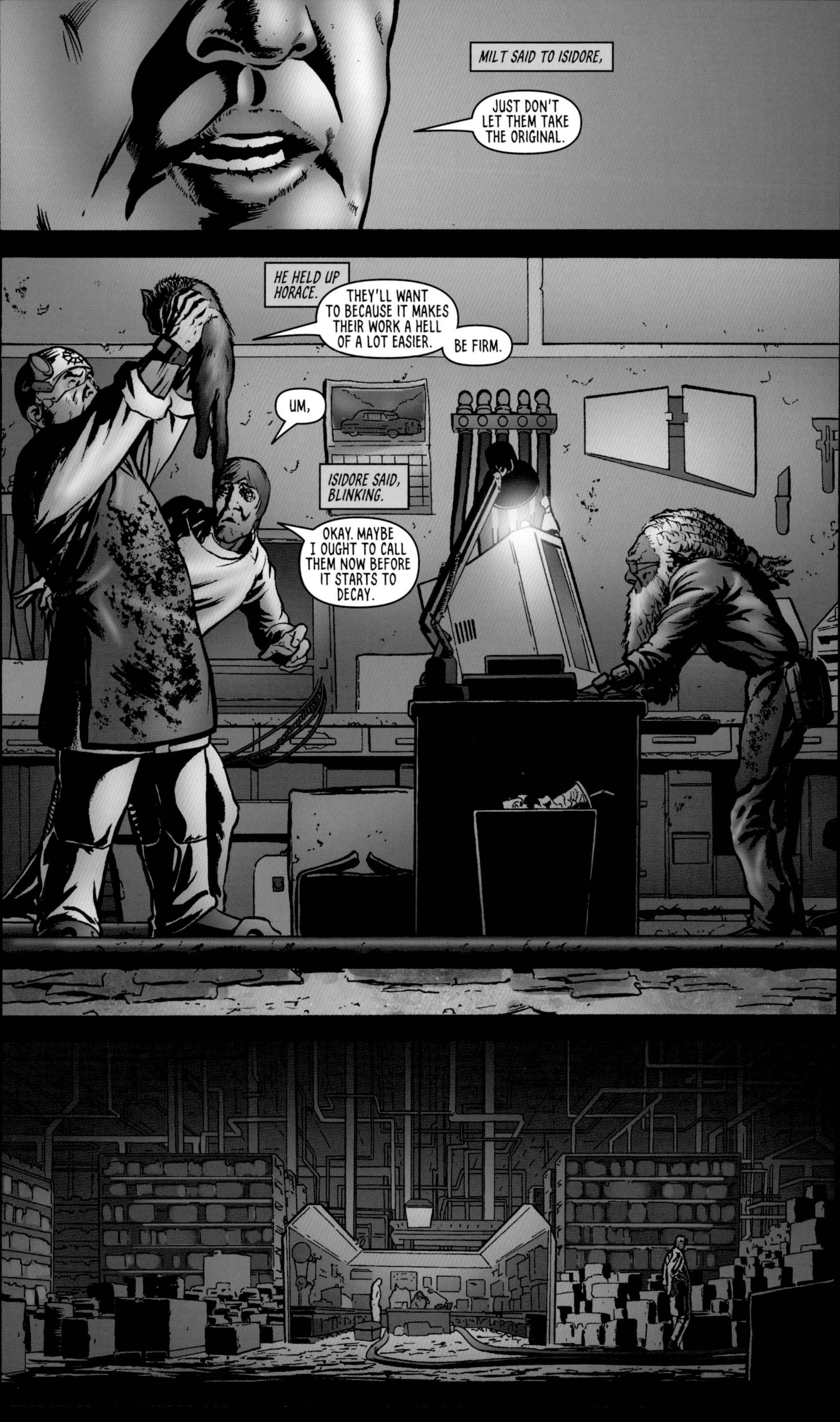
MILT SAID TO ISIDORE,
JUST DON'T LET THEM TAKE THE ORIGINAL.
HE HELD UP HORACE.
THEY'LL WANT TO BECAUSE IT MAKES THEIR WORK A HELL OF A LOT EASIER.
BE FIRM.
UM,
ISIDORE SAID, BLINKING.
OKAY. MAYBE I OUGHT TO CALL THEM NOW BEFORE IT STARTS TO DECAY.

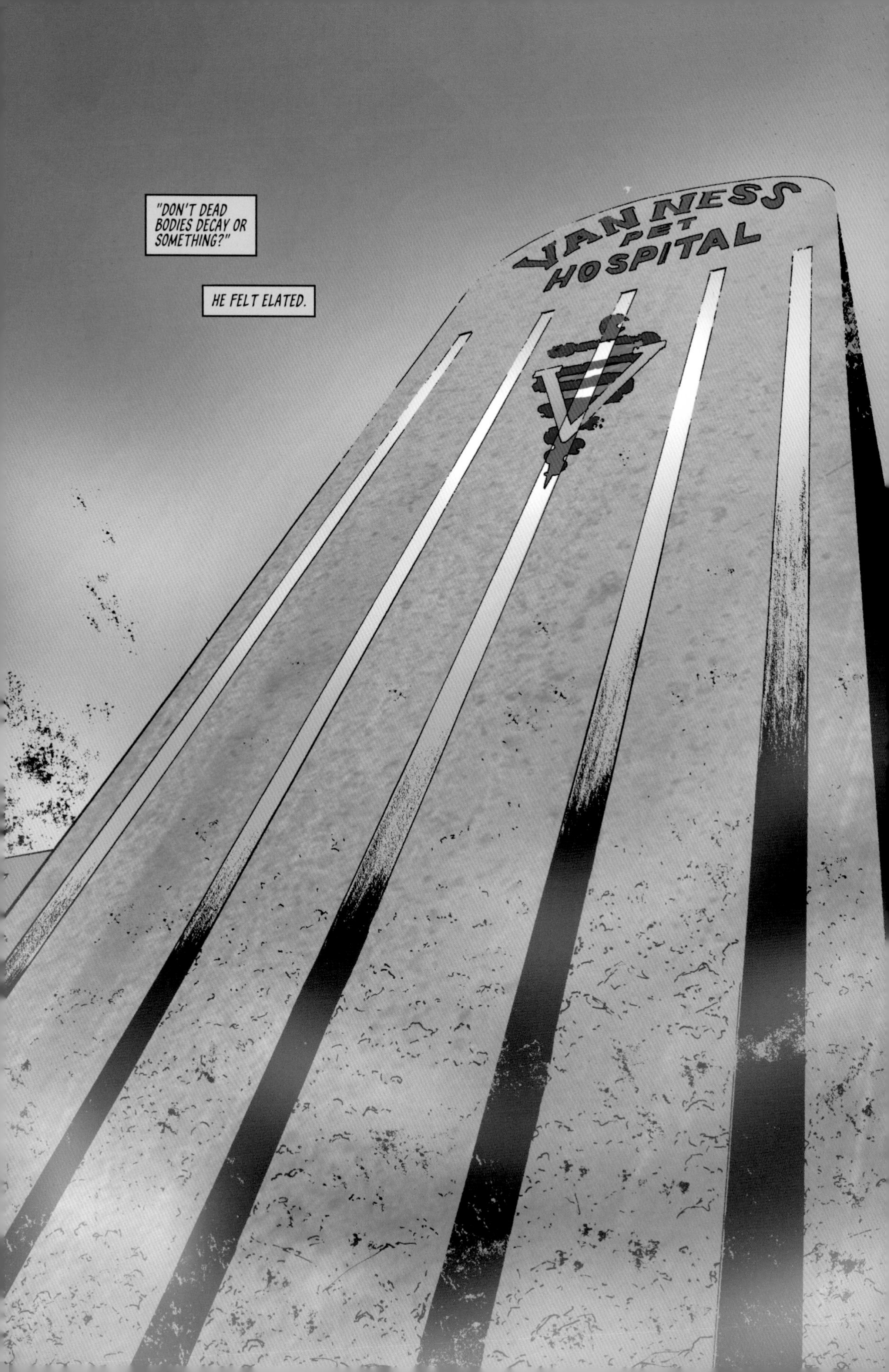
"DON'T DEAD BODIES DECAY OR SOMETHING?"
HE FELT ELATED.
VAN NESS PET HOSPITAL

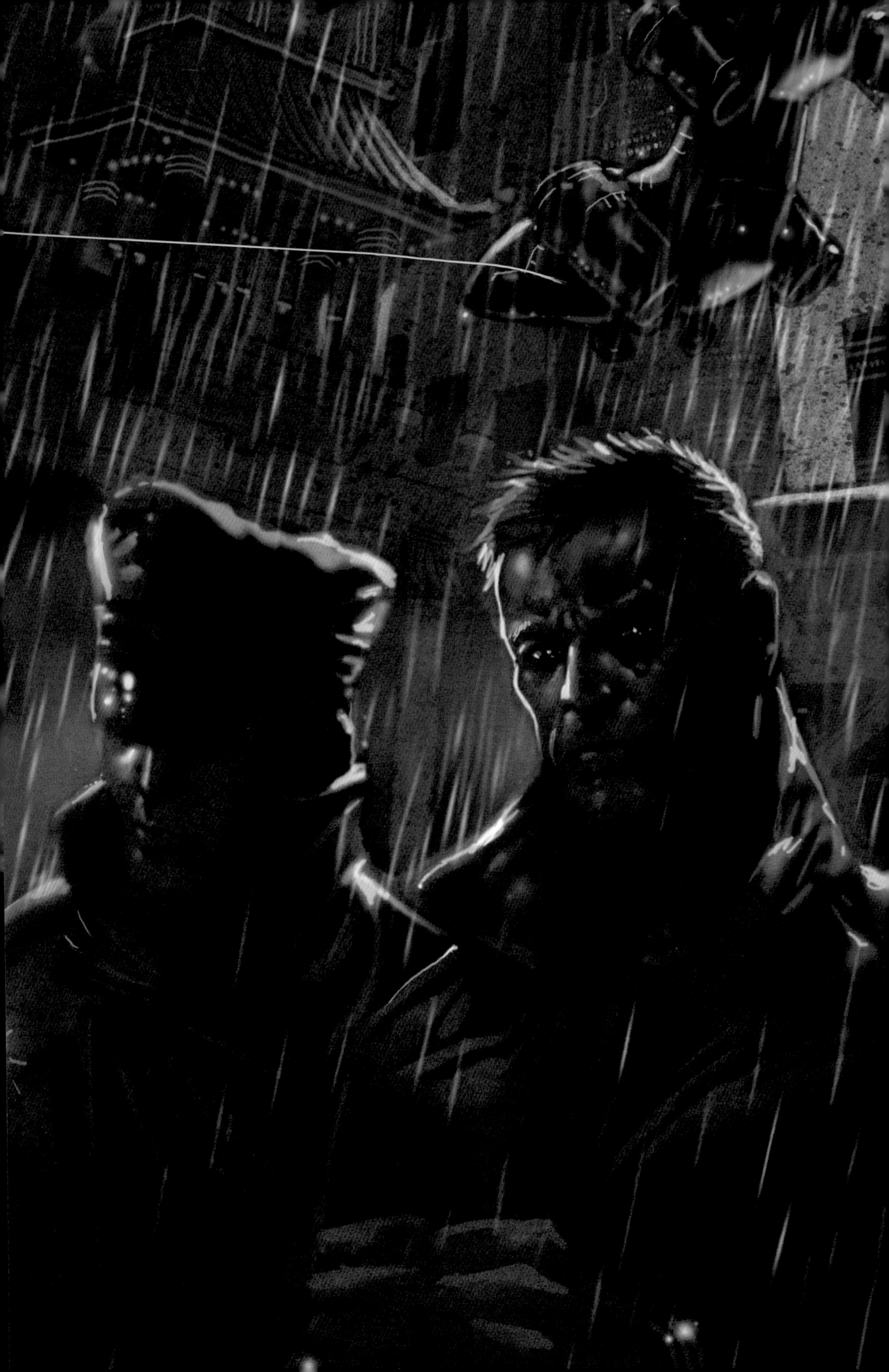

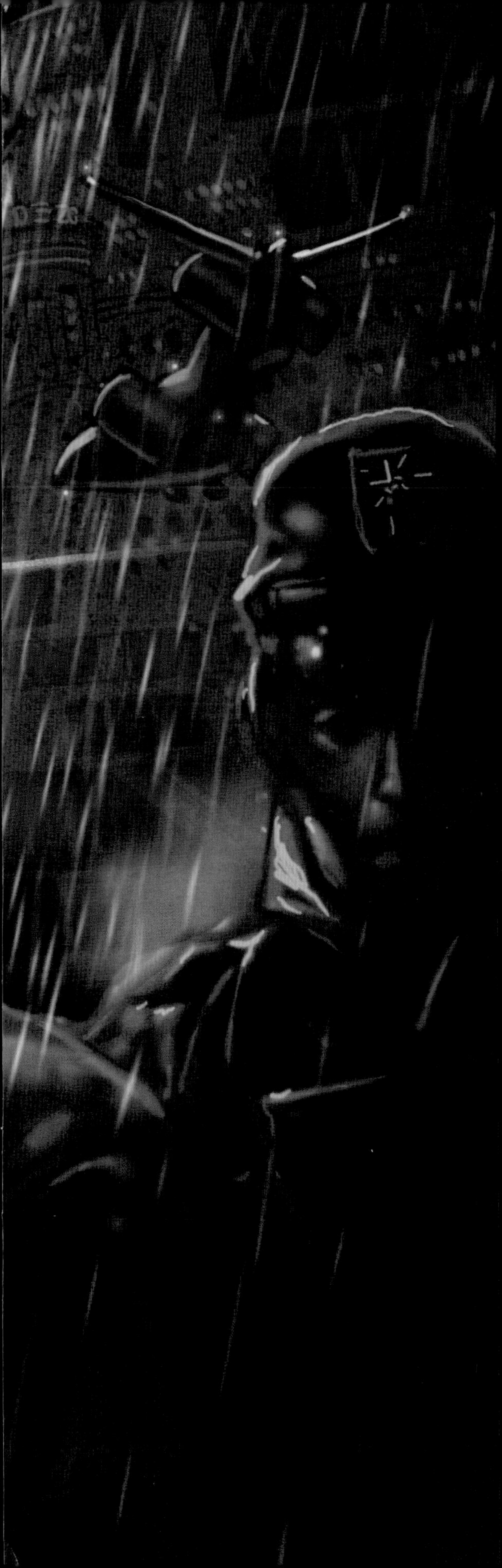

BOOK SIX

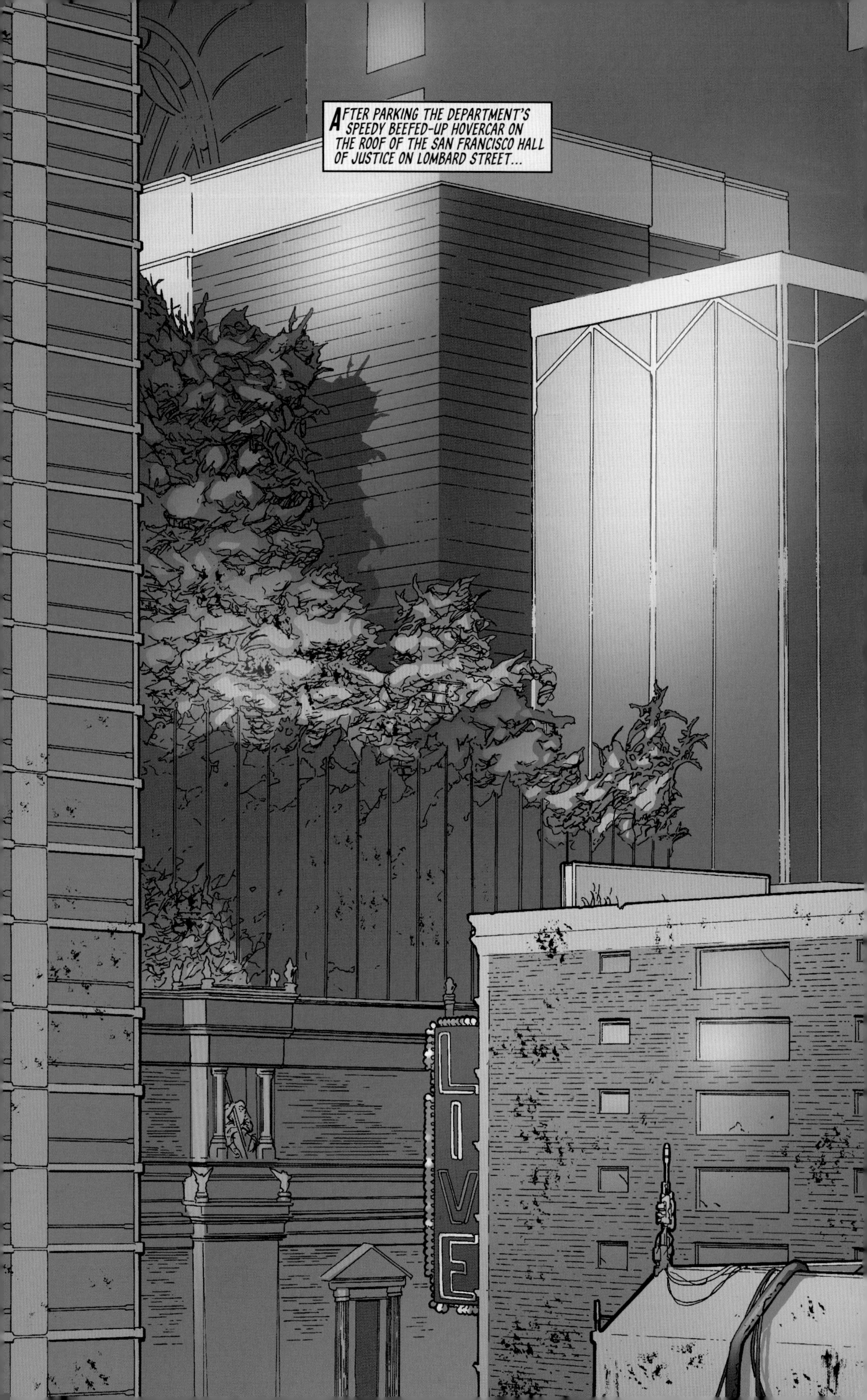
AFTER PARKING THE DEPARTMENT'S SPEEDY BEEFED-UP HOVERCAR ON THE ROOF OF THE SAN FRANCISCO HALL OF JUSTICE ON LOMBARD STREET...
LIVE

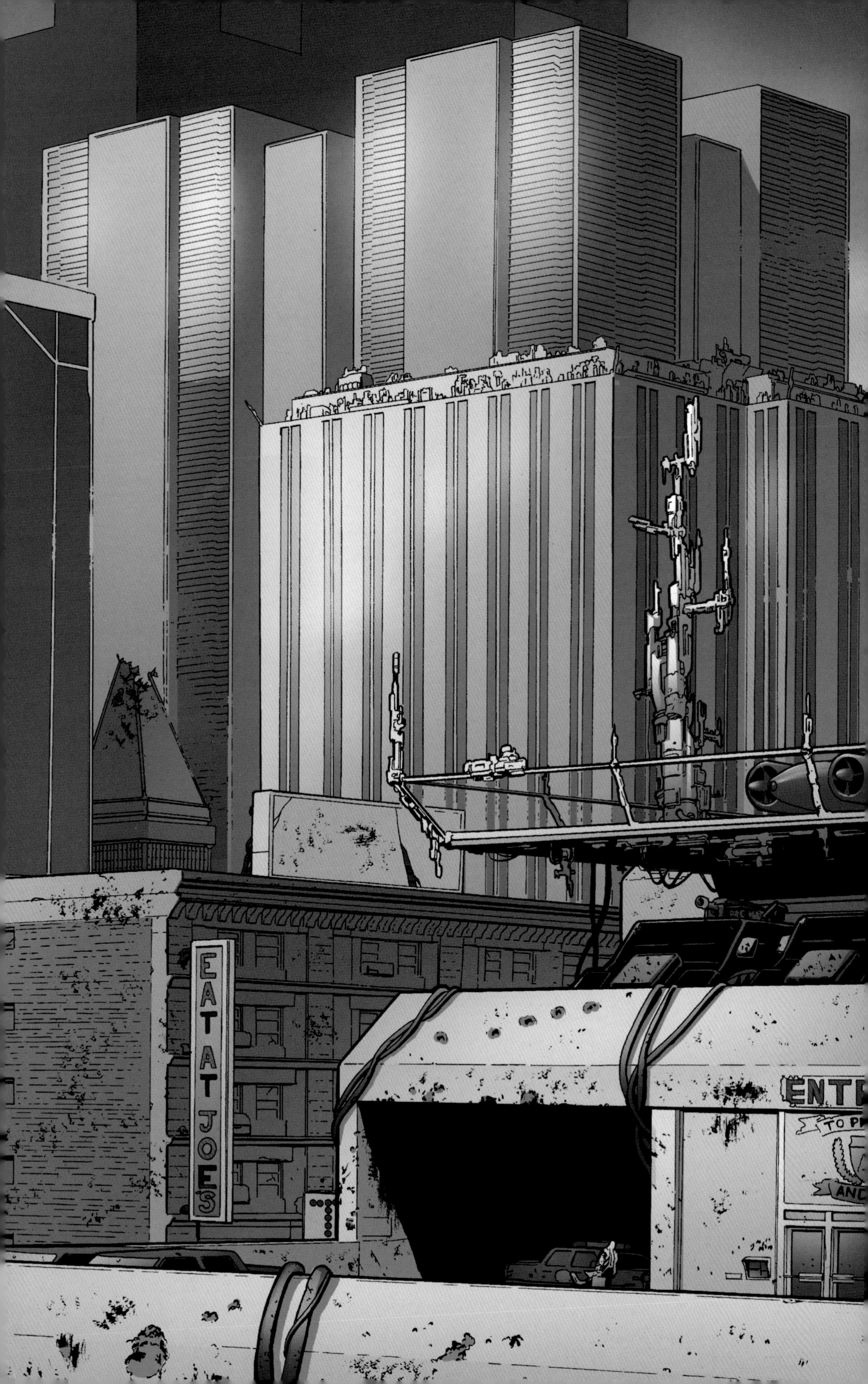
EAT AT JOES

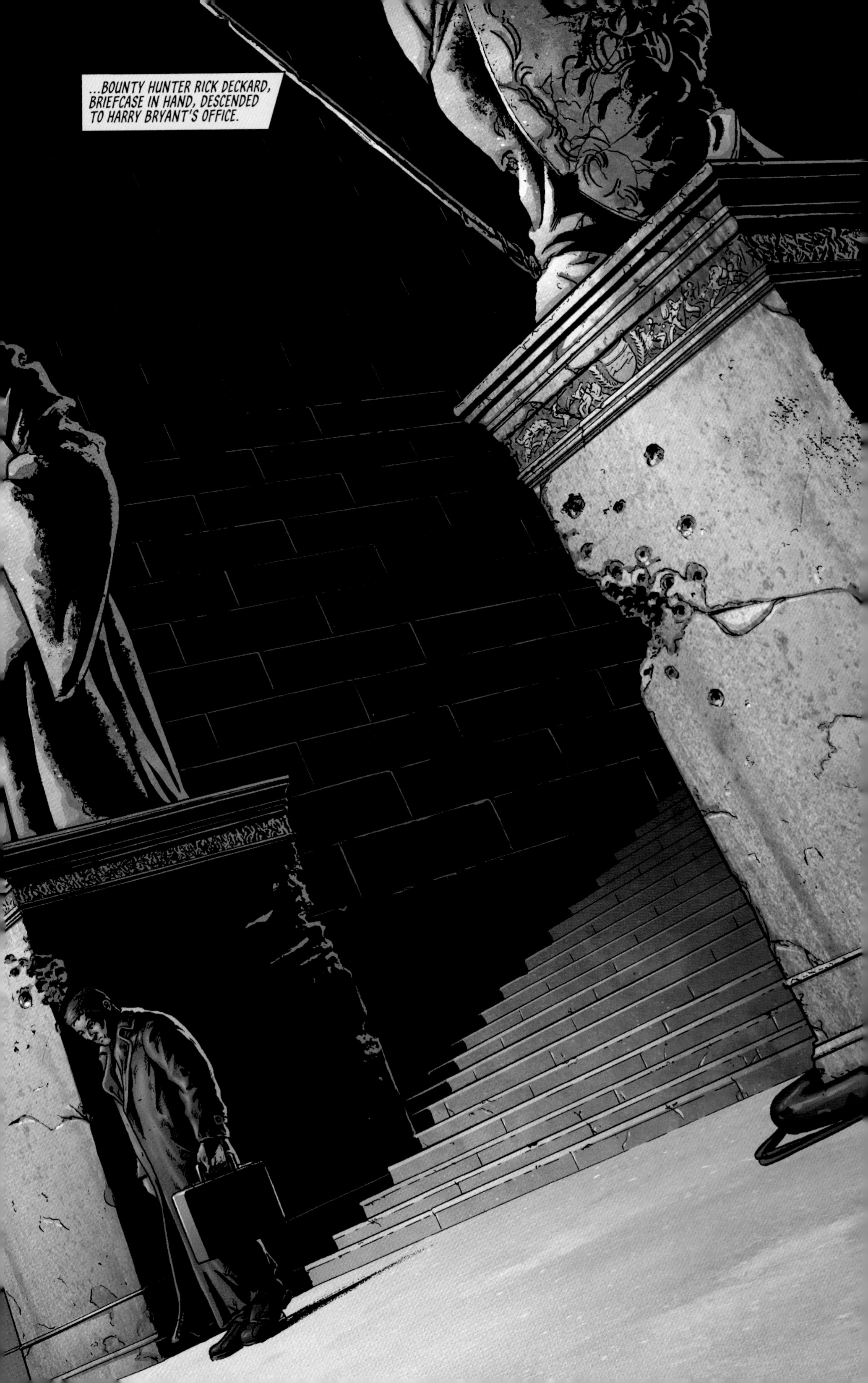
...BOUNTY HUNTER RICK DECKARD, BRIEFCASE IN HAND, DESCENDED TO HARRY BRYANT'S OFFICE.

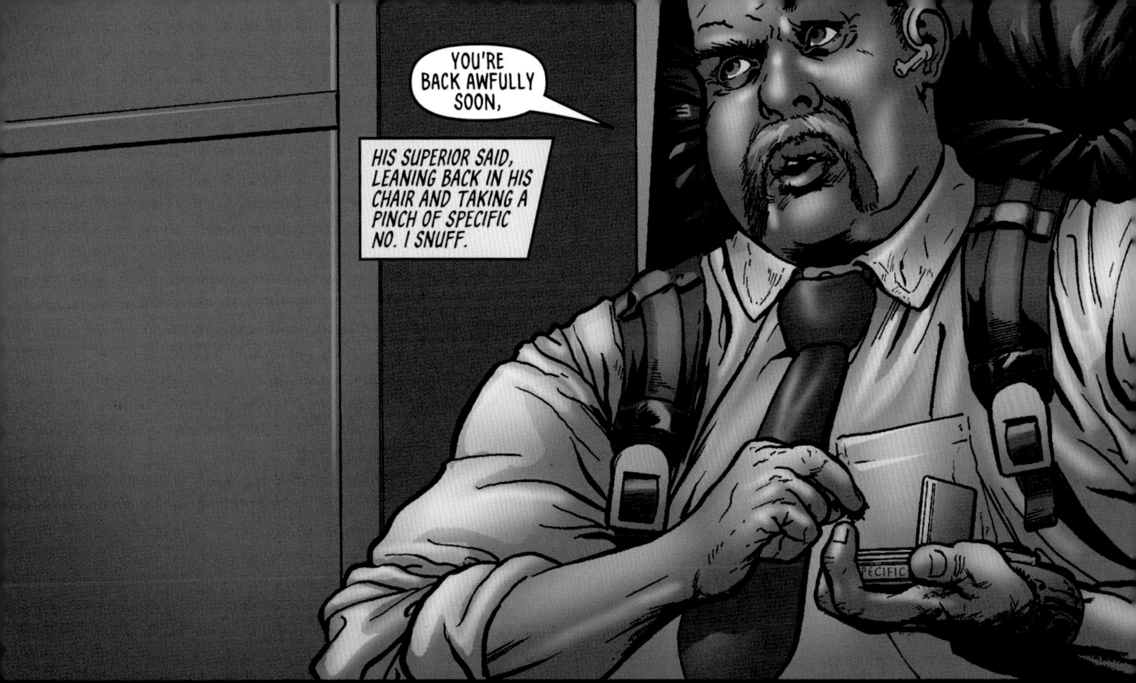
YOU'RE BACK AWFULLY SOON,
HIS SUPERIOR SAID, LEANING BACK IN HIS CHAIR AND TAKING A PINCH OF SPECIFIC NO. 1 SNUFF.
SPECIFIC

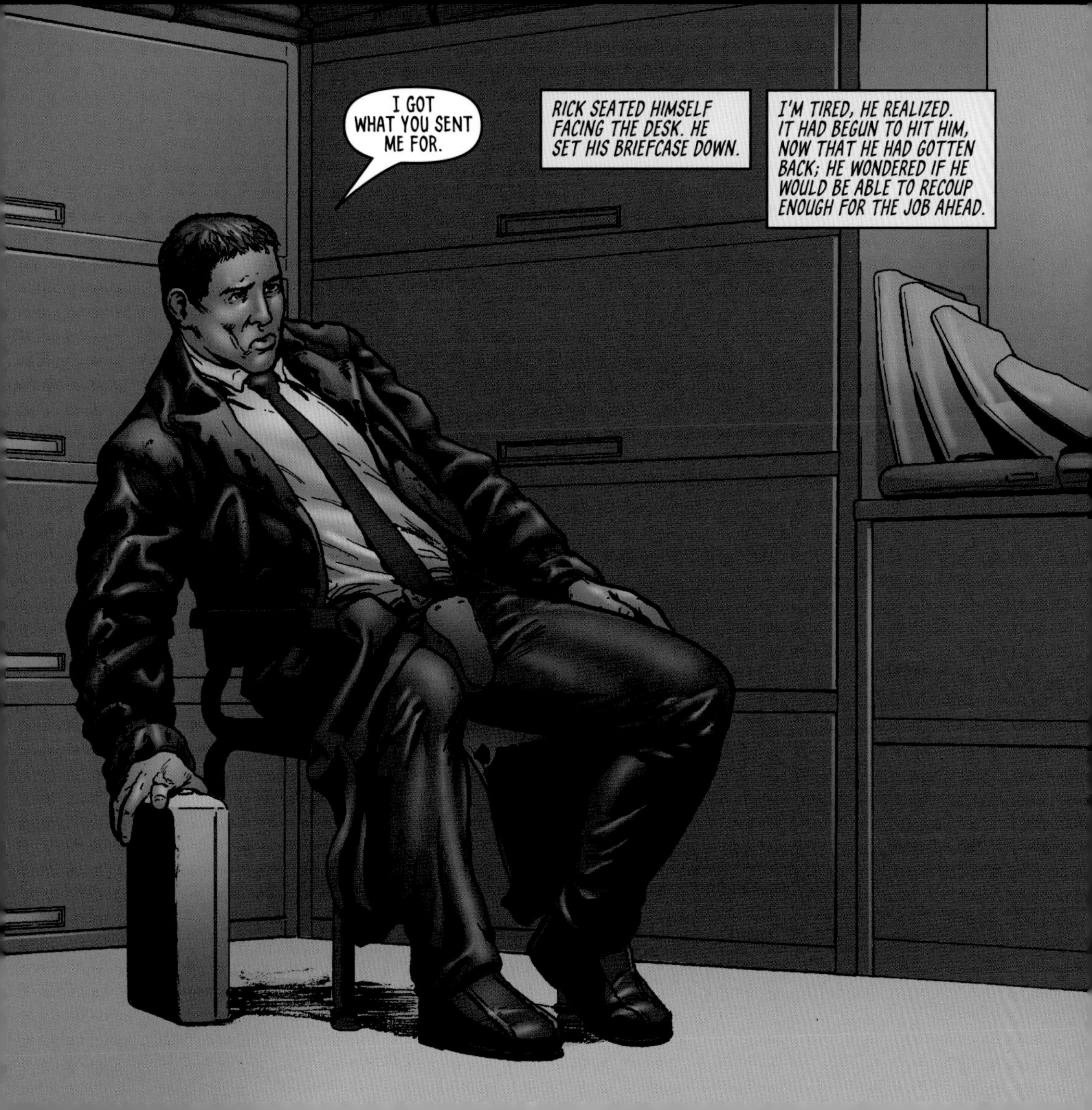
I GOT WHAT YOU SENT ME FOR.
RICK SEATED HIMSELF FACING THE DESK. HE SET HIS BRIEFCASE DOWN.
I'M TIRED, HE REALIZED. IT HAD BEGUN TO HIT HIM, NOW THAT HE HAD GOTTEN BACK; HE WONDERED IF HE WOULD BE ABLE TO RECOUP ENOUGH FOR THE JOB AHEAD.

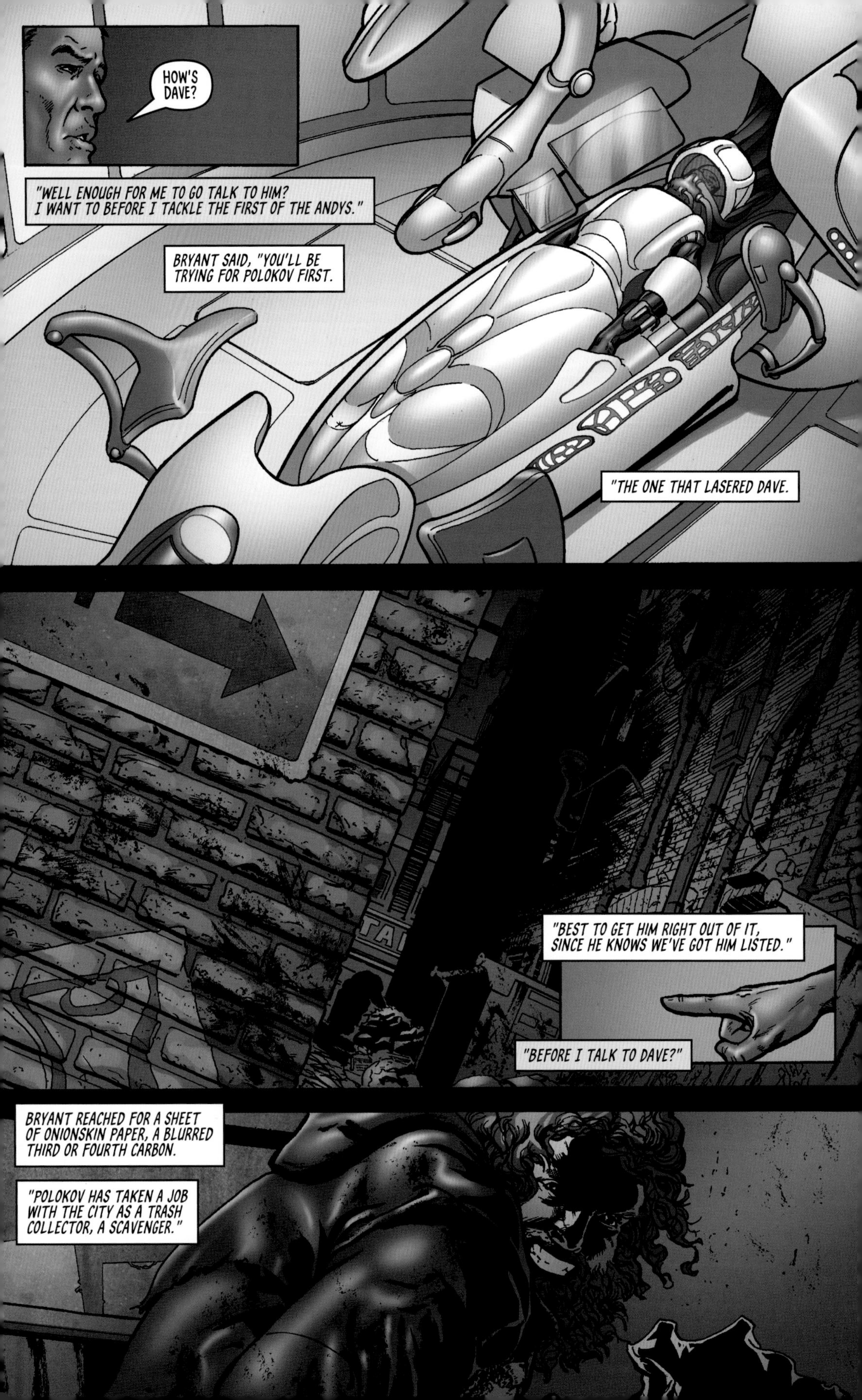
HOW'S DAVE?
"WELL ENOUGH FOR ME TO GO TALK TO HIM? I WANT TO BEFORE I TACKLE THE FIRST OF THE ANDYS."
BRYANT SAID, "YOU'LL BE TRYING FOR POLOKOV FIRST.
"THE ONE THAT LASERED DAVE.
"BEST TO GET HIM RIGHT OUT OF IT, SINCE HE KNOWS WE'VE GOT HIM LISTED."
"BEFORE I TALK TO DAVE?"
BRYANT REACHED FOR A SHEET OF ONIONSKIN PAPER, A BLURRED THIRD OR FOURTH CARBON.
"POLOKOV HAS TAKEN A JOB WITH THE CITY AS A TRASH COLLECTOR, A SCAVENGER."

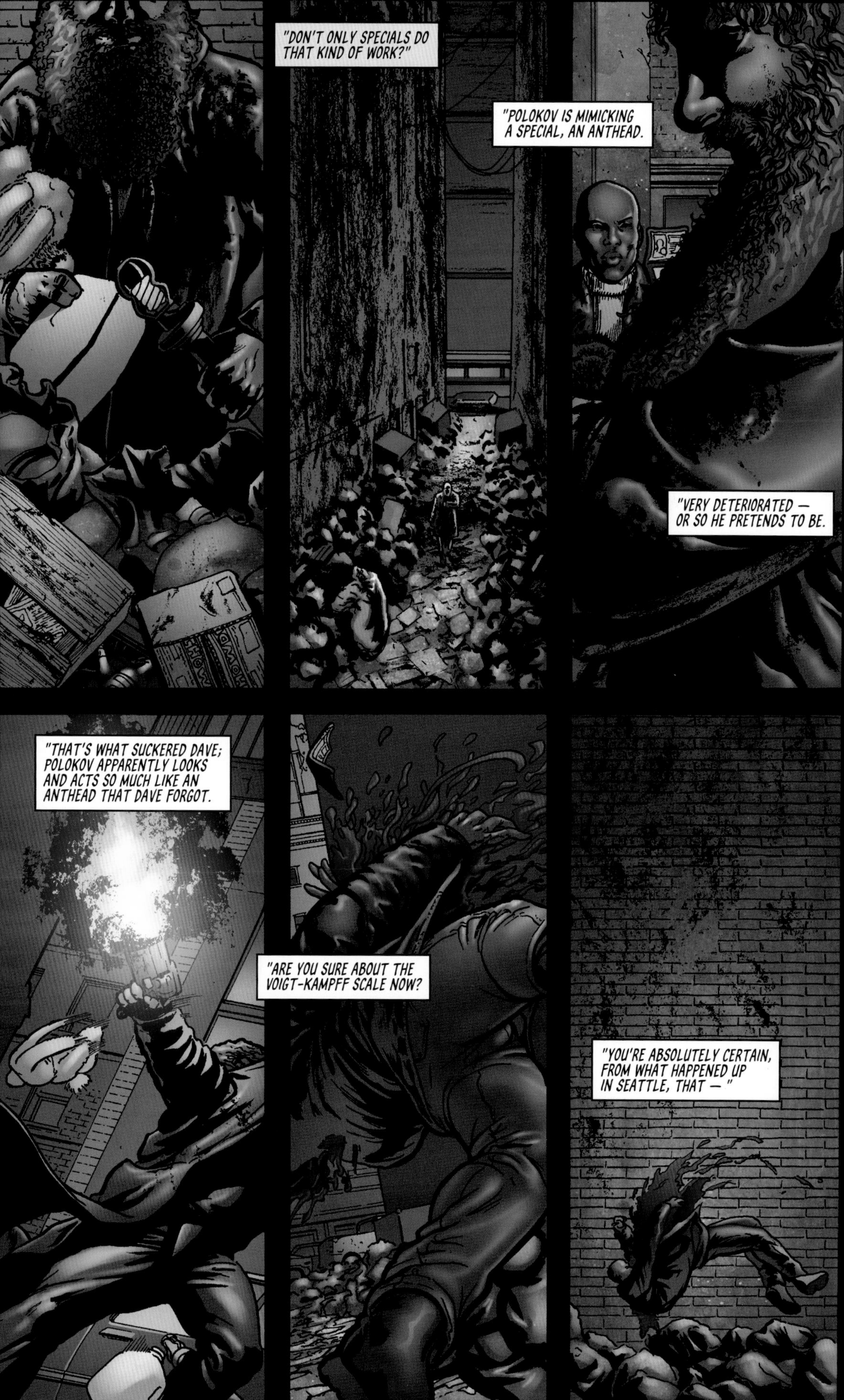
"DON'T ONLY SPECIALS DO THAT KIND OF WORK?"
"POLOKOV IS MIMICKING A SPECIAL, AN ANTHEAD.
"VERY DETERIORATED — OR SO HE PRETENDS TO BE.
"THAT'S WHAT SUCKERED DAVE; POLOKOV APPARENTLY LOOKS AND ACTS SO MUCH LIKE AN ANTHEAD THAT DAVE FORGOT.
"ARE YOU SURE ABOUT THE VOIGT-KAMPFF SCALE NOW?
"YOU'RE ABSOLUTELY CERTAIN, FROM WHAT HAPPENED UP IN SEATTLE, THAT — "

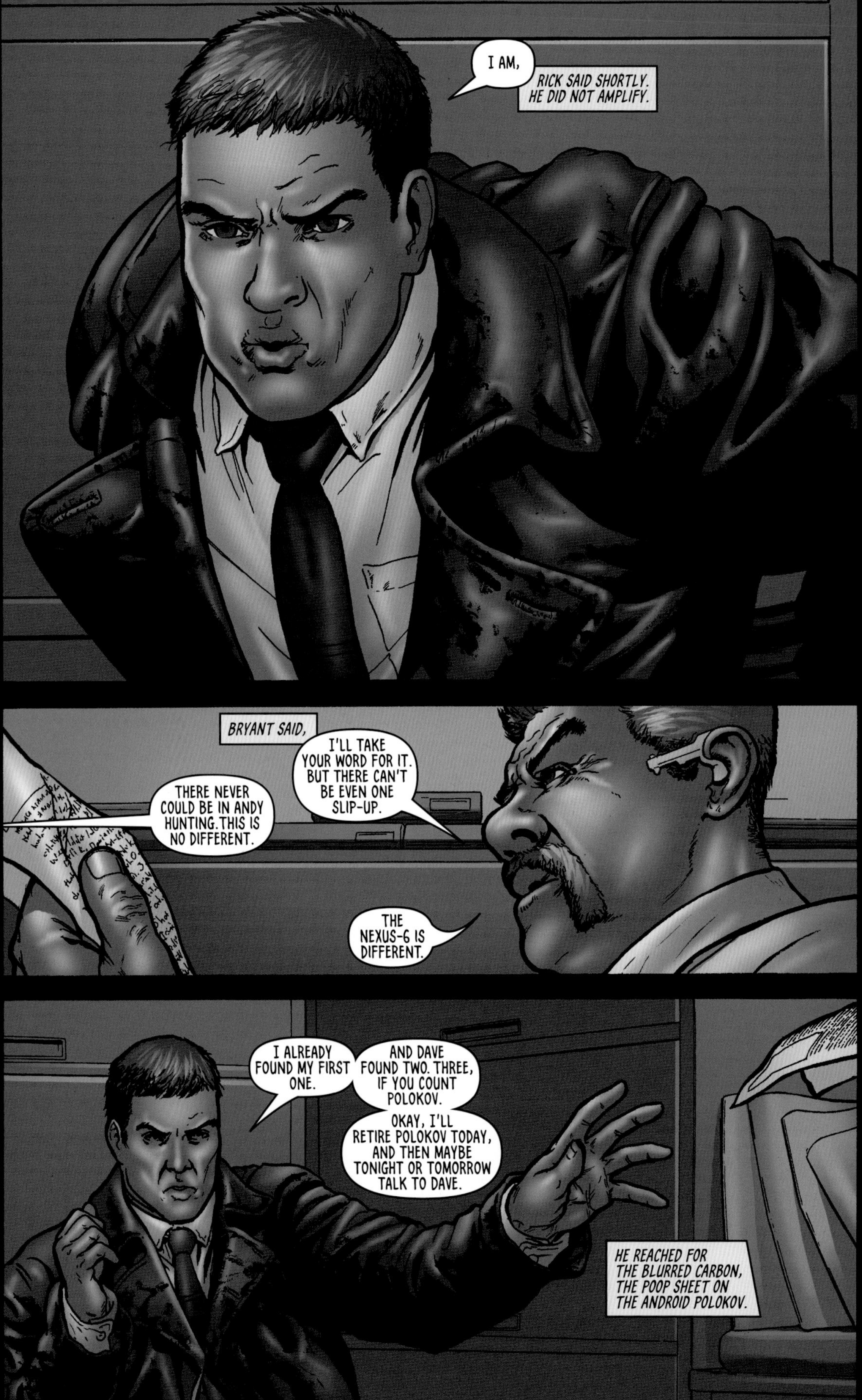
I AM,
RICK SAID SHORTLY. HE DID NOT AMPLIFY.
BRYANT SAID,
I'LL TAKE YOUR WORD FOR IT. BUT THERE CAN'T BE EVEN ONE SLIP-UP.
THERE NEVER COULD BE IN ANDY HUNTING. THIS IS NO DIFFERENT.
THE NEXUS-6 IS DIFFERENT.
I ALREADY FOUND MY FIRST ONE.
AND DAVE FOUND TWO. THREE, IF YOU COUNT POLOKOV.
OKAY, I'LL RETIRE POLOKOV TODAY, AND THEN MAYBE TONIGHT OR TOMORROW TALK TO DAVE.
HE REACHED FOR THE BLURRED CARBON, THE POOP SHEET ON THE ANDROID POLOKOV.

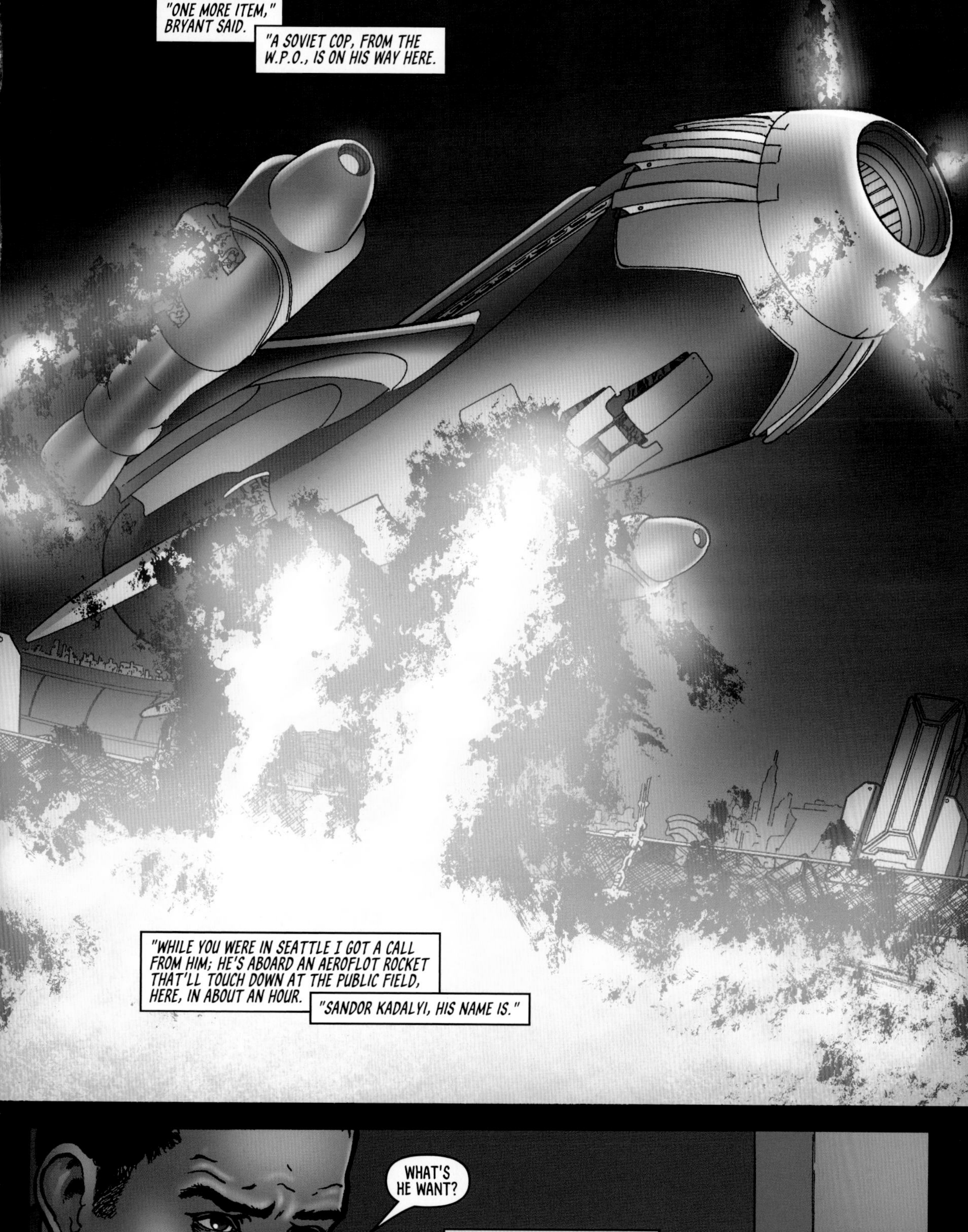
"ONE MORE ITEM," BRYANT SAID.
"A SOVIET COP, FROM THE W.P.O., IS ON HIS WAY HERE.
"WHILE YOU WERE IN SEATTLE I GOT A CALL FROM HIM; HE'S ABOARD AN AEROFLOT ROCKET THAT'LL TOUCH DOWN AT THE PUBLIC FIELD, HERE, IN ABOUT AN HOUR.
"SANDOR KADALYI, HIS NAME IS."
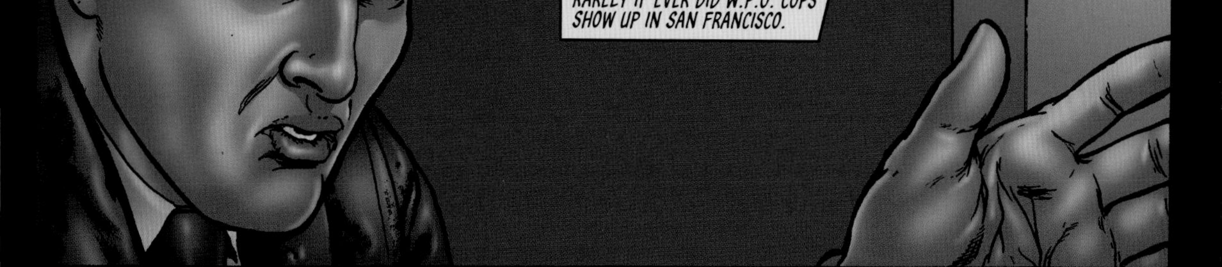
WHAT'S HE WANT?
RARELY IF EVER DID W.P.O. COPS SHOW UP IN SAN FRANCISCO.

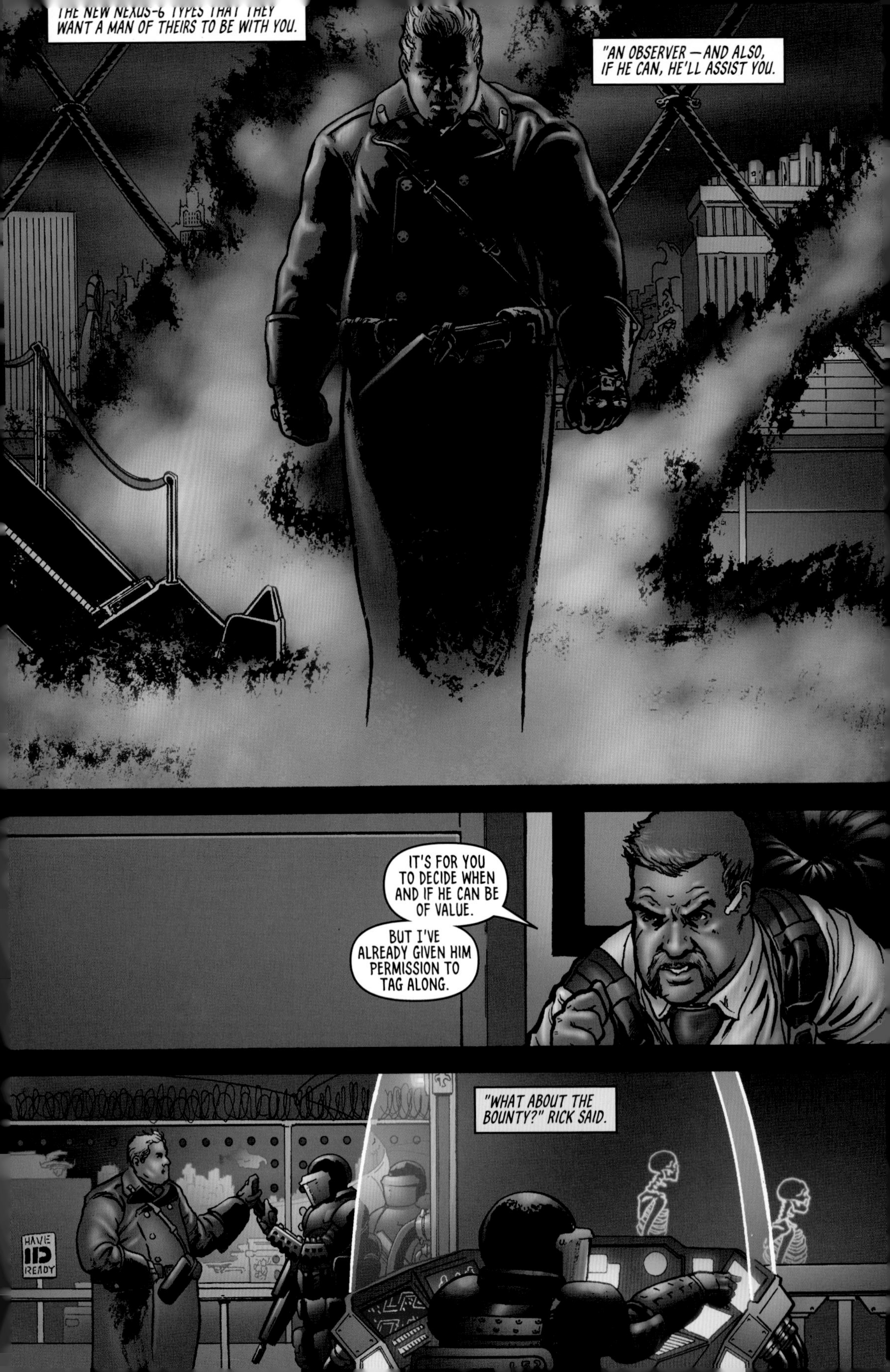
THE NEW NEXUS-6 TYPES THAT THEY WANT A MAN OF THEIRS TO BE WITH YOU.
"AN OBSERVER — AND ALSO, IF HE CAN, HE'LL ASSIST YOU.
IT'S FOR YOU TO DECIDE WHEN AND IF HE CAN BE OF VALUE.
BUT I'VE ALREADY GIVEN HIM PERMISSION TO TAG ALONG.
"WHAT ABOUT THE BOUNTY?" RICK SAID.
HAVE ID READY

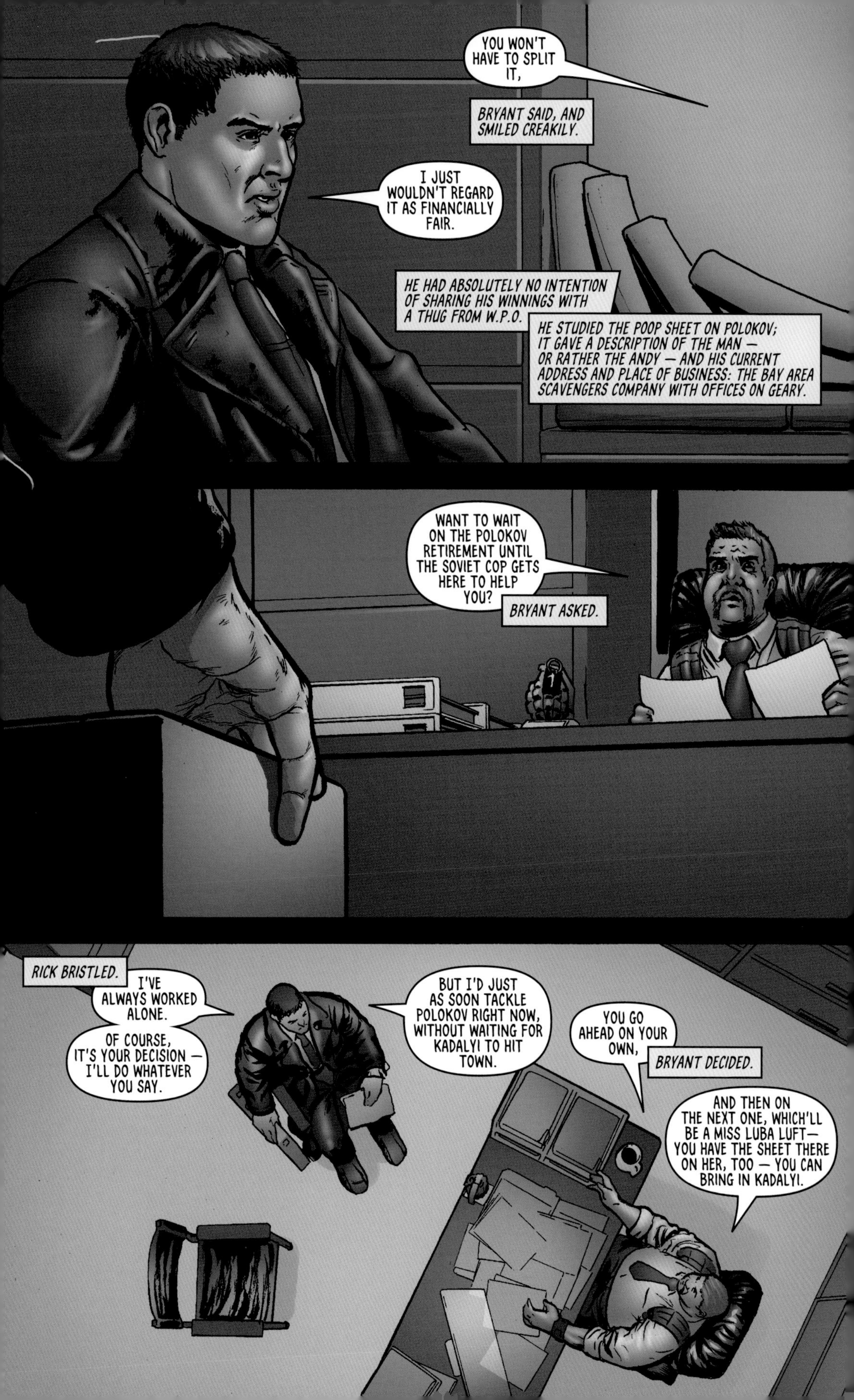
YOU WON'T HAVE TO SPLIT IT,
BRYANT SAID, AND SMILED CREAKILY.
I JUST WOULDN'T REGARD IT AS FINANCIALLY FAIR.
HE HAD ABSOLUTELY NO INTENTION OF SHARING HIS WINNINGS WITH A THUG FROM W.P.O.
HE STUDIED THE POOP SHEET ON POLOKOV; IT GAVE A DESCRIPTION OF THE MAN — OR RATHER THE ANDY — AND HIS CURRENT ADDRESS AND PLACE OF BUSINESS: THE BAY AREA SCAVENGERS COMPANY WITH OFFICES ON GEARY.
WANT TO WAIT ON THE POLOKOV RETIREMENT UNTIL THE SOVIET COP GETS HERE TO HELP YOU?
BRYANT ASKED.
RICK BRISTLED.
I'VE ALWAYS WORKED ALONE.
OF COURSE, IT'S YOUR DECISION — I'LL DO WHATEVER YOU SAY.
BUT I'D JUST AS SOON TACKLE POLOKOV RIGHT NOW, WITHOUT WAITING FOR KADALYI TO HIT TOWN.
YOU GO AHEAD ON YOUR OWN,
BRYANT DECIDED.
AND THEN ON THE NEXT ONE, WHICH'LL BE A MISS LUBA LUFT— YOU HAVE THE SHEET THERE ON HER, TOO — YOU CAN BRING IN KADALYI.

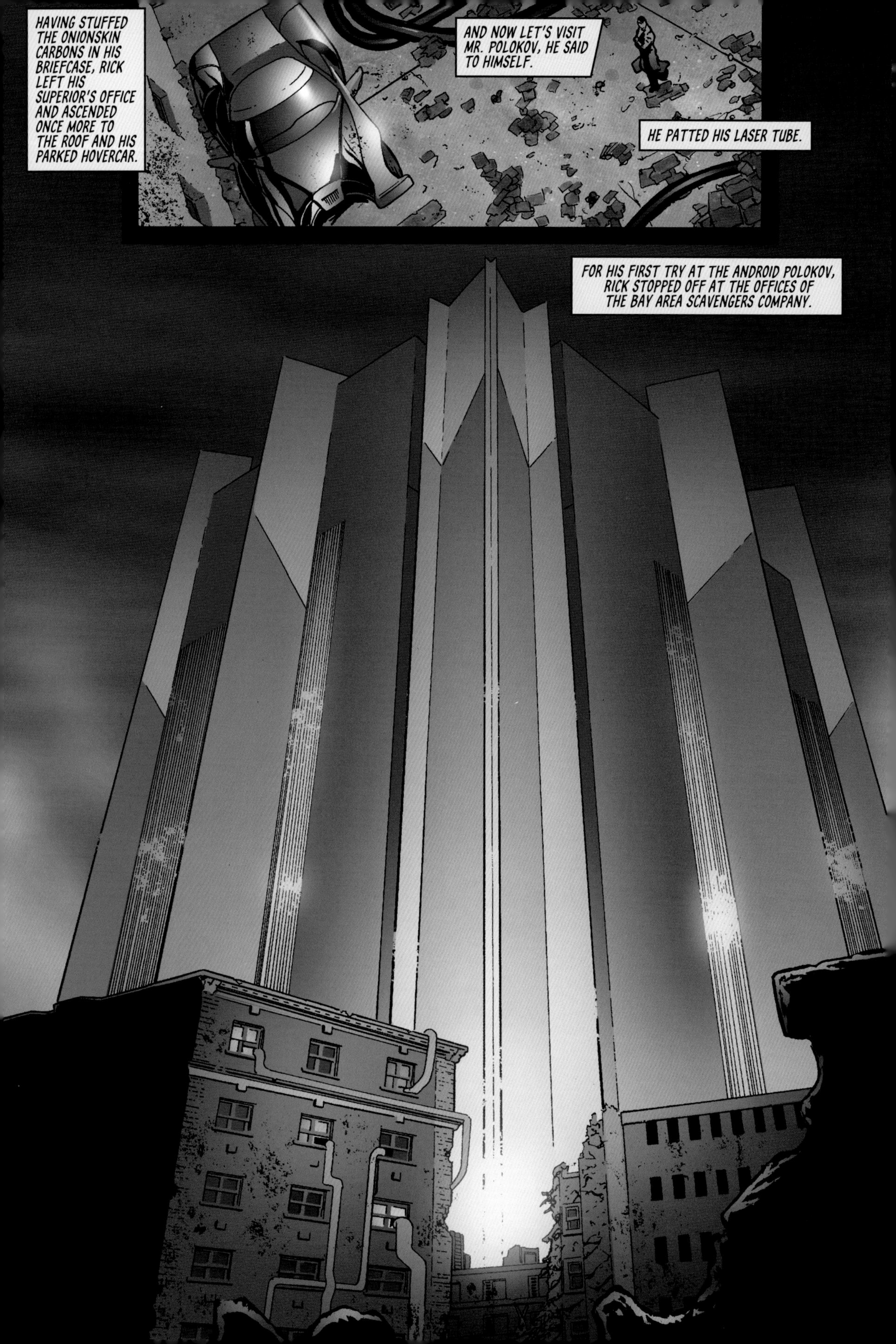
HAVING STUFFED THE ONIONSKIN CARBONS IN HIS BRIEFCASE, RICK LEFT HIS SUPERIOR'S OFFICE AND ASCENDED ONCE MORE TO THE ROOF AND HIS PARKED HOVERCAR.
AND NOW LET'S VISIT MR. POLOKOV, HE SAID TO HIMSELF.
HE PATTED HIS LASER TUBE.
FOR HIS FIRST TRY AT THE ANDROID POLOKOV, RICK STOPPED OFF AT THE OFFICES OF THE BAY AREA SCAVENGERS COMPANY.

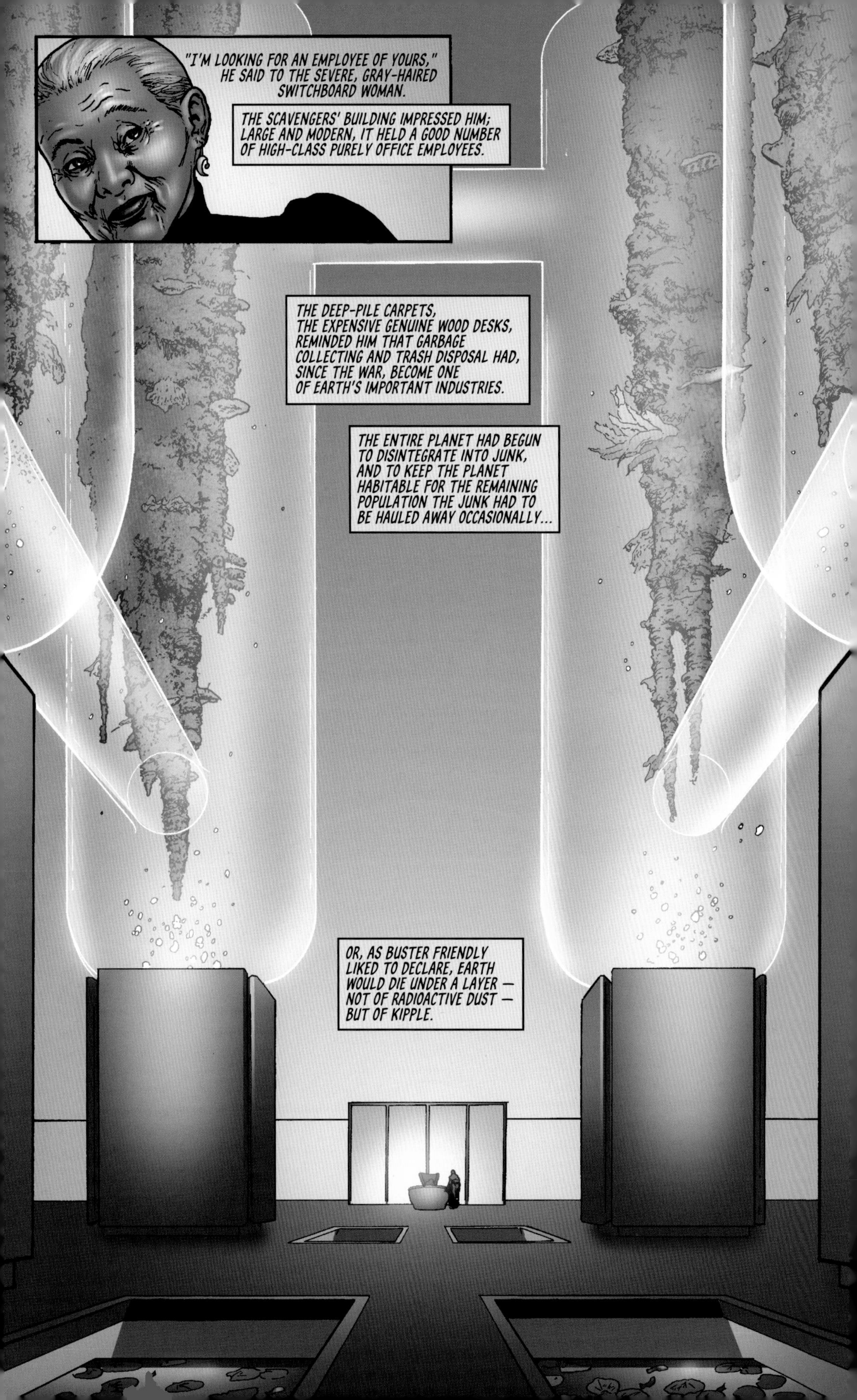
"I'M LOOKING FOR AN EMPLOYEE OF YOURS," HE SAID TO THE SEVERE, GRAY-HAIRED SWITCHBOARD WOMAN.
THE SCAVENGERS' BUILDING IMPRESSED HIM; LARGE AND MODERN, IT HELD A GOOD NUMBER OF HIGH-CLASS PURELY OFFICE EMPLOYEES.
THE DEEP-PILE CARPETS, THE EXPENSIVE GENUINE WOOD DESKS, REMINDED HIM THAT GARBAGE COLLECTING AND TRASH DISPOSAL HAD, SINCE THE WAR, BECOME ONE OF EARTH'S IMPORTANT INDUSTRIES.
THE ENTIRE PLANET HAD BEGUN TO DISINTEGRATE INTO JUNK, AND TO KEEP THE PLANET HABITABLE FOR THE REMAINING POPULATION THE JUNK HAD TO BE HAULED AWAY OCCASIONALLY...
OR, AS BUSTER FRIENDLY LIKED TO DECLARE, EARTH WOULD DIE UNDER A LAYER — NOT OF RADIOACTIVE DUST — BUT OF KIPPLE.

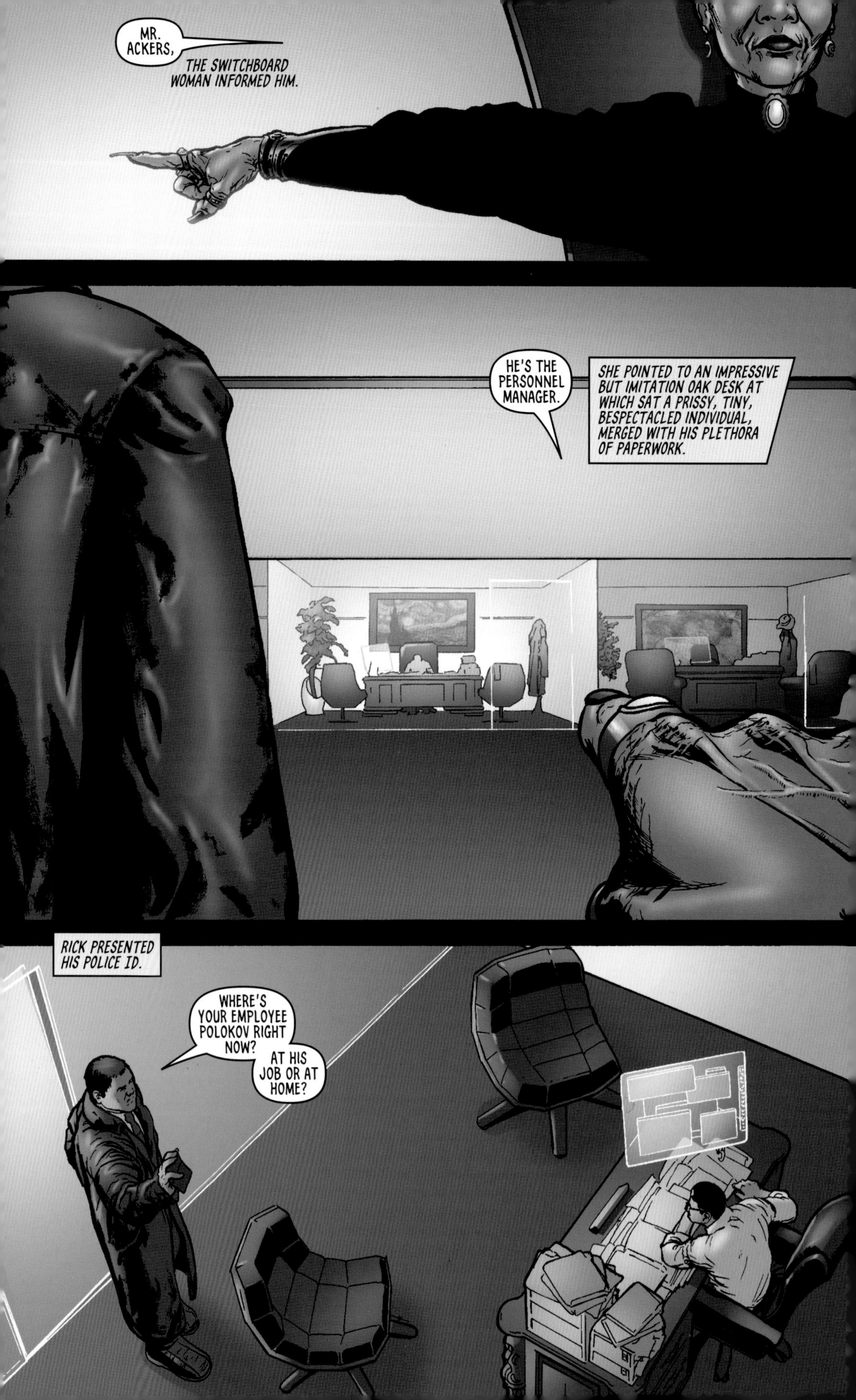
MR. ACKERS,
THE SWITCHBOARD WOMAN INFORMED HIM.
HE'S THE PERSONNEL MANAGER.
SHE POINTED TO AN IMPRESSIVE BUT IMITATION OAK DESK AT WHICH SAT A PRISSY, TINY, BESPECTACLED INDIVIDUAL, MERGED WITH HIS PLETHORA OF PAPERWORK.
RICK PRESENTED HIS POLICE ID.
WHERE'S YOUR EMPLOYEE POLOKOV RIGHT NOW?
AT HIS JOB OR AT HOME?

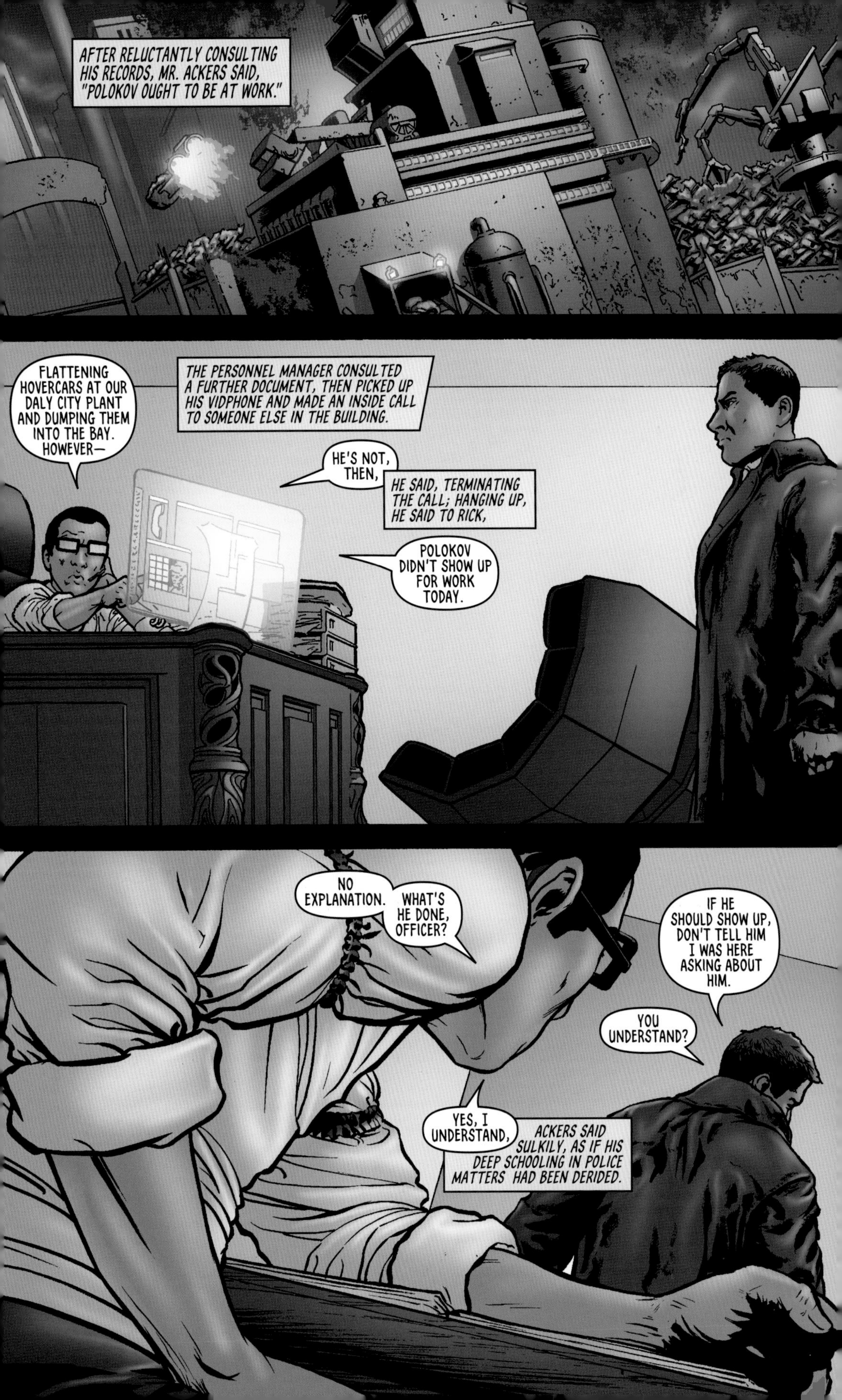
AFTER RELUCTANTLY CONSULTING HIS RECORDS, MR. ACKERS SAID, "POLOKOV OUGHT TO BE AT WORK."
FLATTENING HOVERCARS AT OUR DALY CITY PLANT AND DUMPING THEM INTO THE BAY. HOWEVER—
THE PERSONNEL MANAGER CONSULTED A FURTHER DOCUMENT, THEN PICKED UP HIS VIDPHONE AND MADE AN INSIDE CALL TO SOMEONE ELSE IN THE BUILDING.
HE'S NOT, THEN,
HE SAID, TERMINATING THE CALL; HANGING UP, HE SAID TO RICK,
POLOKOV DIDN'T SHOW UP FOR WORK TODAY.
NO EXPLANATION.
WHAT'S HE DONE, OFFICER?
IF HE SHOULD SHOW UP, DON'T TELL HIM I WAS HERE ASKING ABOUT HIM.
YOU UNDERSTAND?
YES, I UNDERSTAND,
ACKERS SAID SULKILY, AS IF HIS DEEP SCHOOLING IN POLICE MATTERS HAD BEEN DERIDED.

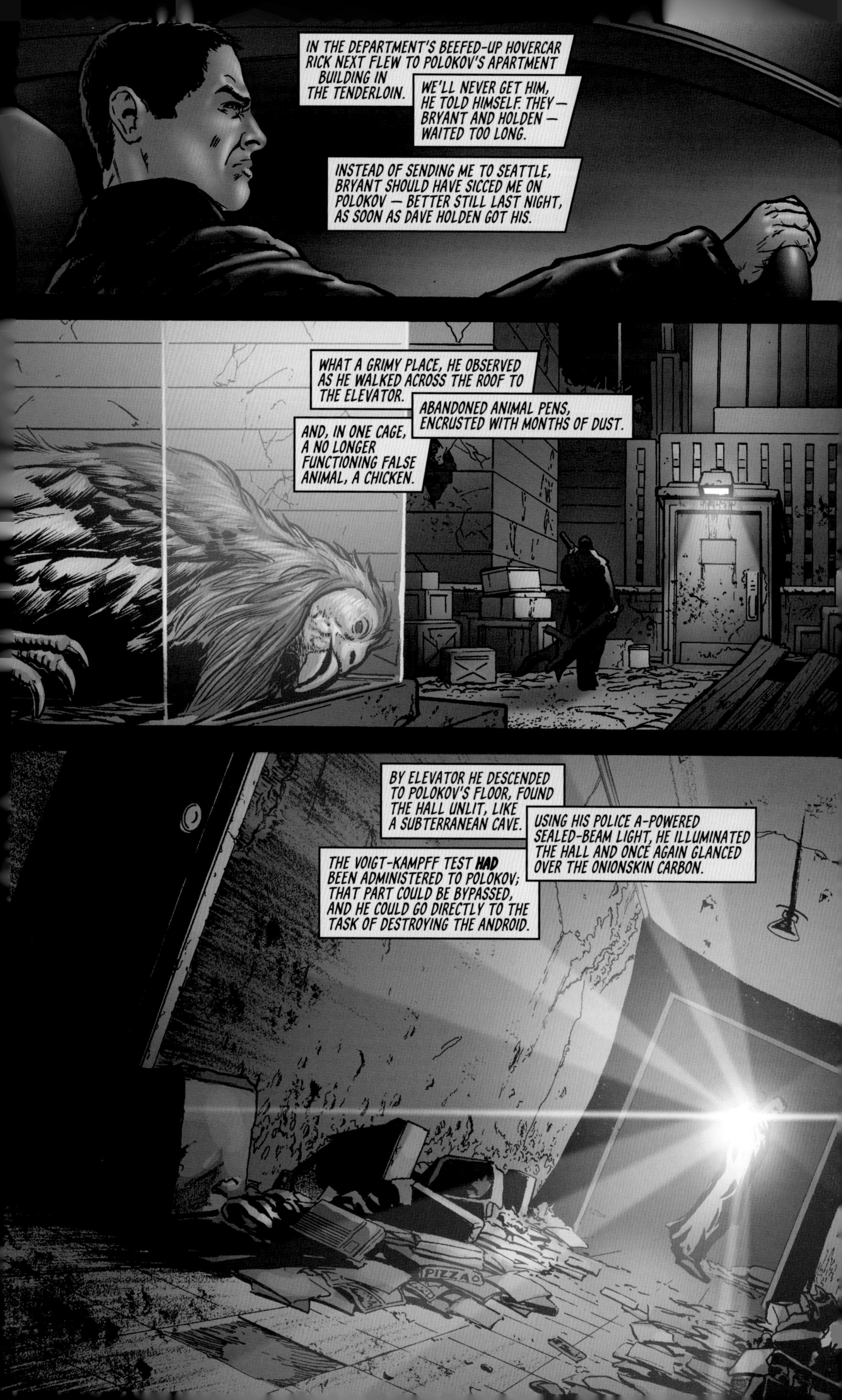
IN THE DEPARTMENT'S BEEFED-UP HOVERCAR RICK NEXT FLEW TO POLOKOV'S APARTMENT BUILDING IN THE TENDERLOIN.
WE'LL NEVER GET HIM, HE TOLD HIMSELF. THEY — BRYANT AND HOLDEN — WAITED TOO LONG.
INSTEAD OF SENDING ME TO SEATTLE, BRYANT SHOULD HAVE SICCED ME ON POLOKOV — BETTER STILL LAST NIGHT, AS SOON AS DAVE HOLDEN GOT HIS.
WHAT A GRIMY PLACE, HE OBSERVED AS HE WALKED ACROSS THE ROOF TO THE ELEVATOR.
ABANDONED ANIMAL PENS, ENCRUSTED WITH MONTHS OF DUST.
AND, IN ONE CAGE, A NO LONGER FUNCTIONING FALSE ANIMAL, A CHICKEN.
BY ELEVATOR HE DESCENDED TO POLOKOV'S FLOOR, FOUND THE HALL UNLIT, LIKE A SUBTERRANEAN CAVE.
USING HIS POLICE A-POWERED SEALED-BEAM LIGHT, HE ILLUMINATED THE HALL AND ONCE AGAIN GLANCED OVER THE ONIONSKIN CARBON.
THE VOIGT-KAMPFF TEST **HAD** BEEN ADMINISTERED TO POLOKOV; THAT PART COULD BE BYPASSED, AND HE COULD GO DIRECTLY TO THE TASK OF DESTROYING THE ANDROID.
PIZZA

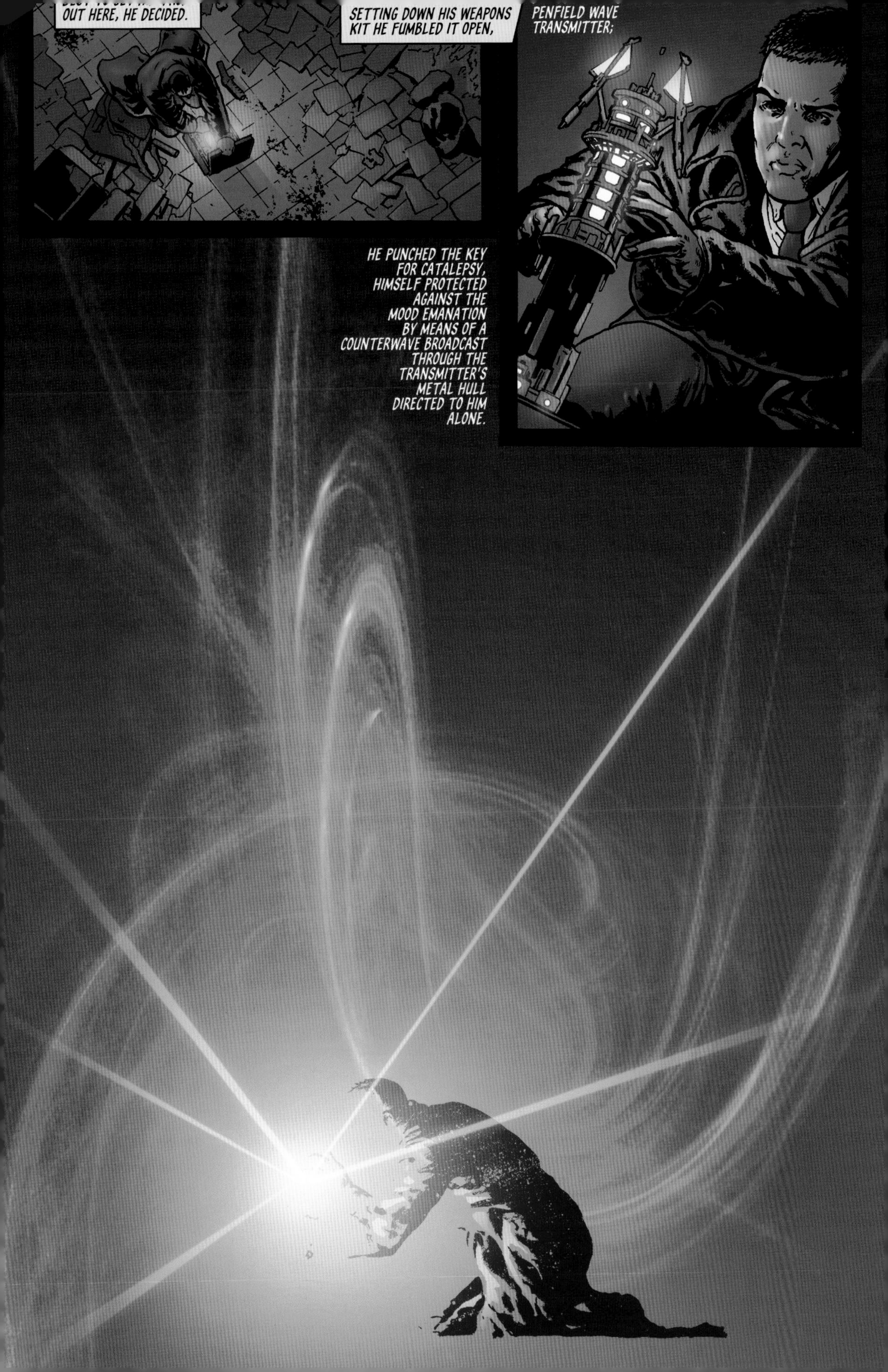
OUT HERE, HE DECIDED.
SETTING DOWN HIS WEAPONS KIT HE FUMBLED IT OPEN,
PENFIELD WAVE TRANSMITTER;
HE PUNCHED THE KEY FOR CATALEPSY, HIMSELF PROTECTED AGAINST THE MOOD EMANATION BY MEANS OF A COUNTERWAVE BROADCAST THROUGH THE TRANSMITTER'S METAL HULL DIRECTED TO HIM ALONE.

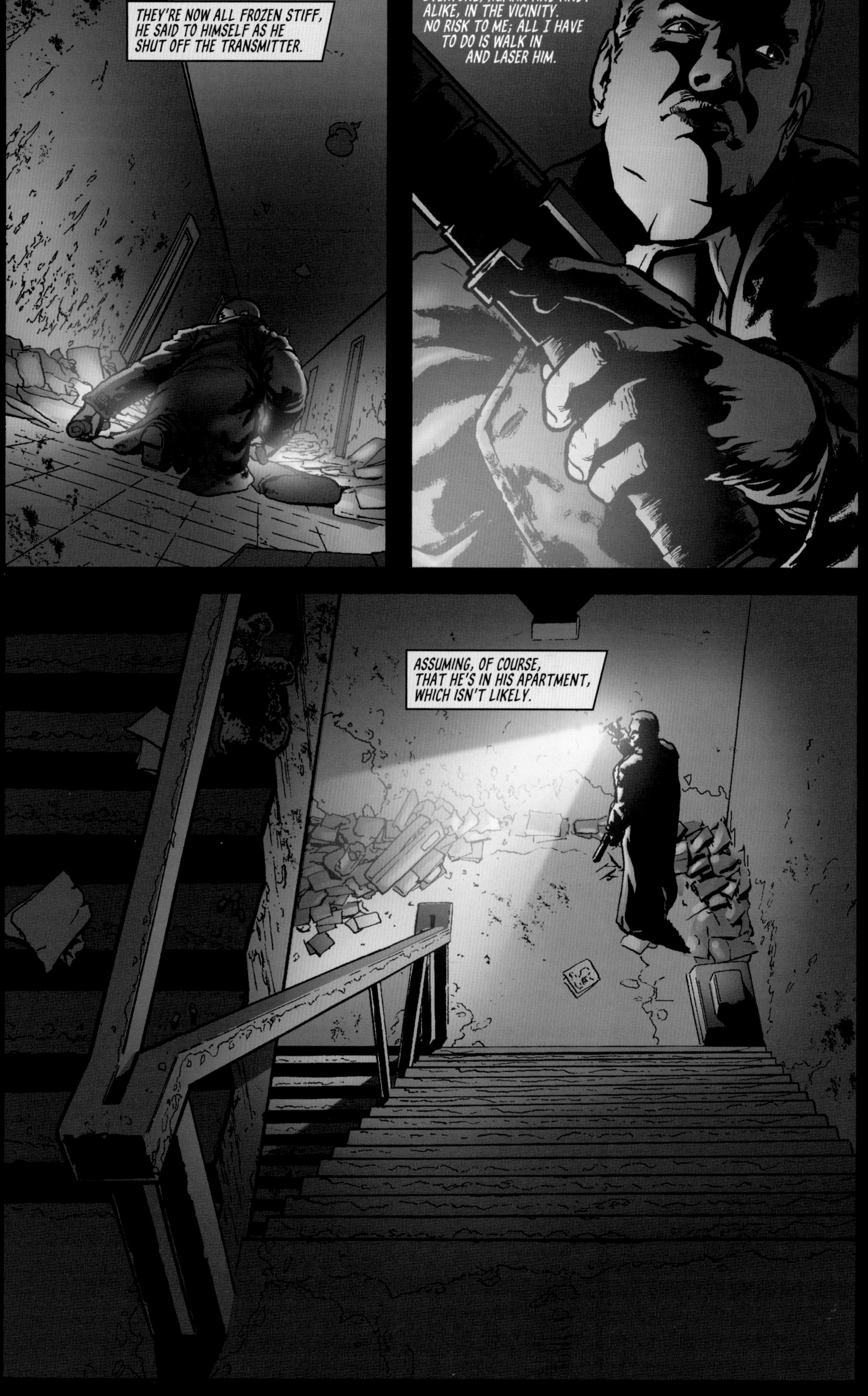
THEY'RE NOW ALL FROZEN STIFF, HE SAID TO HIMSELF AS HE SHUT OFF THE TRANSMITTER.
ALIKE, IN THE VICINITY. NO RISK TO ME; ALL I HAVE TO DO IS WALK IN AND LASER HIM.
ASSUMING, OF COURSE, THAT HE'S IN HIS APARTMENT, WHICH ISN'T LIKELY.

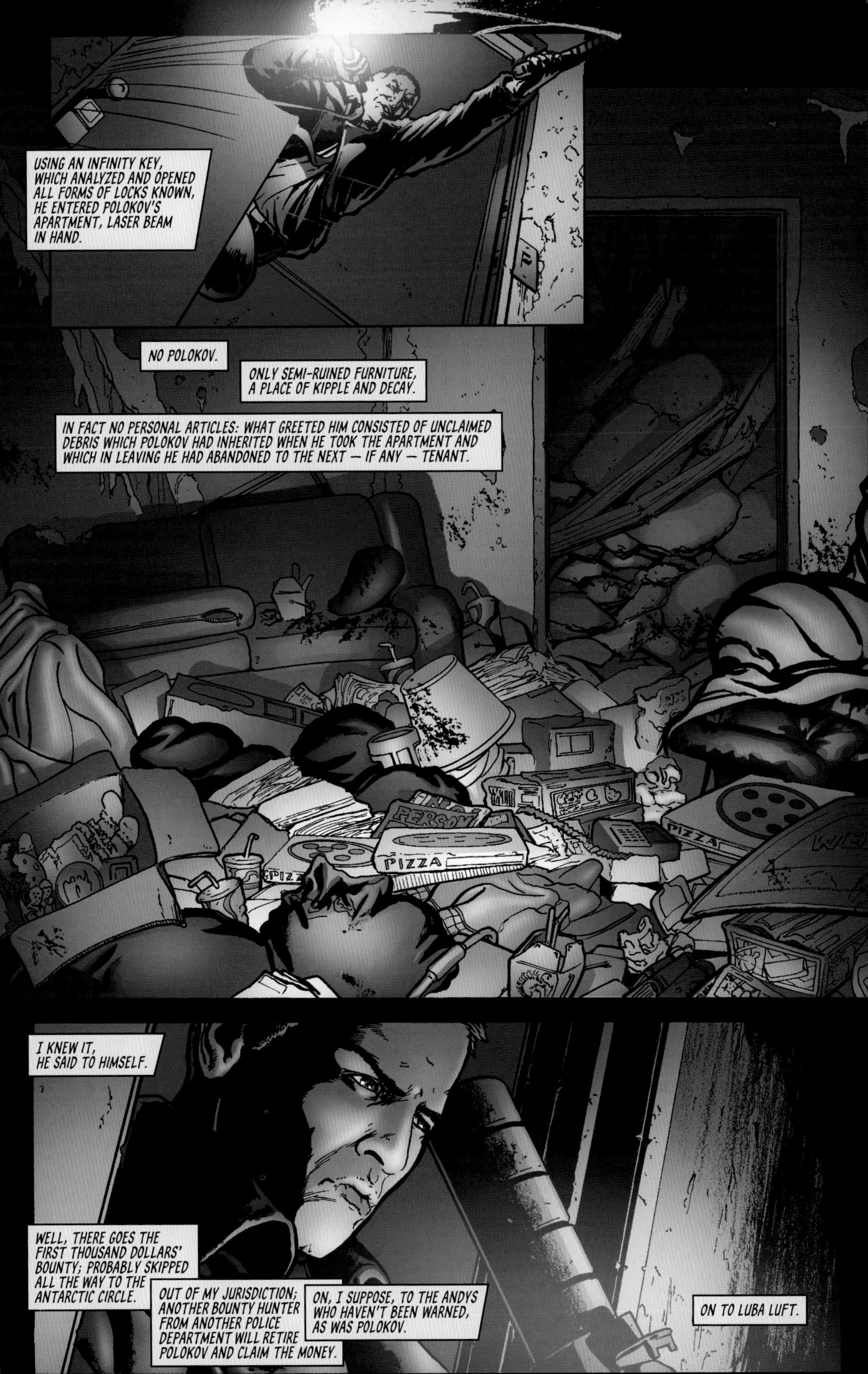
USING AN INFINITY KEY, WHICH ANALYZED AND OPENED ALL FORMS OF LOCKS KNOWN, HE ENTERED POLOKOV'S APARTMENT, LASER BEAM IN HAND.
NO POLOKOV.
ONLY SEMI-RUINED FURNITURE, A PLACE OF KIPPLE AND DECAY.
IN FACT NO PERSONAL ARTICLES: WHAT GREETED HIM CONSISTED OF UNCLAIMED DEBRIS WHICH POLOKOV HAD INHERITED WHEN HE TOOK THE APARTMENT AND WHICH IN LEAVING HE HAD ABANDONED TO THE NEXT — IF ANY — TENANT.
PIZZA
PIZZA
I KNEW IT, HE SAID TO HIMSELF.
WELL, THERE GOES THE FIRST THOUSAND DOLLARS' BOUNTY; PROBABLY SKIPPED ALL THE WAY TO THE ANTARCTIC CIRCLE.
OUT OF MY JURISDICTION; ANOTHER BOUNTY HUNTER FROM ANOTHER POLICE DEPARTMENT WILL RETIRE POLOKOV AND CLAIM THE MONEY.
ON, I SUPPOSE, TO THE ANDYS WHO HAVEN'T BEEN WARNED, AS WAS POLOKOV.
ON TO LUBA LUFT.

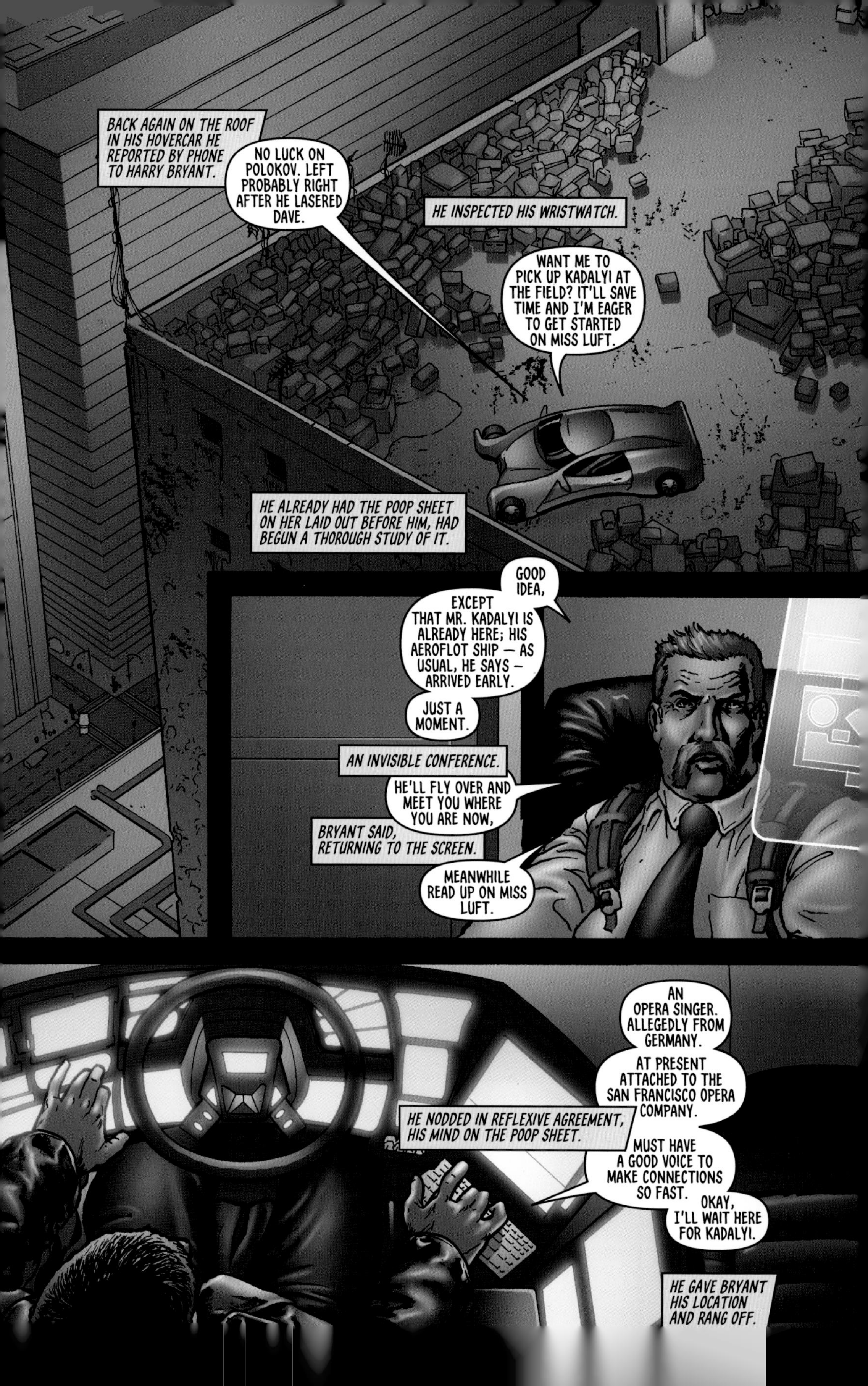
BACK AGAIN ON THE ROOF IN HIS HOVERCAR HE REPORTED BY PHONE TO HARRY BRYANT.
NO LUCK ON POLOKOV. LEFT PROBABLY RIGHT AFTER HE LASERED DAVE.
HE INSPECTED HIS WRISTWATCH.
WANT ME TO PICK UP KADALYI AT THE FIELD? IT'LL SAVE TIME AND I'M EAGER TO GET STARTED ON MISS LUFT.
HE ALREADY HAD THE POOP SHEET ON HER LAID OUT BEFORE HIM, HAD BEGUN A THOROUGH STUDY OF IT.
GOOD IDEA,
EXCEPT THAT MR. KADALYI IS ALREADY HERE; HIS AEROFLOT SHIP — AS USUAL, HE SAYS — ARRIVED EARLY.
JUST A MOMENT.
AN INVISIBLE CONFERENCE.
HE'LL FLY OVER AND MEET YOU WHERE YOU ARE NOW,
BRYANT SAID, RETURNING TO THE SCREEN.
MEANWHILE READ UP ON MISS LUFT.
AN OPERA SINGER. ALLEGEDLY FROM GERMANY.
AT PRESENT ATTACHED TO THE SAN FRANCISCO OPERA COMPANY.
HE NODDED IN REFLEXIVE AGREEMENT, HIS MIND ON THE POOP SHEET.
MUST HAVE A GOOD VOICE TO MAKE CONNECTIONS SO FAST.
OKAY, I'LL WAIT HERE FOR KADALYI.
HE GAVE BRYANT HIS LOCATION AND RANG OFF.

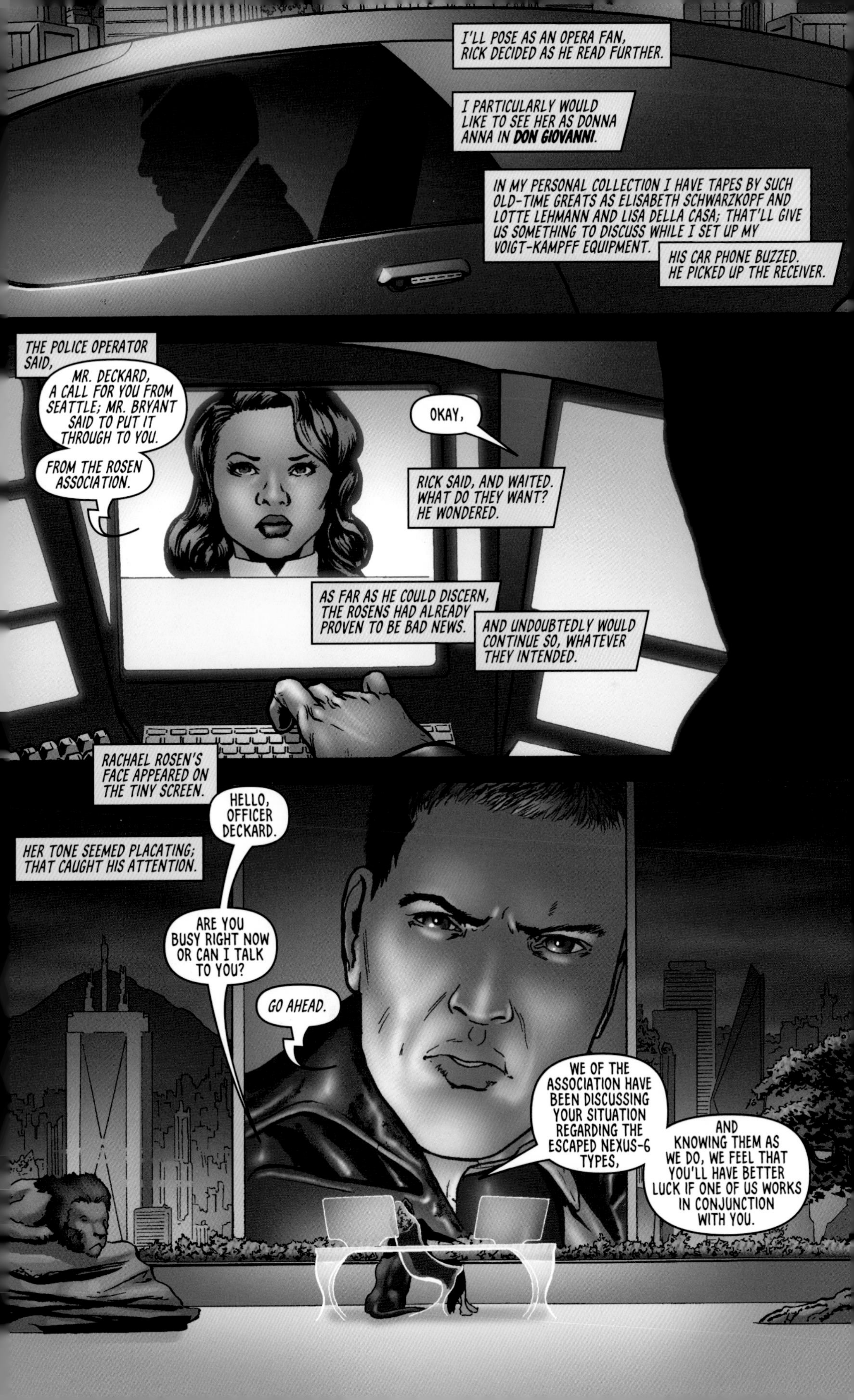
I'LL POSE AS AN OPERA FAN, RICK DECIDED AS HE READ FURTHER.
I PARTICULARLY WOULD LIKE TO SEE HER AS DONNA ANNA IN **DON GIOVANNI**.
IN MY PERSONAL COLLECTION I HAVE TAPES BY SUCH OLD-TIME GREATS AS ELISABETH SCHWARZKOPF AND LOTTE LEHMANN AND LISA DELLA CASA; THAT'LL GIVE US SOMETHING TO DISCUSS WHILE I SET UP MY VOIGT-KAMPFF EQUIPMENT.
HIS CAR PHONE BUZZED. HE PICKED UP THE RECEIVER.
THE POLICE OPERATOR SAID,
MR. DECKARD, A CALL FOR YOU FROM SEATTLE; MR. BRYANT SAID TO PUT IT THROUGH TO YOU.
FROM THE ROSEN ASSOCIATION.
OKAY,
RICK SAID, AND WAITED. WHAT DO THEY WANT? HE WONDERED.
AS FAR AS HE COULD DISCERN, THE ROSENS HAD ALREADY PROVEN TO BE BAD NEWS.
AND UNDOUBTEDLY WOULD CONTINUE SO, WHATEVER THEY INTENDED.
RACHAEL ROSEN'S FACE APPEARED ON THE TINY SCREEN.
HELLO, OFFICER DECKARD.
HER TONE SEEMED PLACATING; THAT CAUGHT HIS ATTENTION.
ARE YOU BUSY RIGHT NOW OR CAN I TALK TO YOU?
GO AHEAD.
WE OF THE ASSOCIATION HAVE BEEN DISCUSSING YOUR SITUATION REGARDING THE ESCAPED NEXUS-6 TYPES,
AND KNOWING THEM AS WE DO, WE FEEL THAT YOU'LL HAVE BETTER LUCK IF ONE OF US WORKS IN CONJUNCTION WITH YOU.

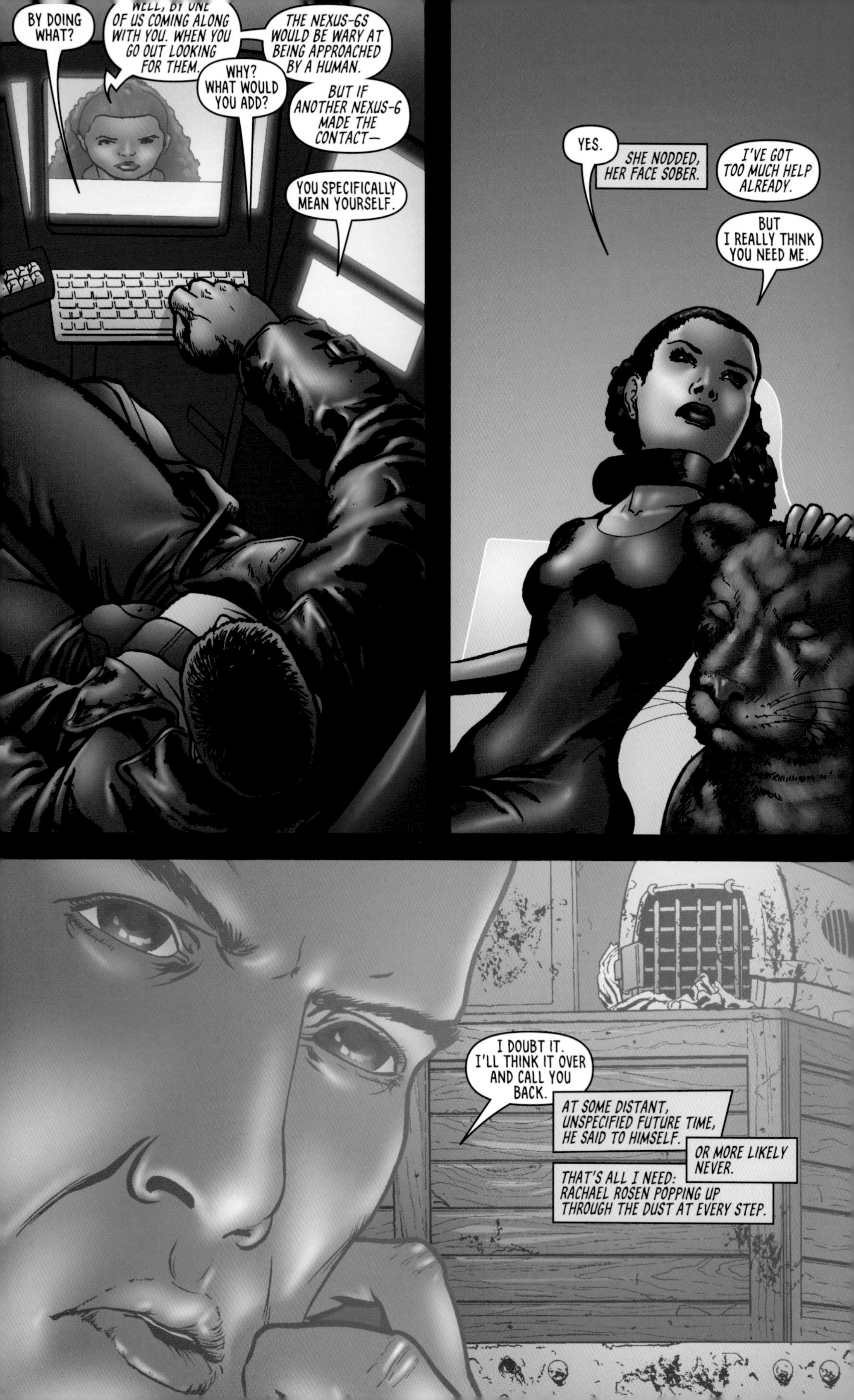
BY DOING WHAT?
WELL, BY ONE OF US COMING ALONG WITH YOU. WHEN YOU GO OUT LOOKING FOR THEM.
THE NEXUS-6S WOULD BE WARY AT BEING APPROACHED BY A HUMAN.
WHY? WHAT WOULD YOU ADD?
BUT IF ANOTHER NEXUS-6 MADE THE CONTACT—
YOU SPECIFICALLY MEAN YOURSELF.
YES.
SHE NODDED, HER FACE SOBER.
I'VE GOT TOO MUCH HELP ALREADY.
BUT I REALLY THINK YOU NEED ME.
I DOUBT IT. I'LL THINK IT OVER AND CALL YOU BACK.
AT SOME DISTANT, UNSPECIFIED FUTURE TIME, HE SAID TO HIMSELF.
OR MORE LIKELY NEVER.
THAT'S ALL I NEED: RACHAEL ROSEN POPPING UP THROUGH THE DUST AT EVERY STEP.

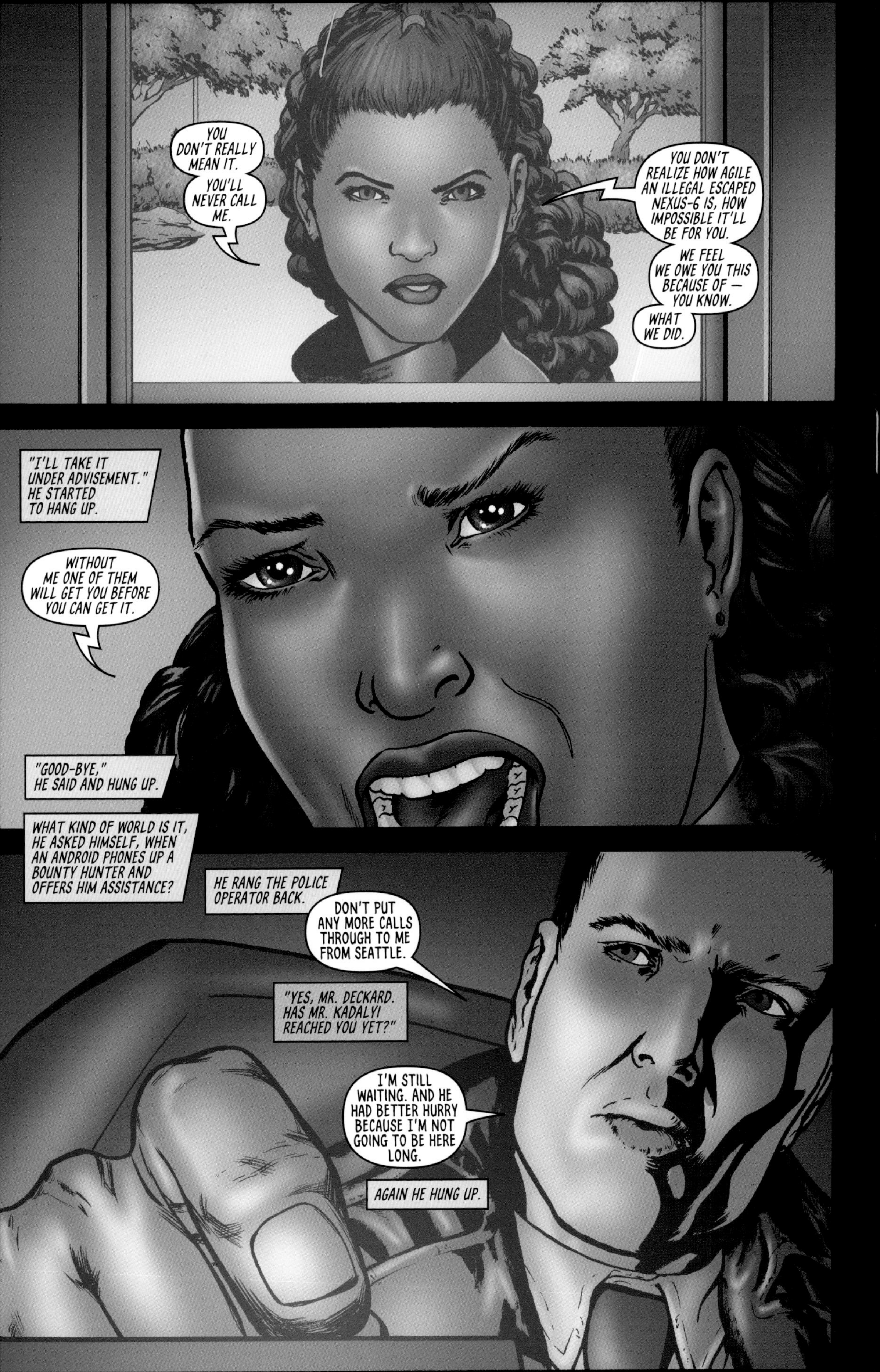
YOU DON'T REALLY MEAN IT.
YOU'LL NEVER CALL ME.
YOU DON'T REALIZE HOW AGILE AN ILLEGAL ESCAPED NEXUS-6 IS, HOW IMPOSSIBLE IT'LL BE FOR YOU.
WE FEEL WE OWE YOU THIS BECAUSE OF — YOU KNOW.
WHAT WE DID.
"I'LL TAKE IT UNDER ADVISEMENT." HE STARTED TO HANG UP.
WITHOUT ME ONE OF THEM WILL GET YOU BEFORE YOU CAN GET IT.
"GOOD-BYE," HE SAID AND HUNG UP.
WHAT KIND OF WORLD IS IT, HE ASKED HIMSELF, WHEN AN ANDROID PHONES UP A BOUNTY HUNTER AND OFFERS HIM ASSISTANCE?
HE RANG THE POLICE OPERATOR BACK.
DON'T PUT ANY MORE CALLS THROUGH TO ME FROM SEATTLE.
"YES, MR. DECKARD. HAS MR. KADALYI REACHED YOU YET?"
I'M STILL WAITING. AND HE HAD BETTER HURRY BECAUSE I'M NOT GOING TO BE HERE LONG.
AGAIN HE HUNG UP.

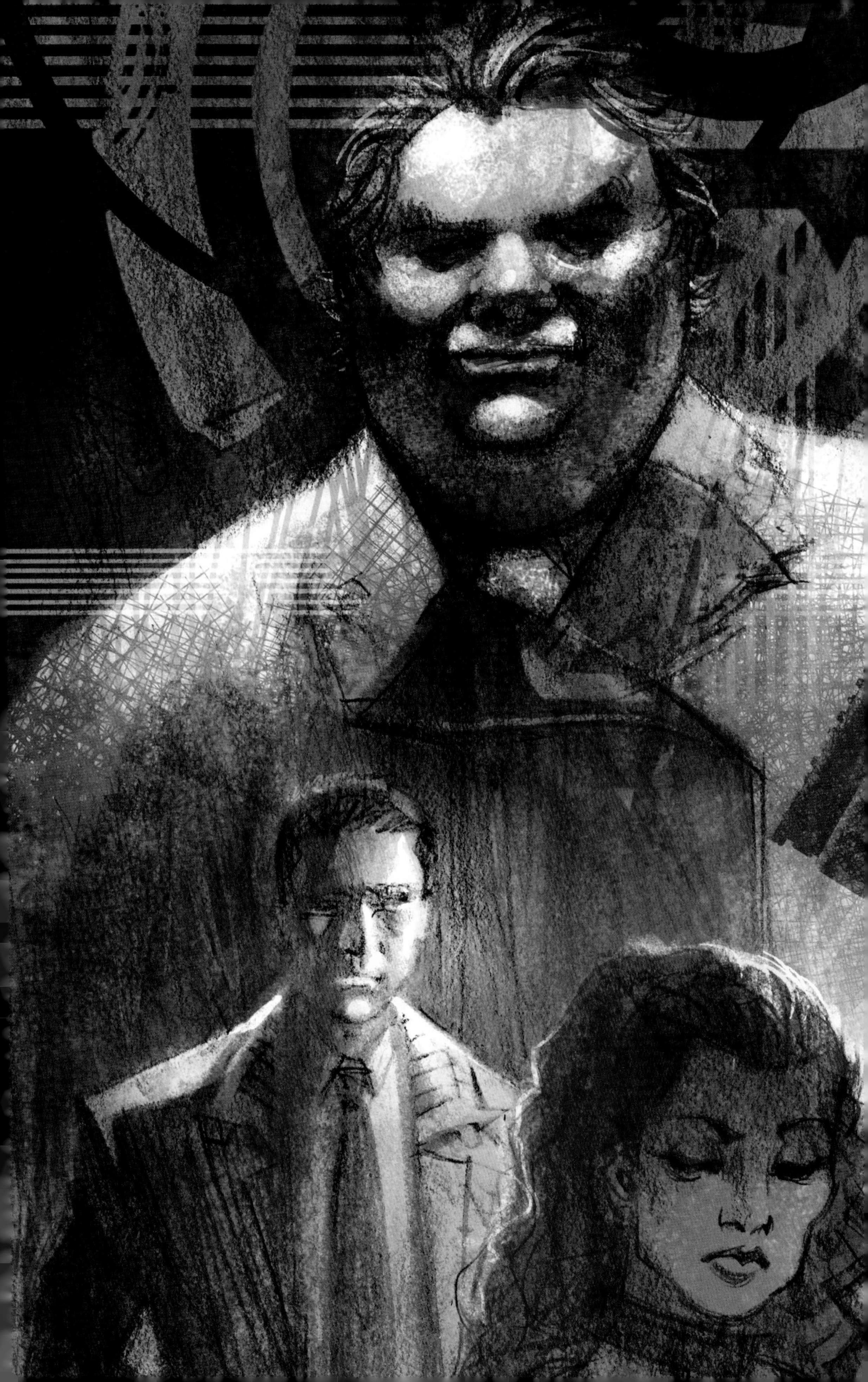

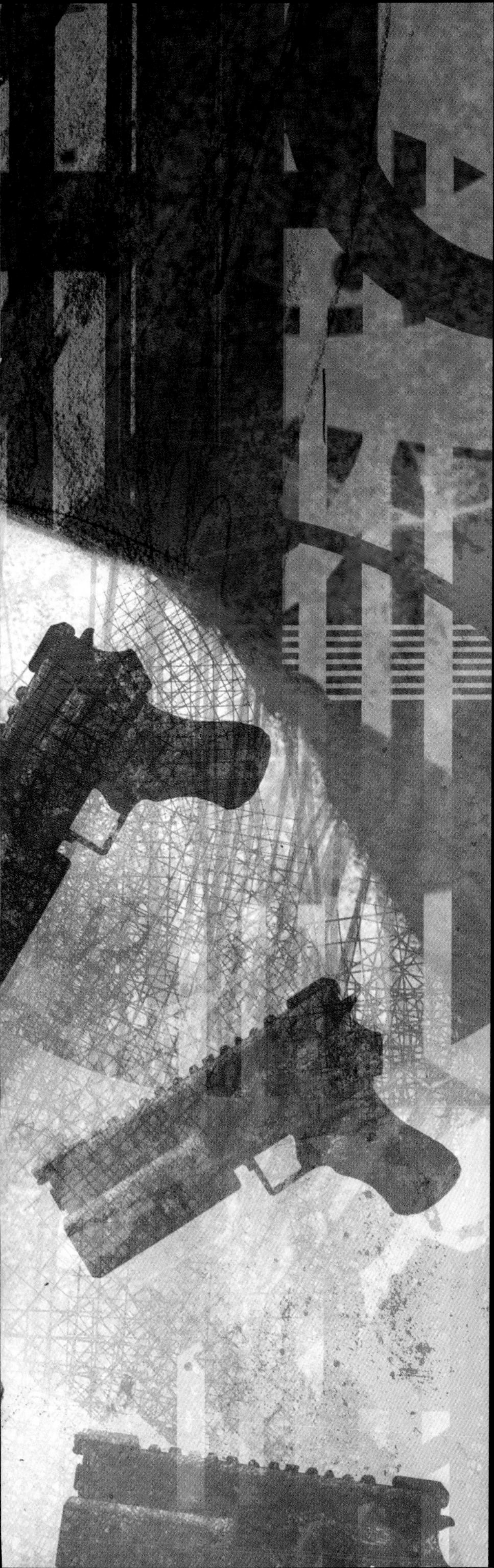

BOOK SEVEN

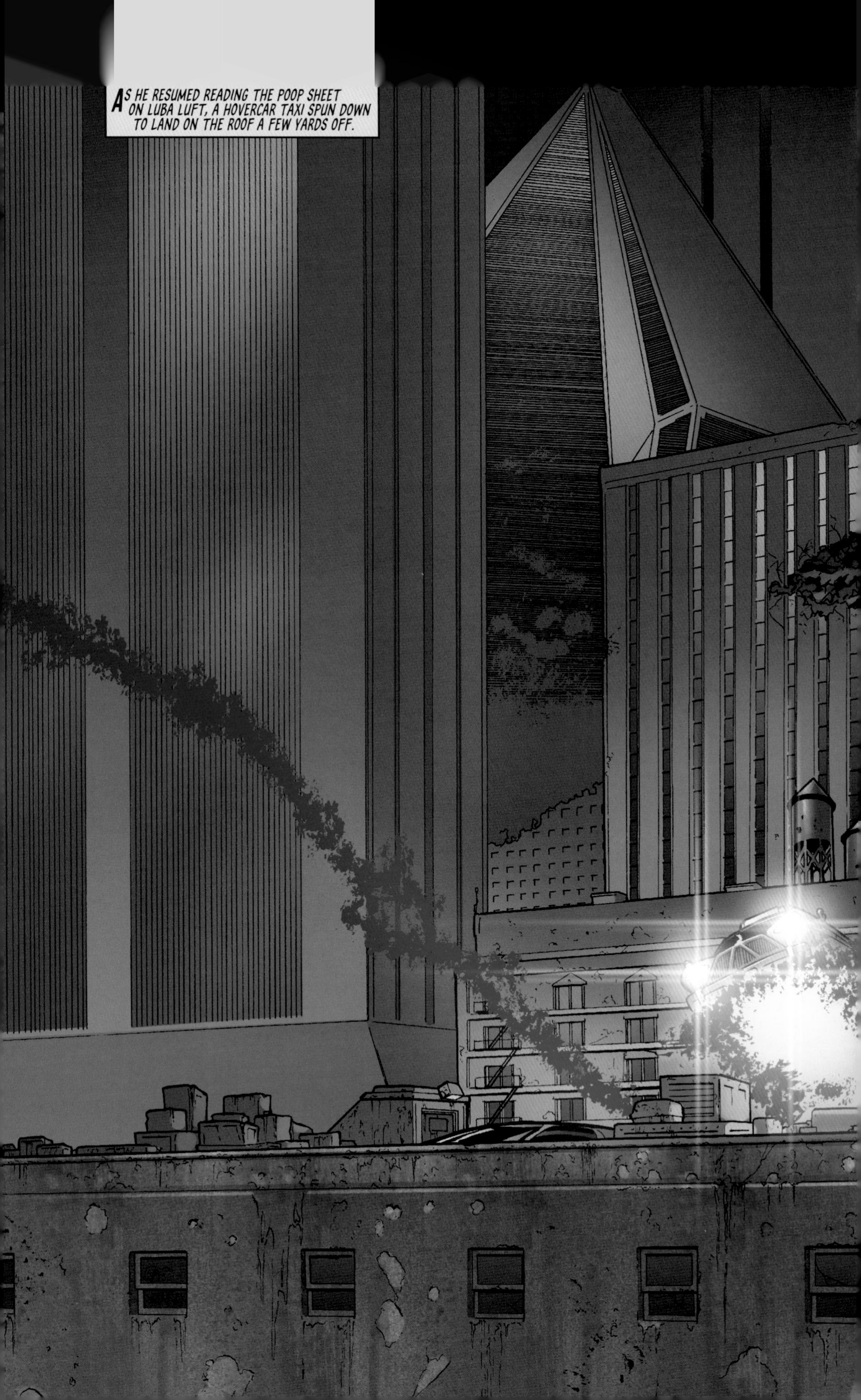
As he resumed reading the poop sheet on Luba Luft, a hovercar taxi spun down to land on the roof a few yards off.

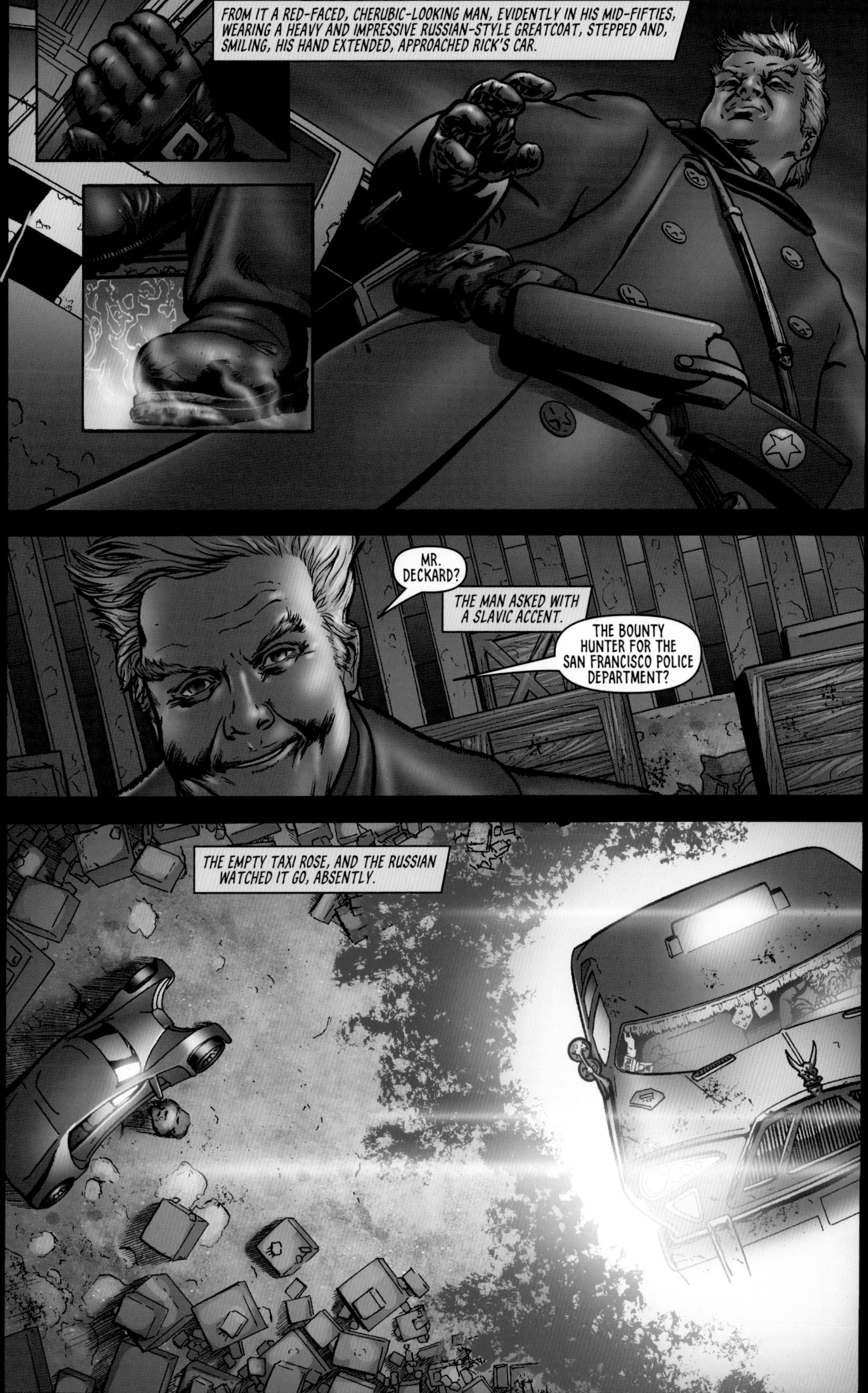
FROM IT A RED-FACED, CHERUBIC-LOOKING MAN, EVIDENTLY IN HIS MID-FIFTIES, WEARING A HEAVY AND IMPRESSIVE RUSSIAN-STYLE GREATCOAT, STEPPED AND, SMILING, HIS HAND EXTENDED, APPROACHED RICK'S CAR.
MR. DECKARD?
THE MAN ASKED WITH A SLAVIC ACCENT.
THE BOUNTY HUNTER FOR THE SAN FRANCISCO POLICE DEPARTMENT?
THE EMPTY TAXI ROSE, AND THE RUSSIAN WATCHED IT GO, ABSENTLY.

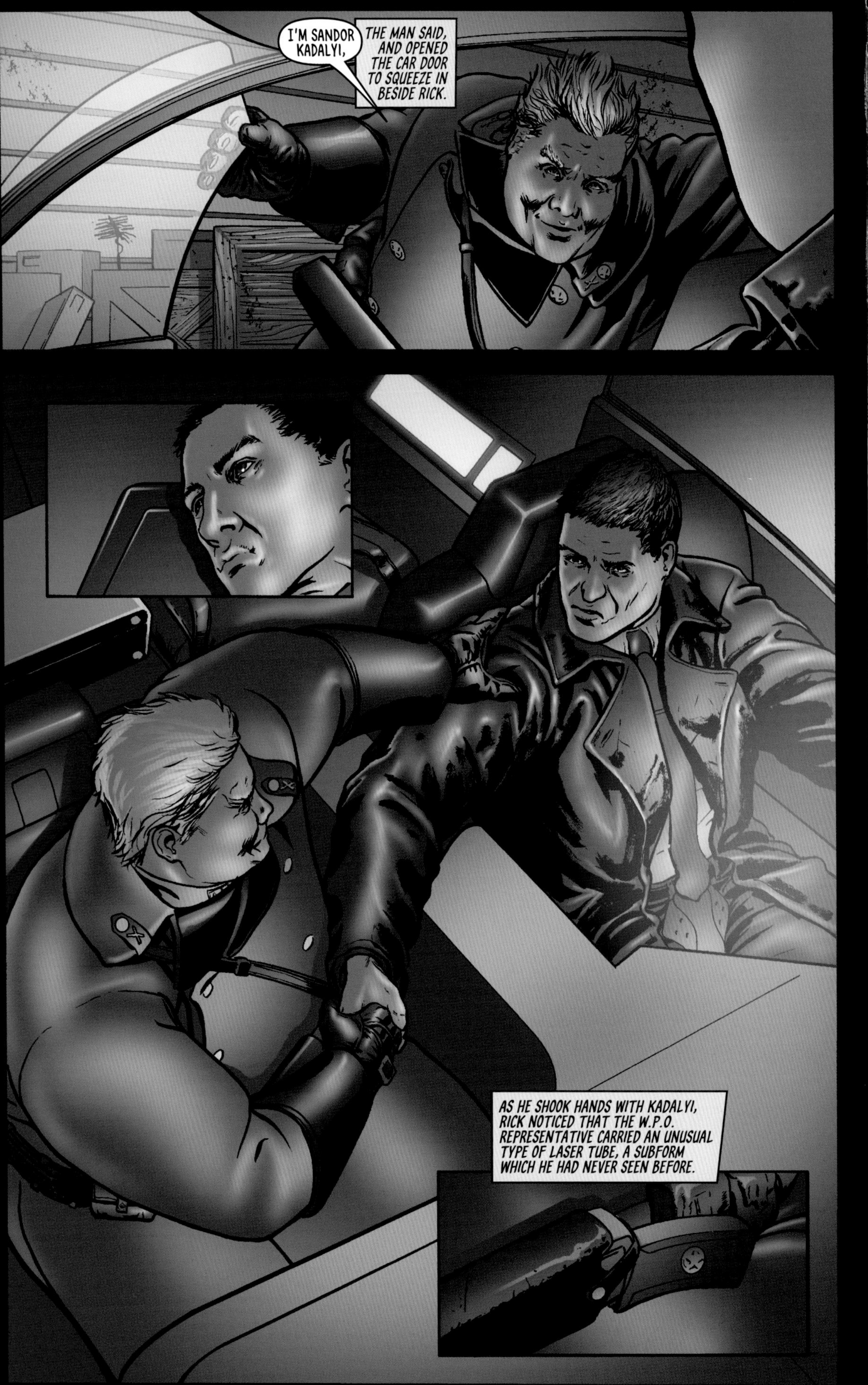
I'M SANDOR KADALYI,
THE MAN SAID, AND OPENED THE CAR DOOR TO SQUEEZE IN BESIDE RICK.
AS HE SHOOK HANDS WITH KADALYI, RICK NOTICED THAT THE W.P.O. REPRESENTATIVE CARRIED AN UNUSUAL TYPE OF LASER TUBE, A SUBFORM WHICH HE HAD NEVER SEEN BEFORE.

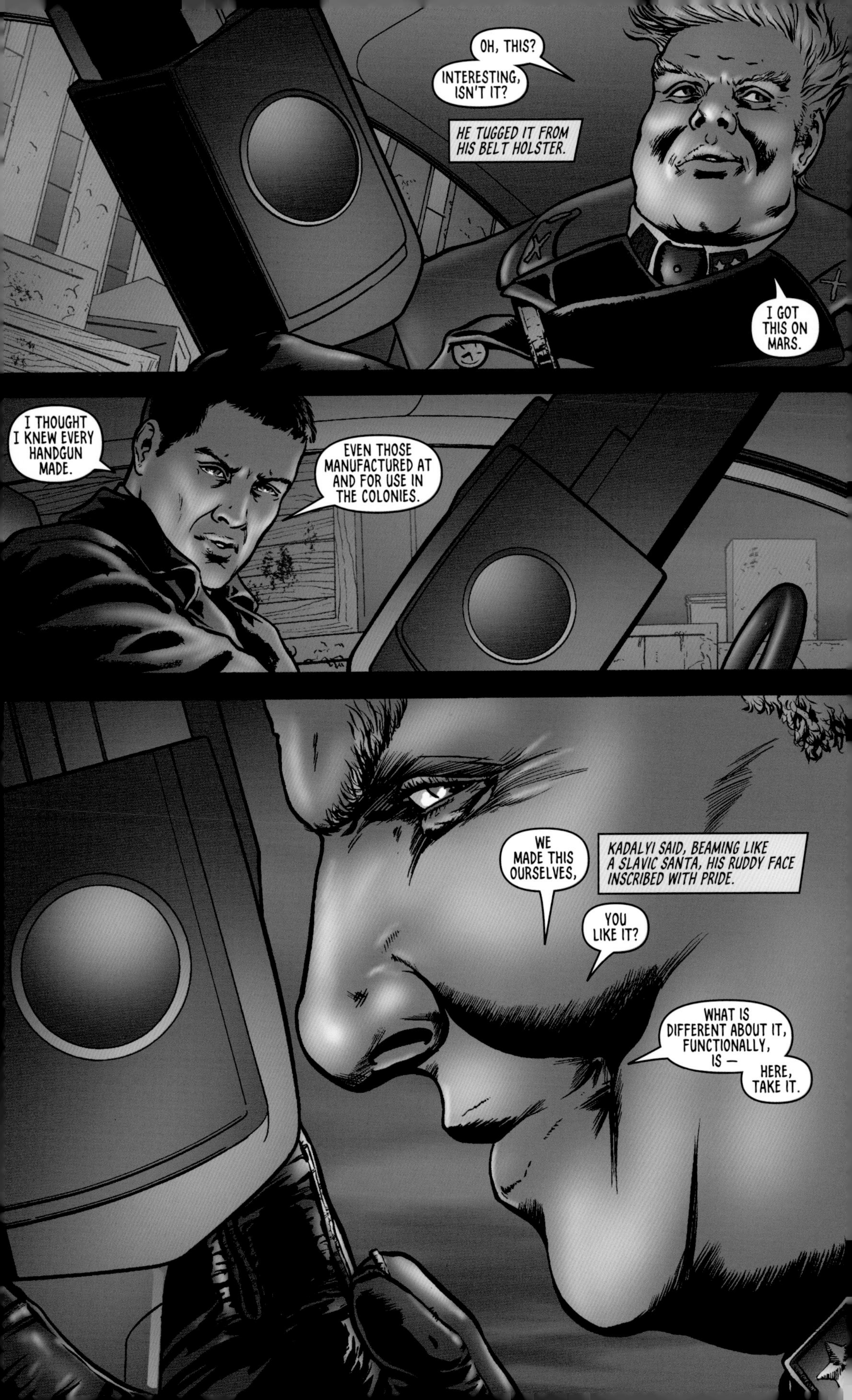
OH, THIS?
INTERESTING, ISN'T IT?
HE TUGGED IT FROM HIS BELT HOLSTER.
I GOT THIS ON MARS.
I THOUGHT I KNEW EVERY HANDGUN MADE.
EVEN THOSE MANUFACTURED AT AND FOR USE IN THE COLONIES.
WE MADE THIS OURSELVES,
KADALYI SAID, BEAMING LIKE A SLAVIC SANTA, HIS RUDDY FACE INSCRIBED WITH PRIDE.
YOU LIKE IT?
WHAT IS DIFFERENT ABOUT IT, FUNCTIONALLY, IS —
HERE, TAKE IT.

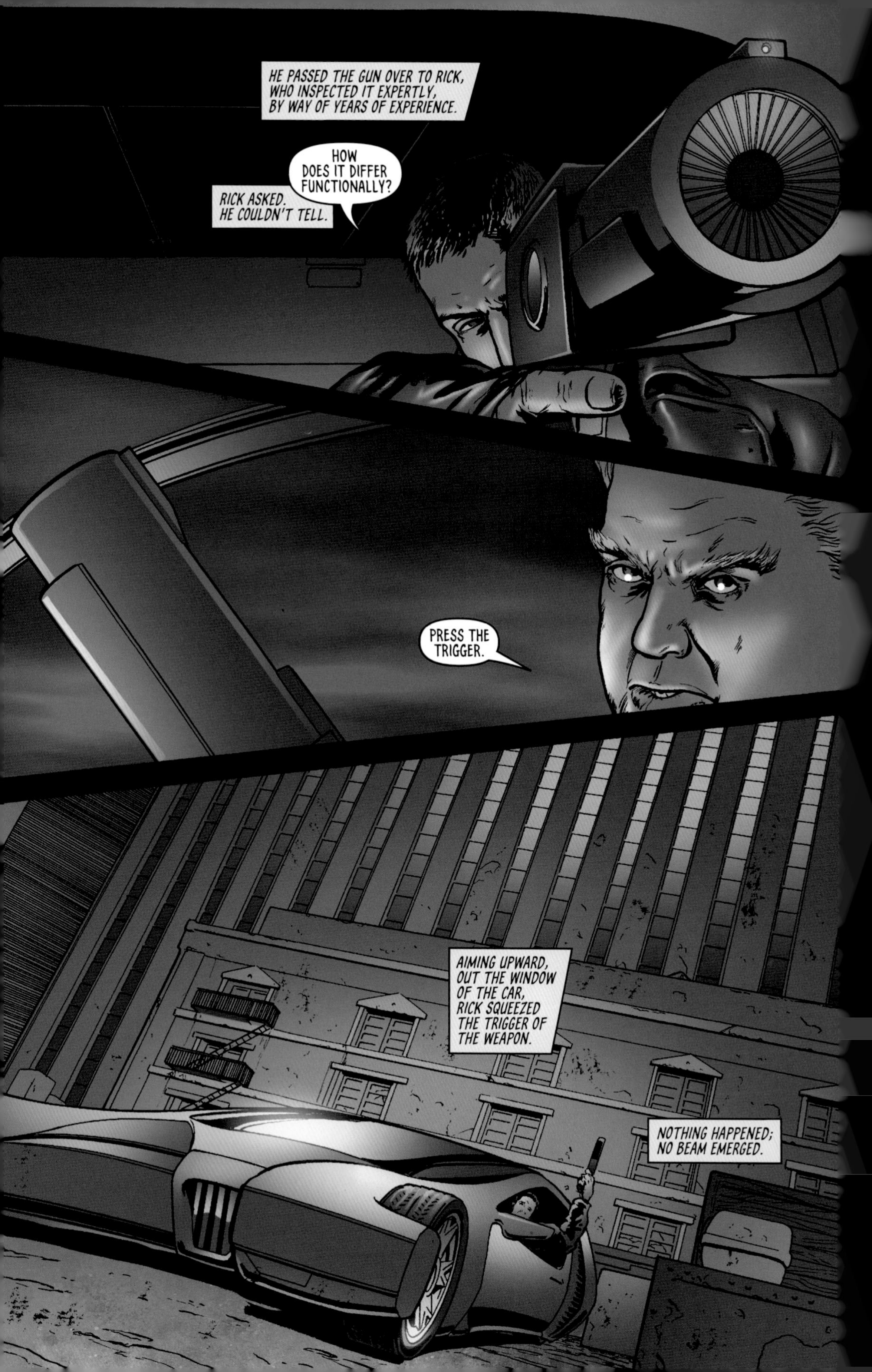
HE PASSED THE GUN OVER TO RICK, WHO INSPECTED IT EXPERTLY, BY WAY OF YEARS OF EXPERIENCE.
HOW DOES IT DIFFER FUNCTIONALLY?
RICK ASKED. HE COULDN'T TELL.
PRESS THE TRIGGER.
AIMING UPWARD, OUT THE WINDOW OF THE CAR, RICK SQUEEZED THE TRIGGER OF THE WEAPON.
NOTHING HAPPENED; NO BEAM EMERGED.

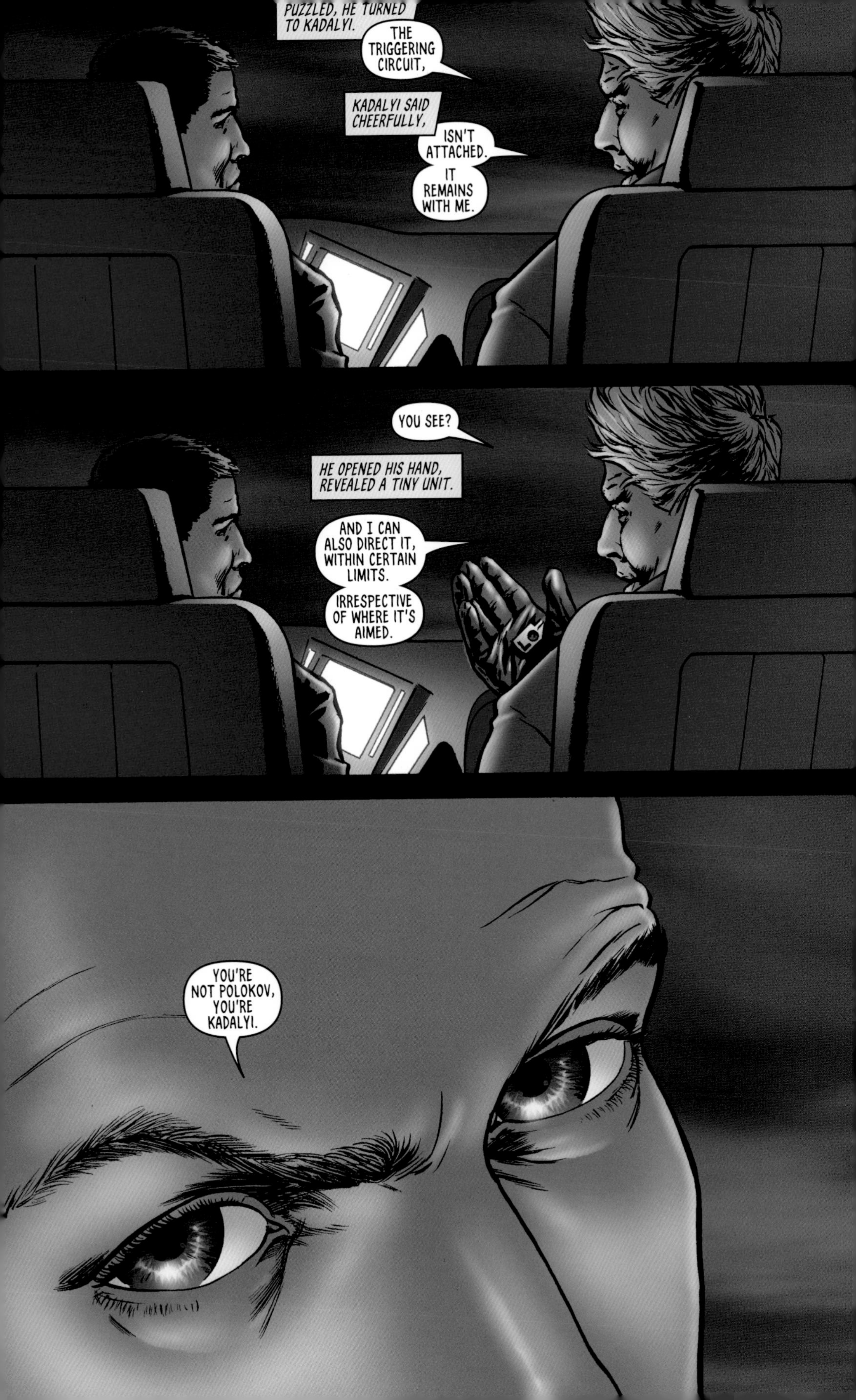
PUZZLED, HE TURNED TO KADALYI.
THE TRIGGERING CIRCUIT,
KADALYI SAID CHEERFULLY,
ISN'T ATTACHED.
IT REMAINS WITH ME.
YOU SEE?
HE OPENED HIS HAND, REVEALED A TINY UNIT.
AND I CAN ALSO DIRECT IT, WITHIN CERTAIN LIMITS.
IRRESPECTIVE OF WHERE IT'S AIMED.
YOU'RE NOT POLOKOV, YOU'RE KADALYI.

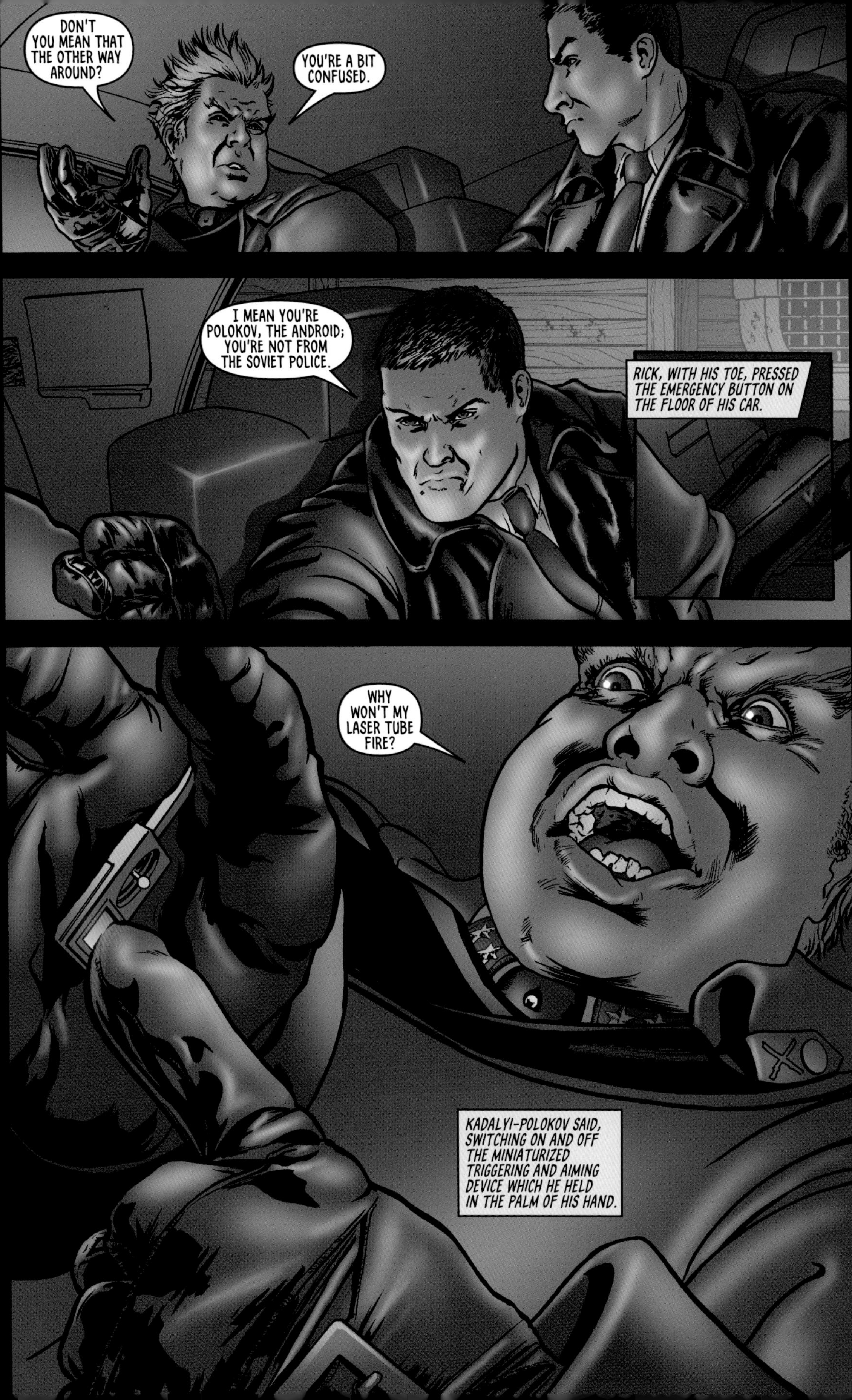
DON'T YOU MEAN THAT THE OTHER WAY AROUND?
YOU'RE A BIT CONFUSED.
I MEAN YOU'RE POLOKOV, THE ANDROID; YOU'RE NOT FROM THE SOVIET POLICE.
RICK, WITH HIS TOE, PRESSED THE EMERGENCY BUTTON ON THE FLOOR OF HIS CAR.
WHY WON'T MY LASER TUBE FIRE?
KADALYI-POLOKOV SAID, SWITCHING ON AND OFF THE MINIATURIZED TRIGGERING AND AIMING DEVICE WHICH HE HELD IN THE PALM OF HIS HAND.

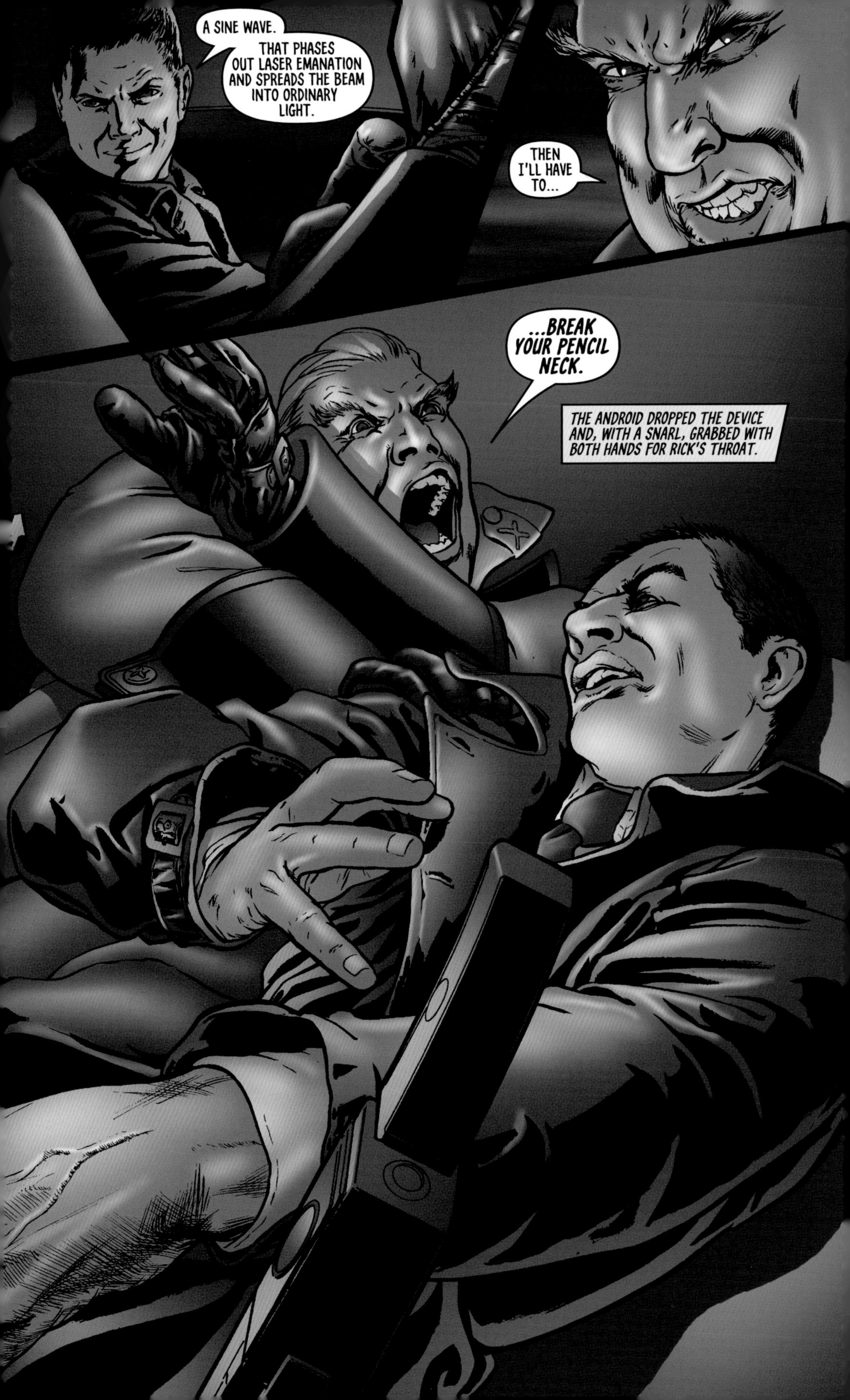
A SINE WAVE.
THAT PHASES OUT LASER EMANATION AND SPREADS THE BEAM INTO ORDINARY LIGHT.
THEN I'LL HAVE TO...
...BREAK YOUR PENCIL NECK.
THE ANDROID DROPPED THE DEVICE AND, WITH A SNARL, GRABBED WITH BOTH HANDS FOR RICK'S THROAT.

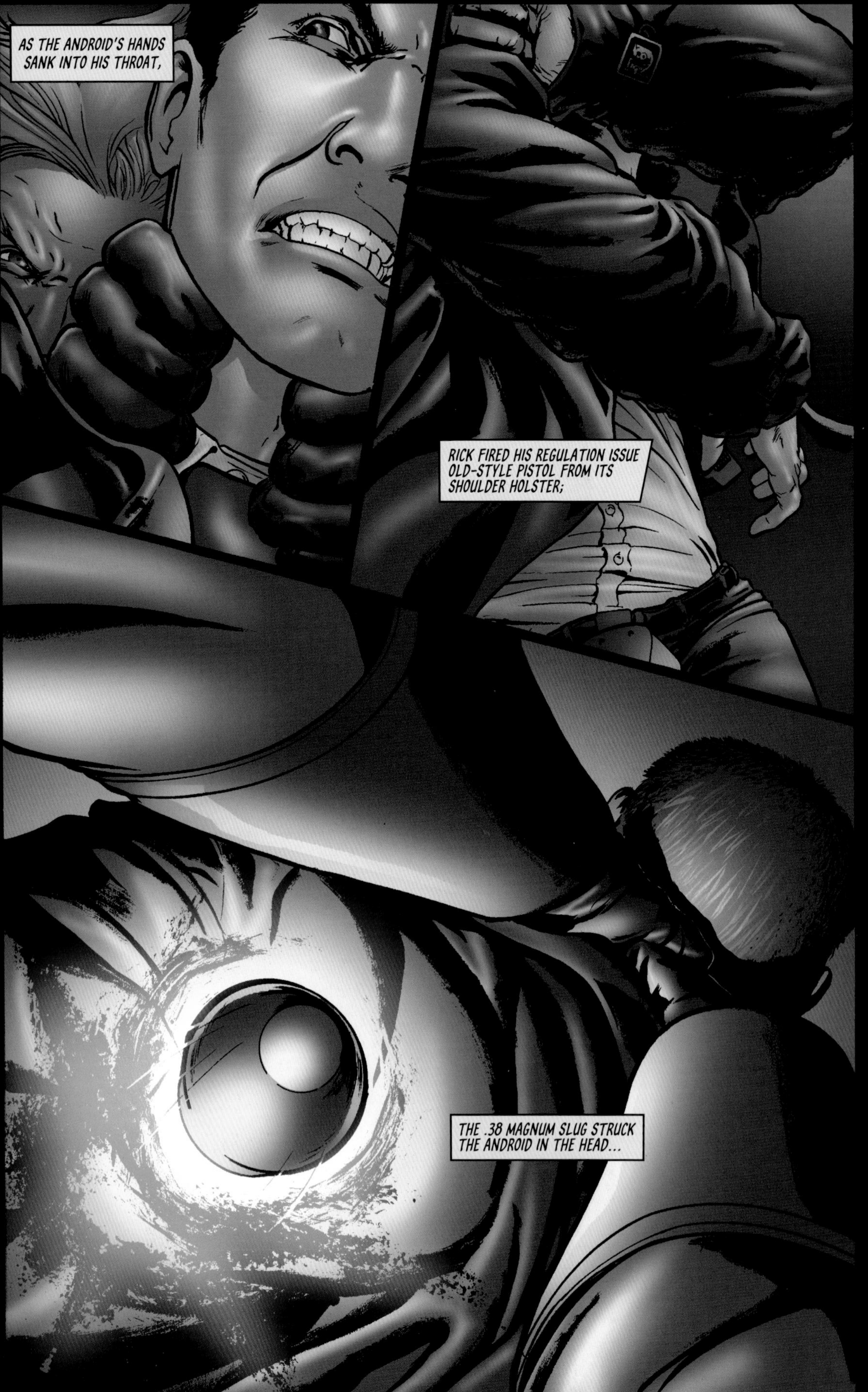
AS THE ANDROID'S HANDS SANK INTO HIS THROAT,
RICK FIRED HIS REGULATION ISSUE OLD-STYLE PISTOL FROM ITS SHOULDER HOLSTER;
THE .38 MAGNUM SLUG STRUCK THE ANDROID IN THE HEAD...

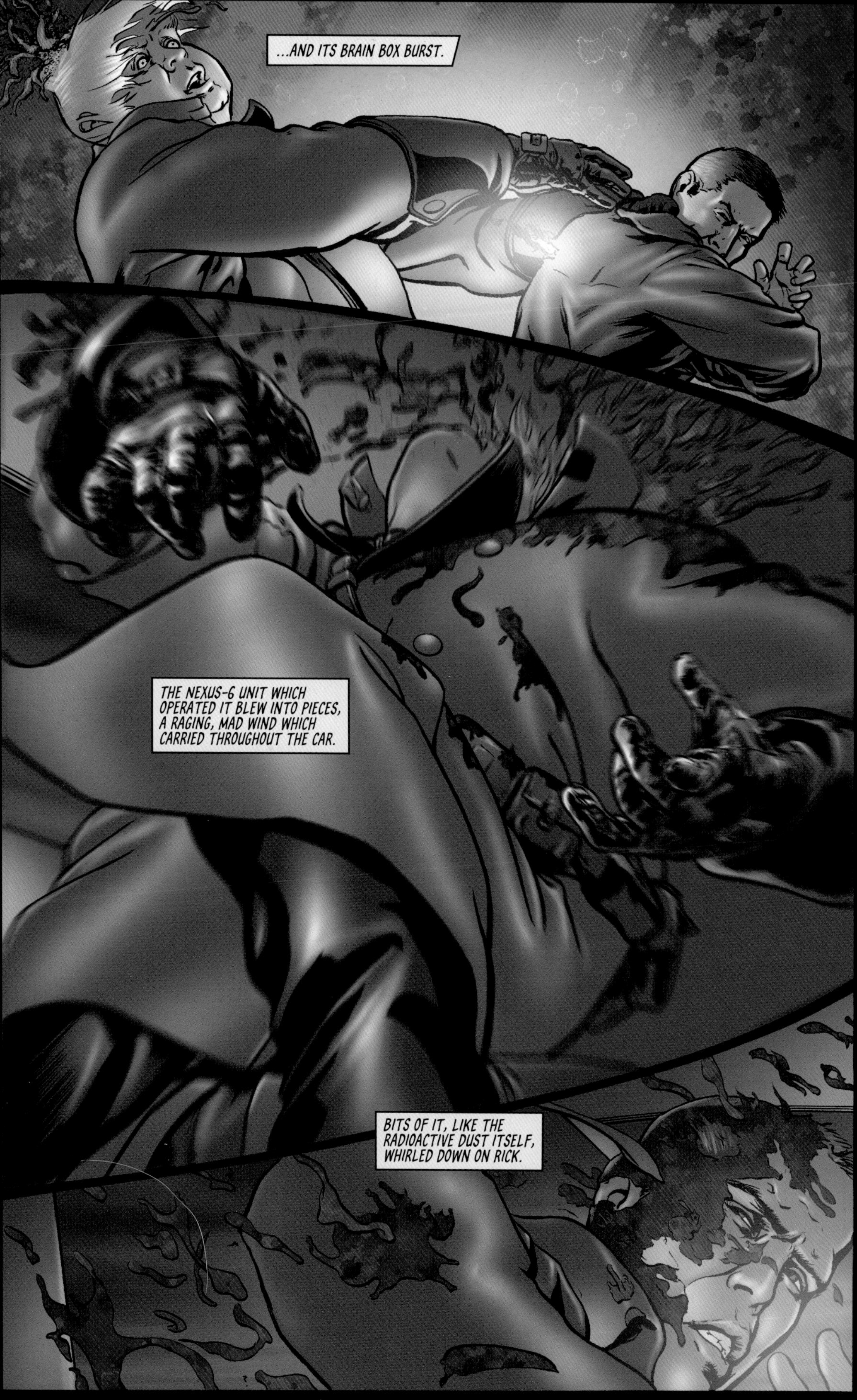

...AND ITS BRAIN BOX BURST.
THE NEXUS-6 UNIT WHICH OPERATED IT BLEW INTO PIECES, A RAGING, MAD WIND WHICH CARRIED THROUGHOUT THE CAR.
BITS OF IT, LIKE THE RADIOACTIVE DUST ITSELF, WHIRLED DOWN ON RICK.

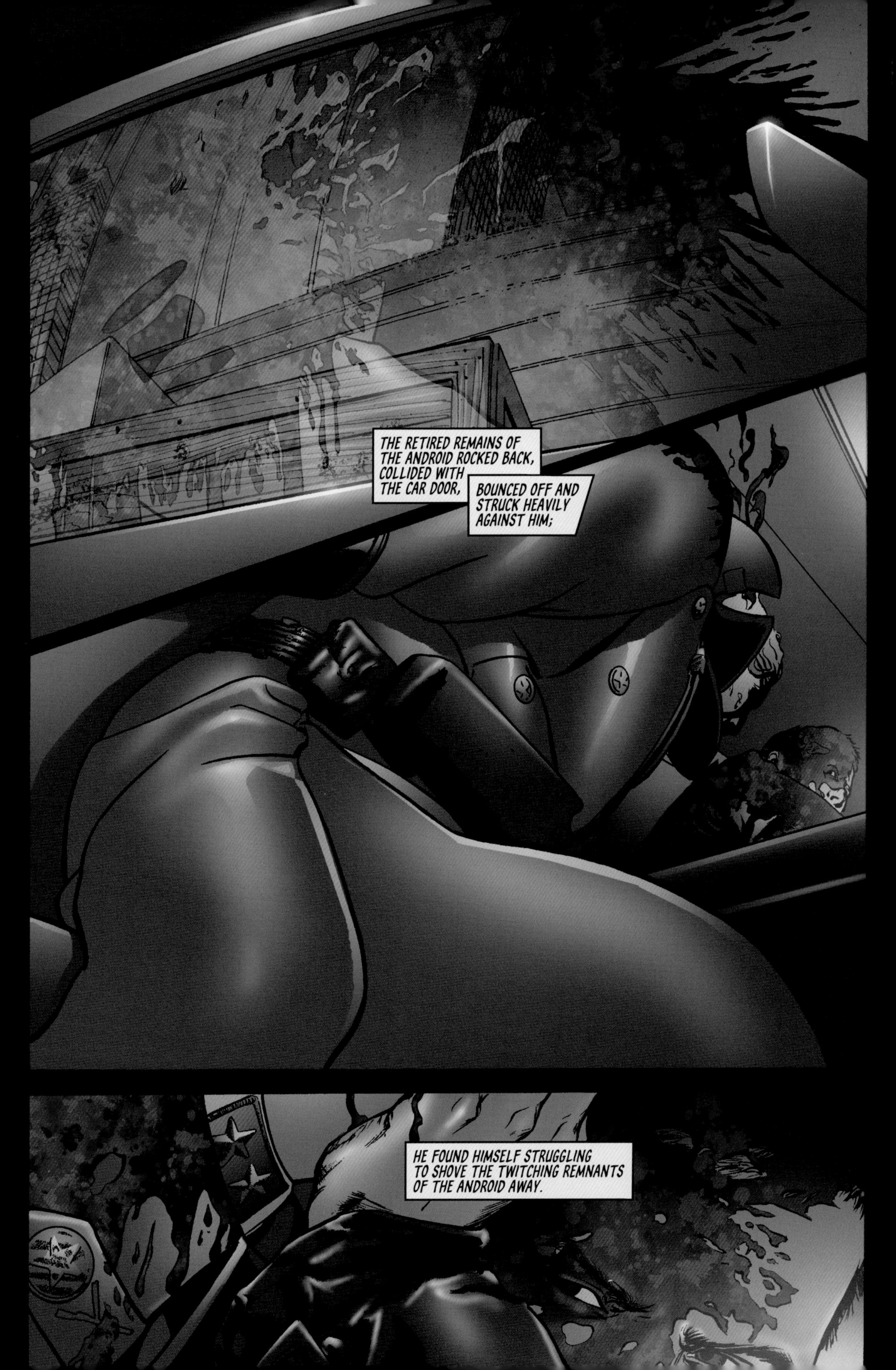
THE RETIRED REMAINS OF THE ANDROID ROCKED BACK, COLLIDED WITH THE CAR DOOR,
BOUNCED OFF AND STRUCK HEAVILY AGAINST HIM;
HE FOUND HIMSELF STRUGGLING TO SHOVE THE TWITCHING REMNANTS OF THE ANDROID AWAY.

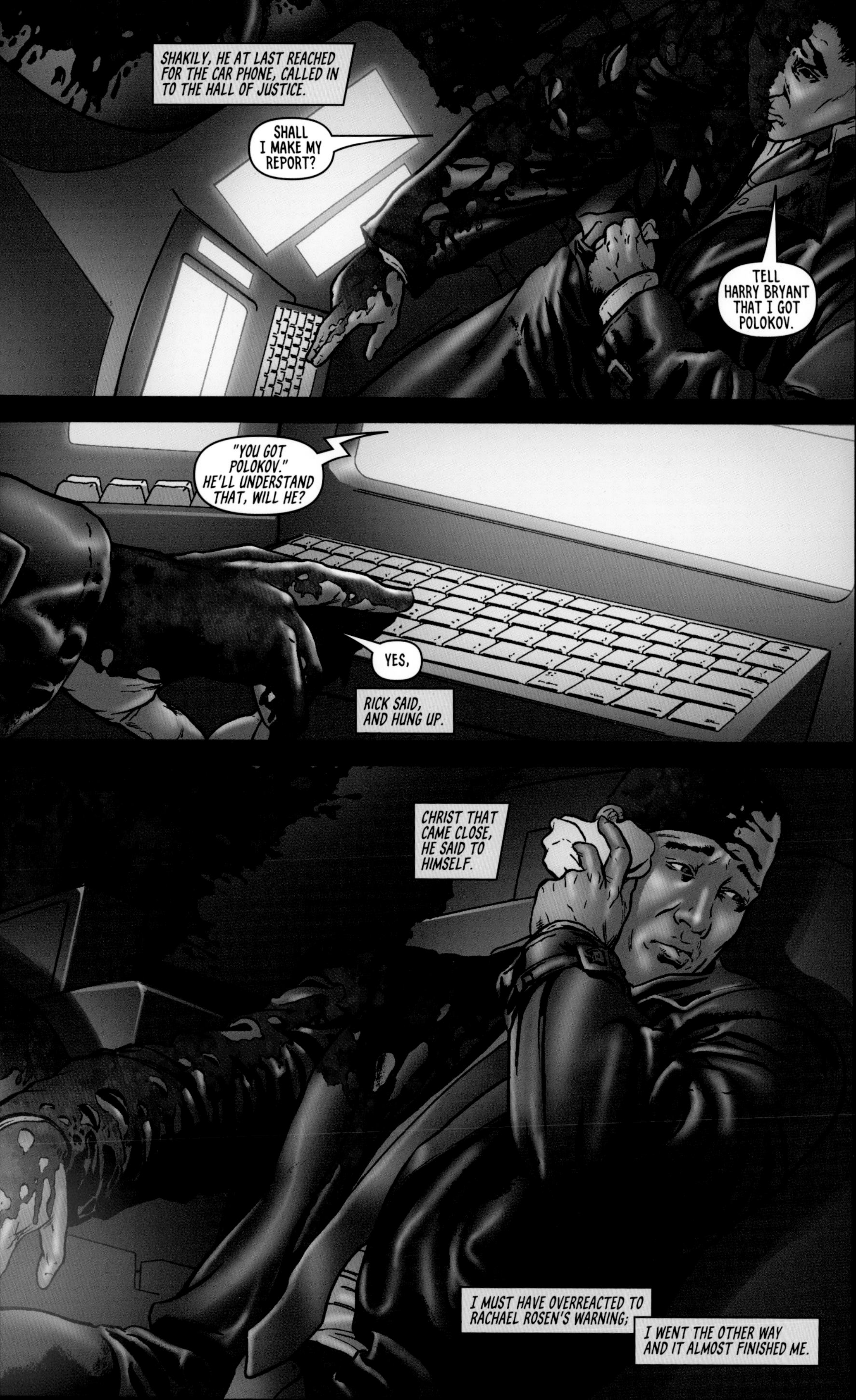
SHAKILY, HE AT LAST REACHED FOR THE CAR PHONE, CALLED IN TO THE HALL OF JUSTICE.
SHALL I MAKE MY REPORT?
TELL HARRY BRYANT THAT I GOT POLOKOV.
"YOU GOT POLOKOV." HE'LL UNDERSTAND THAT, WILL HE?
YES,
RICK SAID, AND HUNG UP.
CHRIST THAT CAME CLOSE, HE SAID TO HIMSELF.
I MUST HAVE OVERREACTED TO RACHAEL ROSEN'S WARNING;
I WENT THE OTHER WAY AND IT ALMOST FINISHED ME.

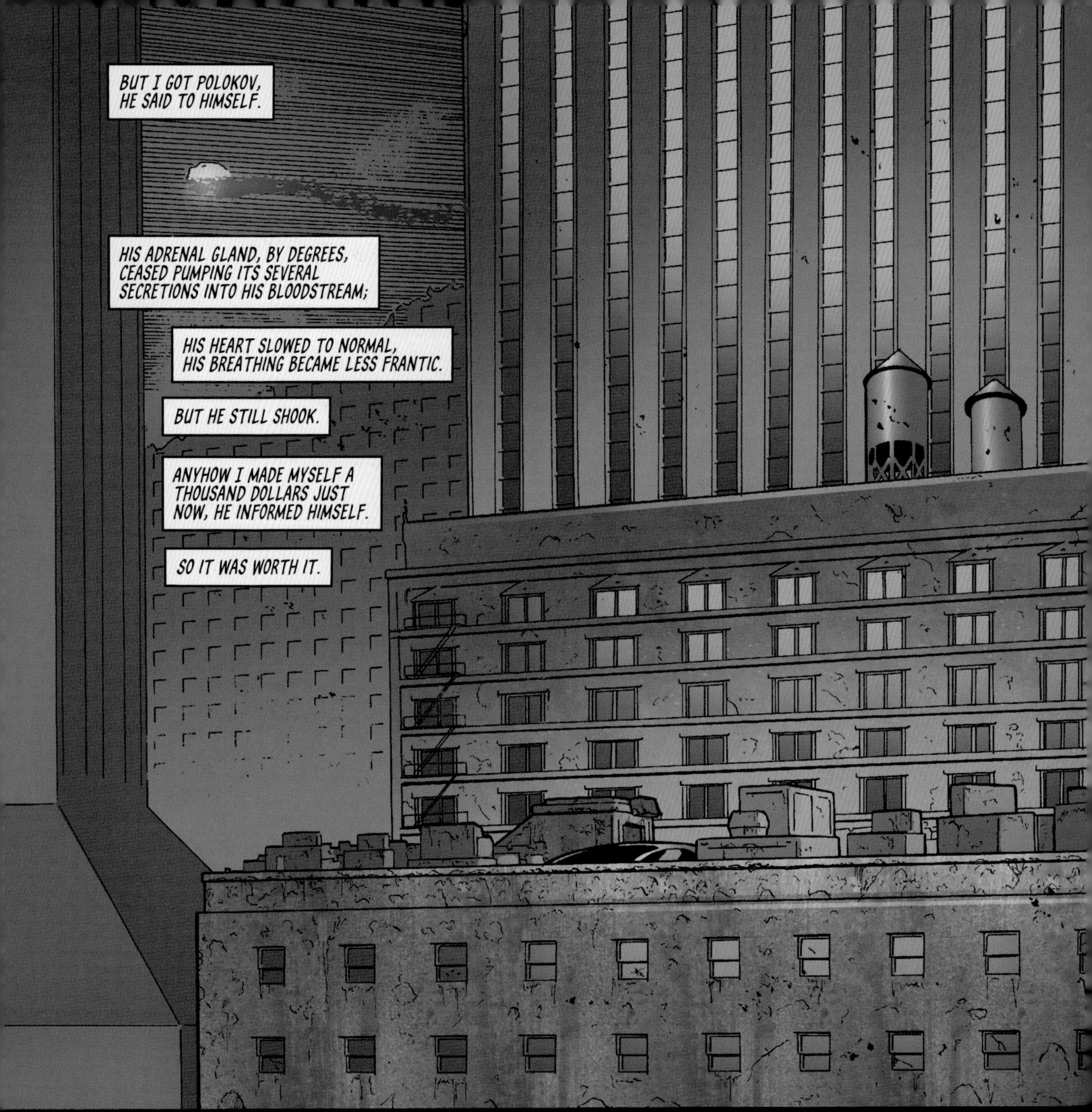
BUT I GOT POLOKOV, HE SAID TO HIMSELF.
HIS ADRENAL GLAND, BY DEGREES, CEASED PUMPING ITS SEVERAL SECRETIONS INTO HIS BLOODSTREAM;
HIS HEART SLOWED TO NORMAL, HIS BREATHING BECAME LESS FRANTIC.
BUT HE STILL SHOOK.
ANYHOW I MADE MYSELF A THOUSAND DOLLARS JUST NOW, HE INFORMED HIMSELF.
SO IT WAS WORTH IT.

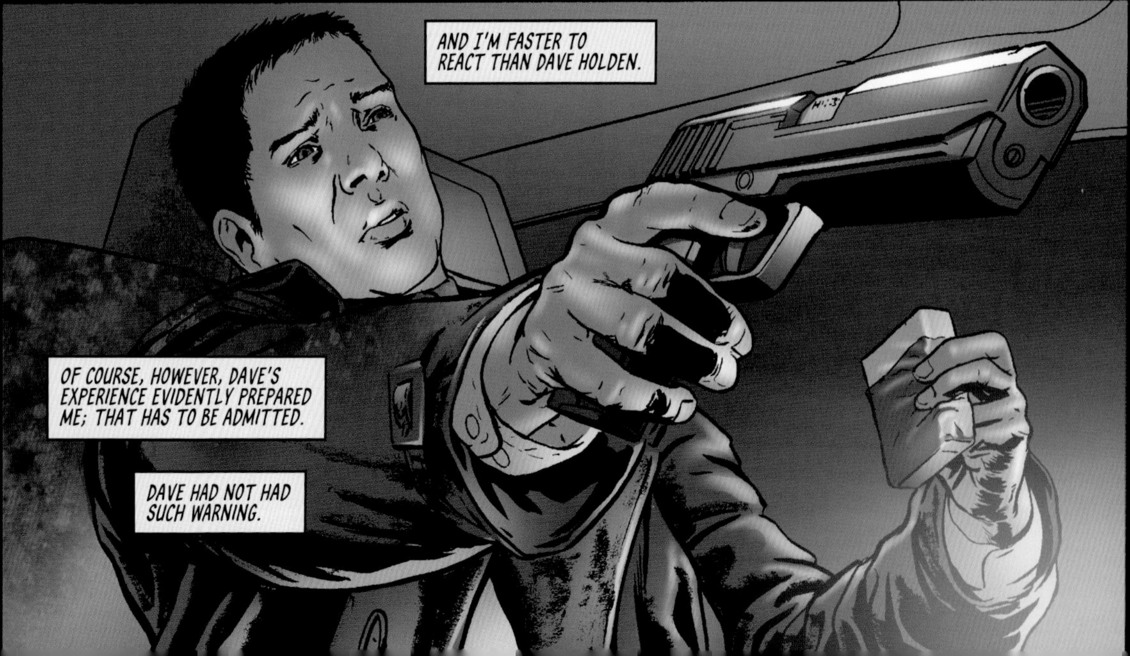
AND I'M FASTER TO REACT THAN DAVE HOLDEN.
OF COURSE, HOWEVER, DAVE'S EXPERIENCE EVIDENTLY PREPARED ME; THAT HAS TO BE ADMITTED.
DAVE HAD NOT HAD SUCH WARNING.

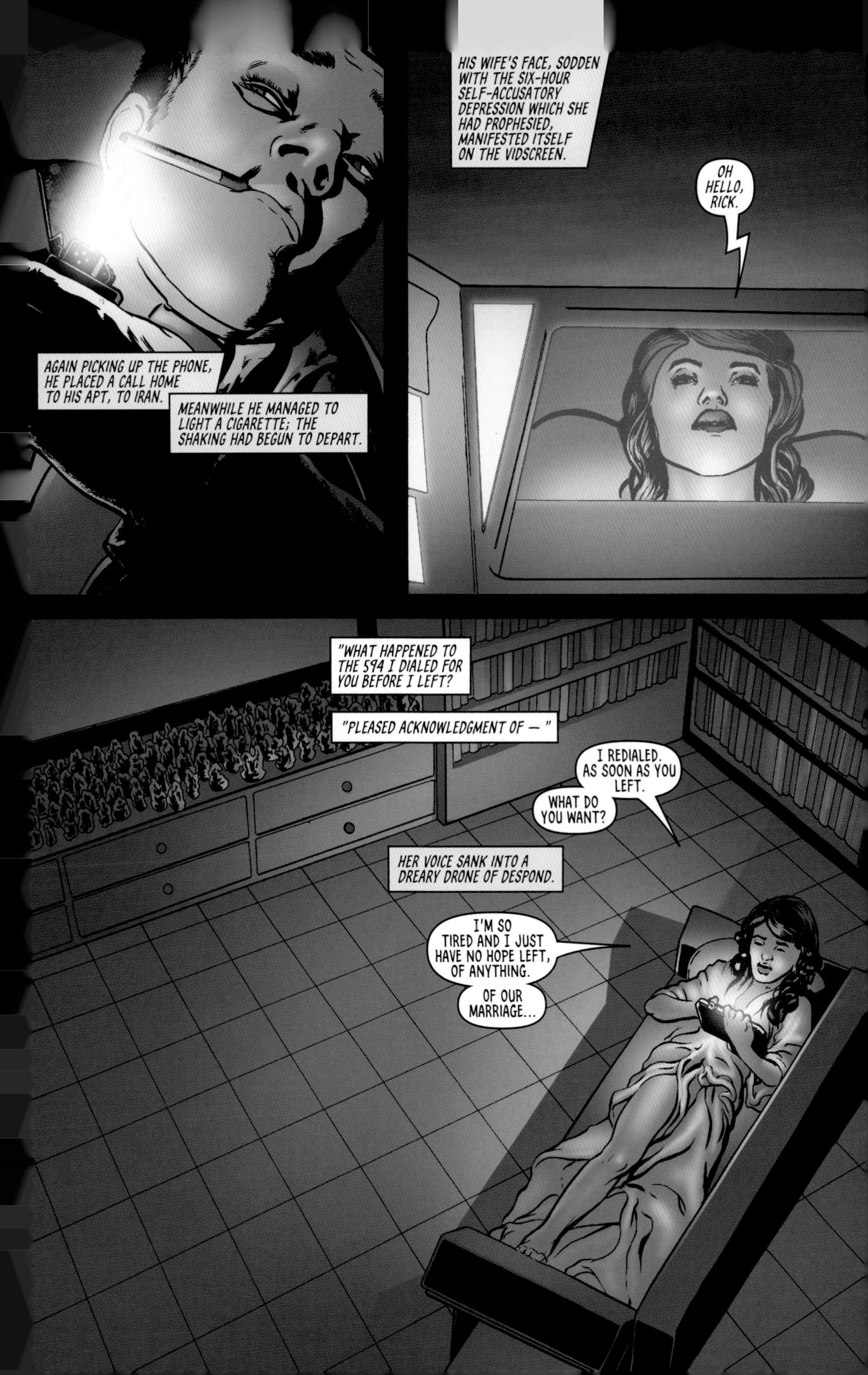
AGAIN PICKING UP THE PHONE, HE PLACED A CALL HOME TO HIS APT, TO IRAN.
MEANWHILE HE MANAGED TO LIGHT A CIGARETTE; THE SHAKING HAD BEGUN TO DEPART.
HIS WIFE'S FACE, SODDEN WITH THE SIX-HOUR SELF-ACCUSATORY DEPRESSION WHICH SHE HAD PROPHESIED, MANIFESTED ITSELF ON THE VIDSCREEN.
OH HELLO, RICK.
"WHAT HAPPENED TO THE 594 I DIALED FOR YOU BEFORE I LEFT?
"PLEASED ACKNOWLEDGMENT OF — "
I REDIALED. AS SOON AS YOU LEFT.
WHAT DO YOU WANT?
HER VOICE SANK INTO A DREARY DRONE OF DESPOND.
I'M SO TIRED AND I JUST HAVE NO HOPE LEFT, OF ANYTHING.
OF OUR MARRIAGE...

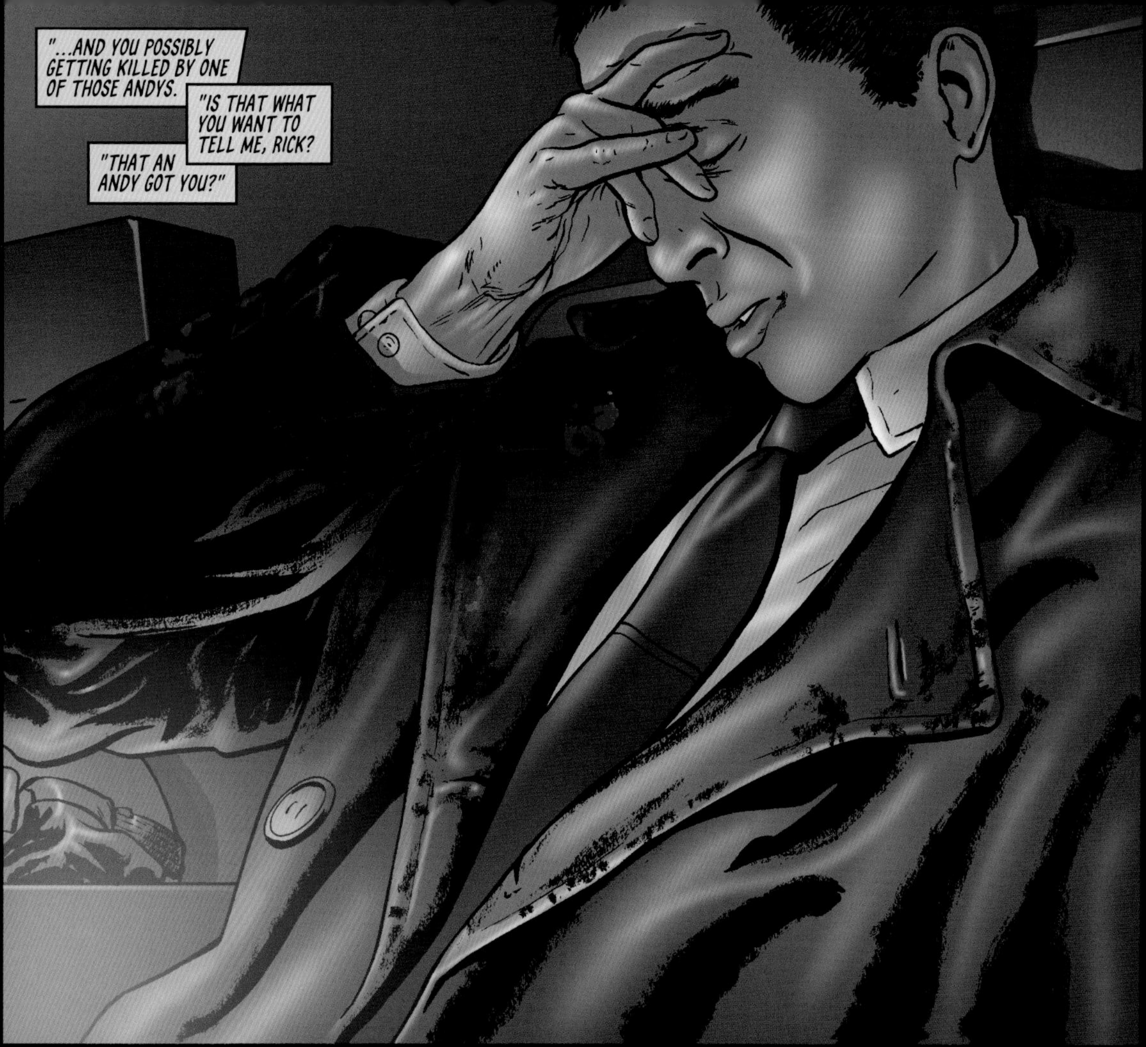
"...AND YOU POSSIBLY GETTING KILLED BY ONE OF THOSE ANDYS.
"IS THAT WHAT YOU WANT TO TELL ME, RICK?
"THAT AN ANDY GOT YOU?"

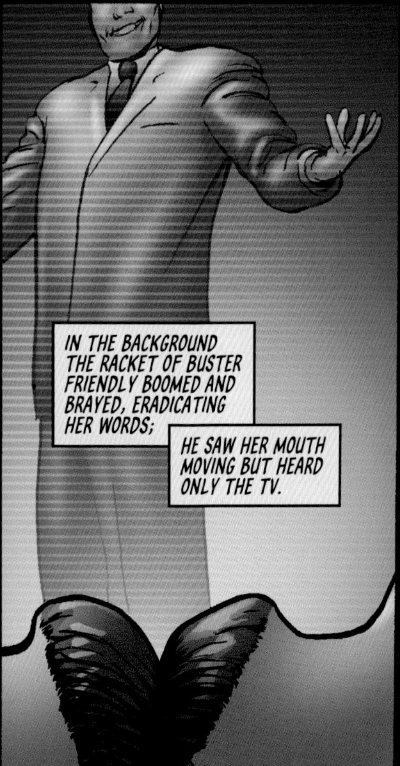
IN THE BACKGROUND THE RACKET OF BUSTER FRIENDLY BOOMED AND BRAYED, ERADICATING HER WORDS;
HE SAW HER MOUTH MOVING BUT HEARD ONLY THE TV.

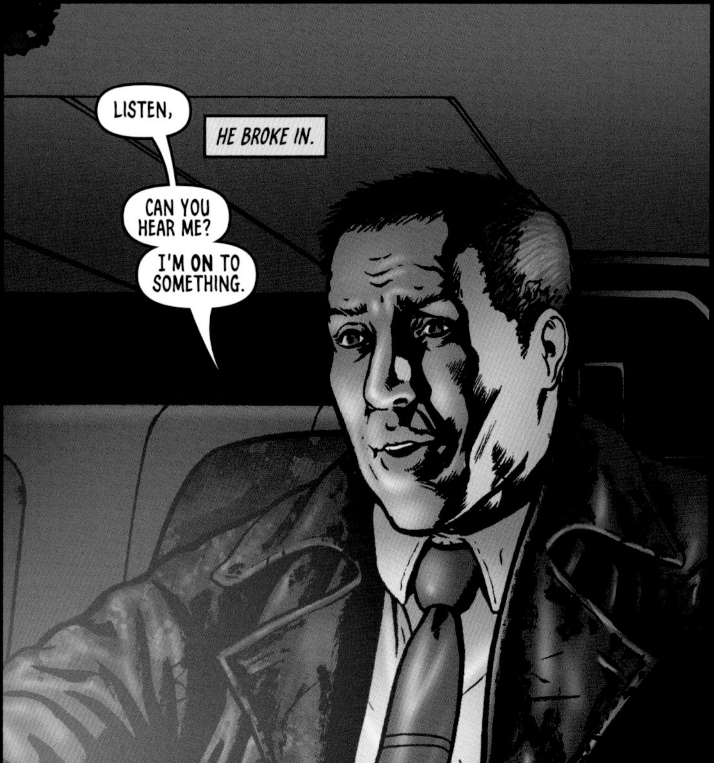
LISTEN,
HE BROKE IN.
CAN YOU HEAR ME?
I'M ON TO SOMETHING.

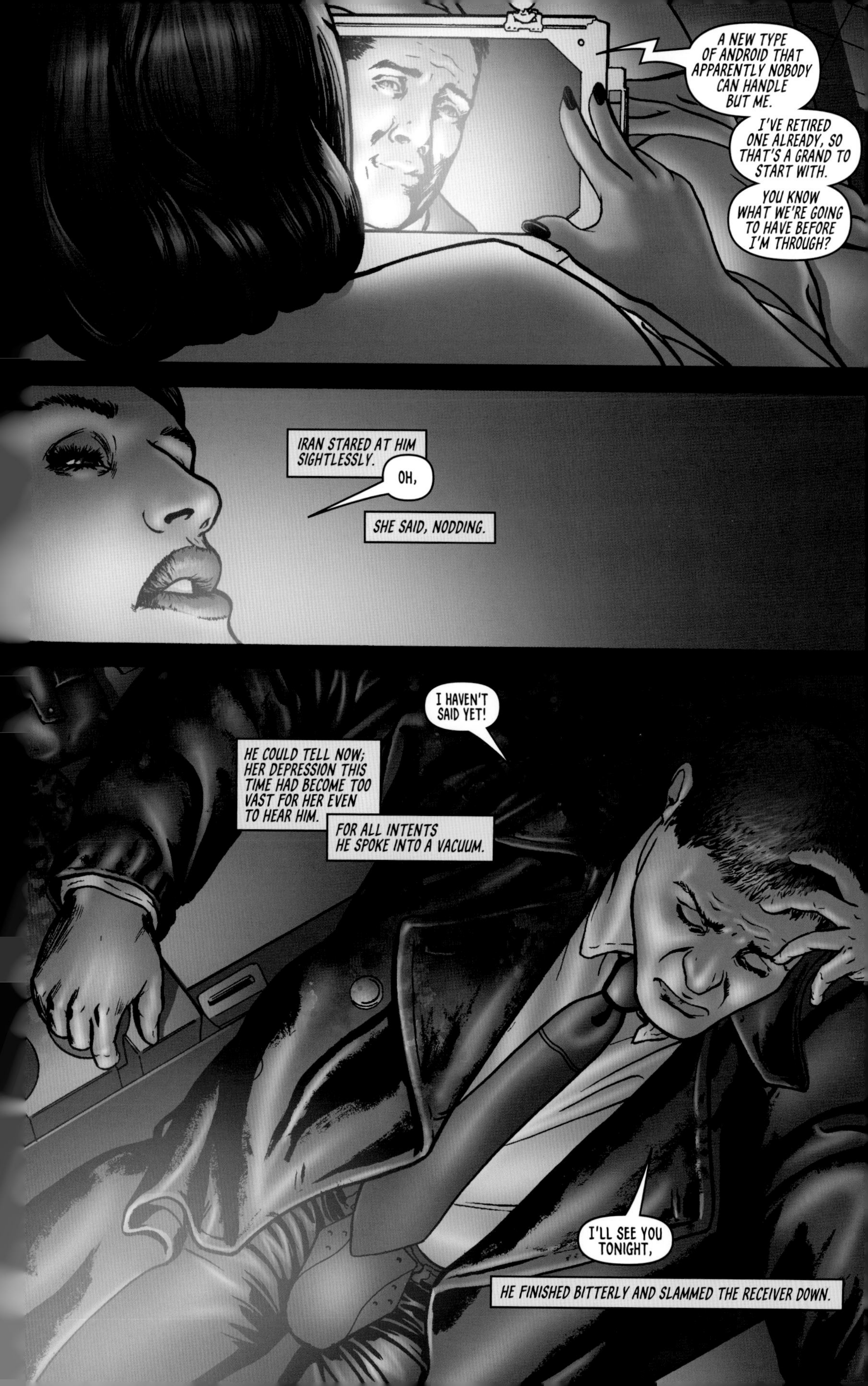
A NEW TYPE OF ANDROID THAT APPARENTLY NOBODY CAN HANDLE BUT ME.
I'VE RETIRED ONE ALREADY, SO THAT'S A GRAND TO START WITH.
YOU KNOW WHAT WE'RE GOING TO HAVE BEFORE I'M THROUGH?
IRAN STARED AT HIM SIGHTLESSLY.
OH,
SHE SAID, NODDING.
I HAVEN'T SAID YET!
HE COULD TELL NOW; HER DEPRESSION THIS TIME HAD BECOME TOO VAST FOR HER EVEN TO HEAR HIM.
FOR ALL INTENTS HE SPOKE INTO A VACUUM.
I'LL SEE YOU TONIGHT,
HE FINISHED BITTERLY AND SLAMMED THE RECEIVER DOWN.

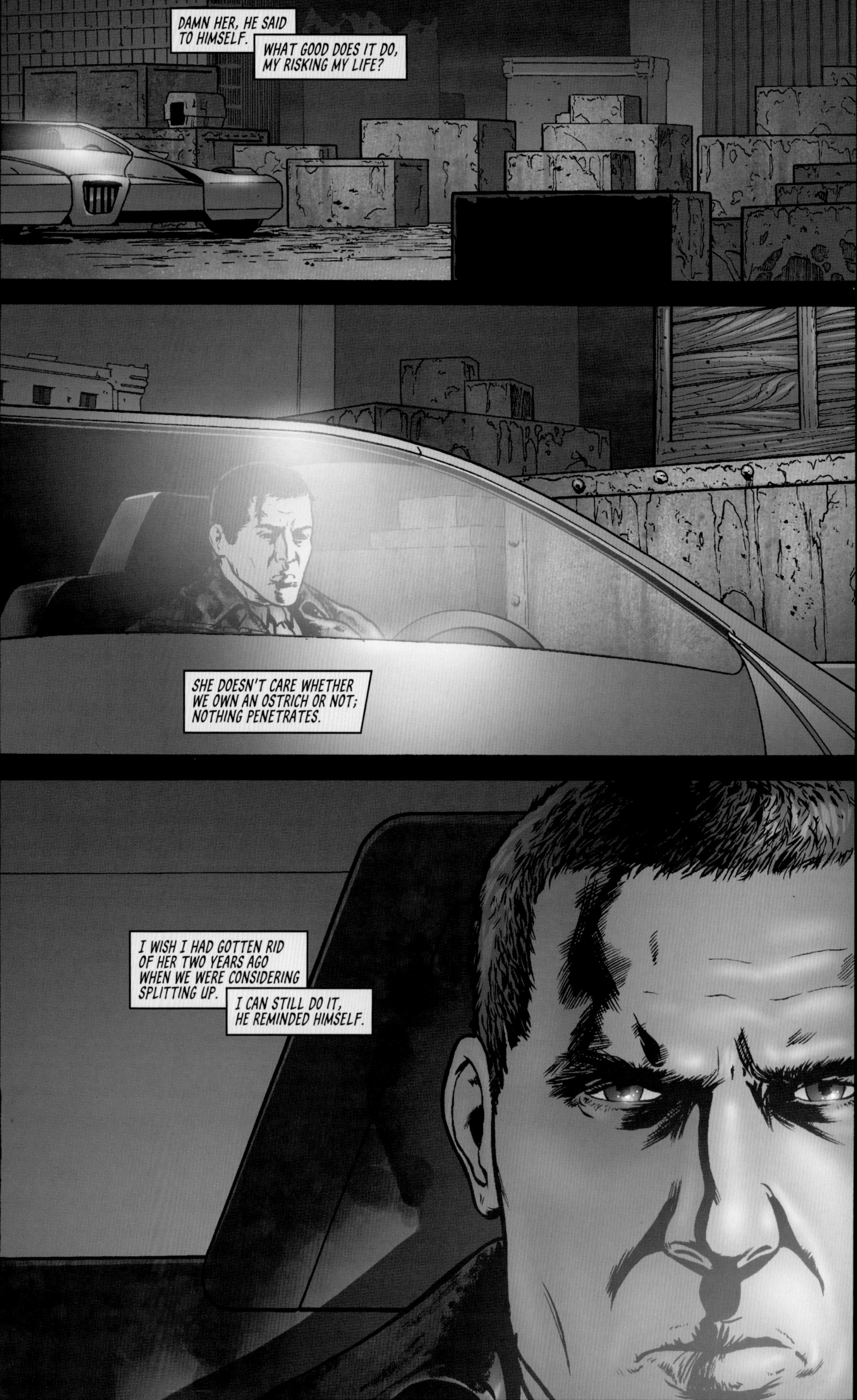
DAMN HER, HE SAID TO HIMSELF.
WHAT GOOD DOES IT DO, MY RISKING MY LIFE?
SHE DOESN'T CARE WHETHER WE OWN AN OSTRICH OR NOT; NOTHING PENETRATES.
I WISH I HAD GOTTEN RID OF HER TWO YEARS AGO WHEN WE WERE CONSIDERING SPLITTING UP.
I CAN STILL DO IT, HE REMINDED HIMSELF.

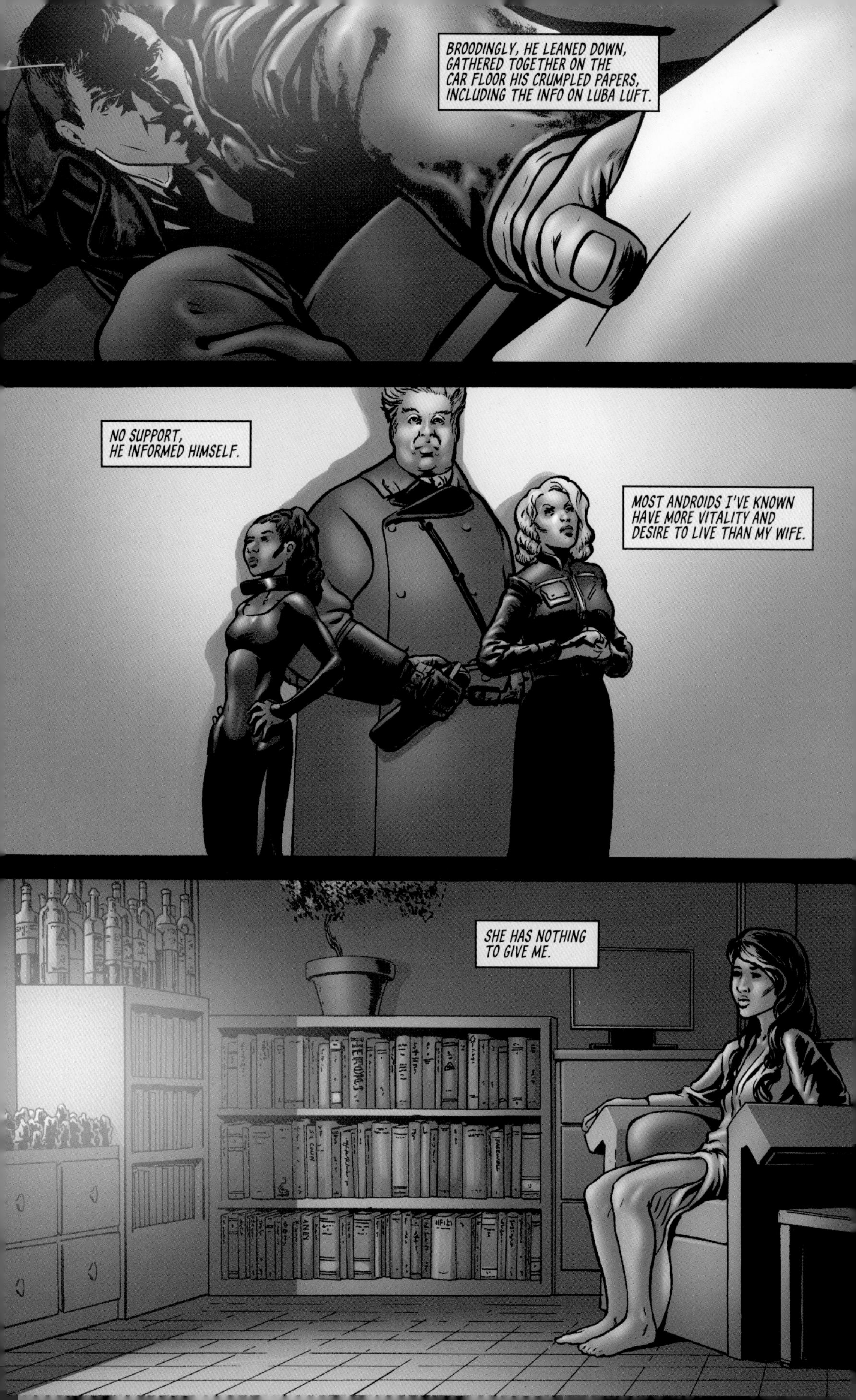
BROODINGLY, HE LEANED DOWN, GATHERED TOGETHER ON THE CAR FLOOR HIS CRUMPLED PAPERS, INCLUDING THE INFO ON LUBA LUFT.
NO SUPPORT, HE INFORMED HIMSELF.
MOST ANDROIDS I'VE KNOWN HAVE MORE VITALITY AND DESIRE TO LIVE THAN MY WIFE.
SHE HAS NOTHING TO GIVE ME.

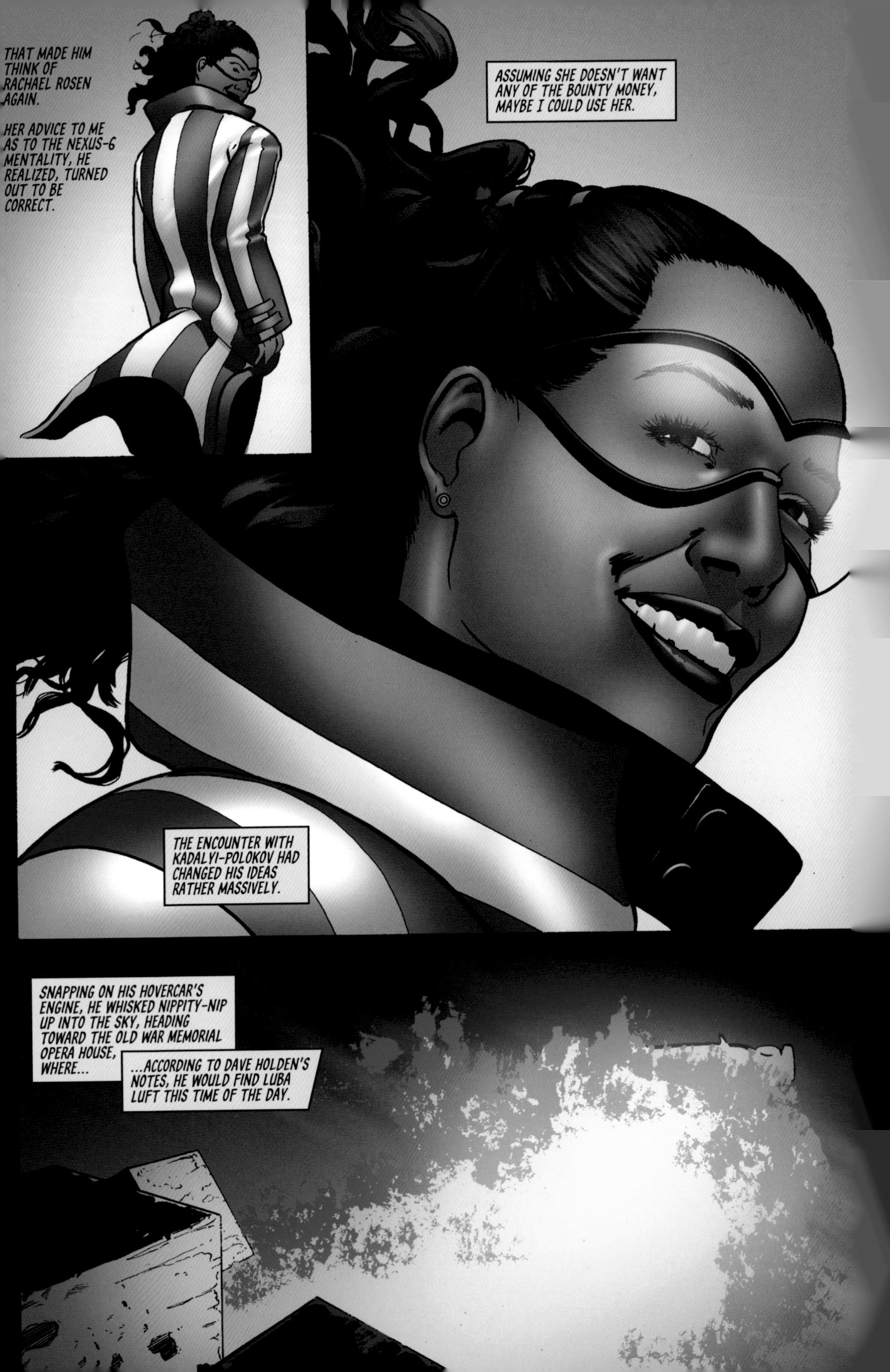

THAT MADE HIM THINK OF RACHAEL ROSEN AGAIN.
HER ADVICE TO ME AS TO THE NEXUS-6 MENTALITY, HE REALIZED, TURNED OUT TO BE CORRECT.
ASSUMING SHE DOESN'T WANT ANY OF THE BOUNTY MONEY, MAYBE I COULD USE HER.
THE ENCOUNTER WITH KADALYI-POLOKOV HAD CHANGED HIS IDEAS RATHER MASSIVELY.
SNAPPING ON HIS HOVERCAR'S ENGINE, HE WHISKED NIPPITY-NIP UP INTO THE SKY, HEADING TOWARD THE OLD WAR MEMORIAL OPERA HOUSE, WHERE...
...ACCORDING TO DAVE HOLDEN'S NOTES, HE WOULD FIND LUBA LUFT THIS TIME OF THE DAY.

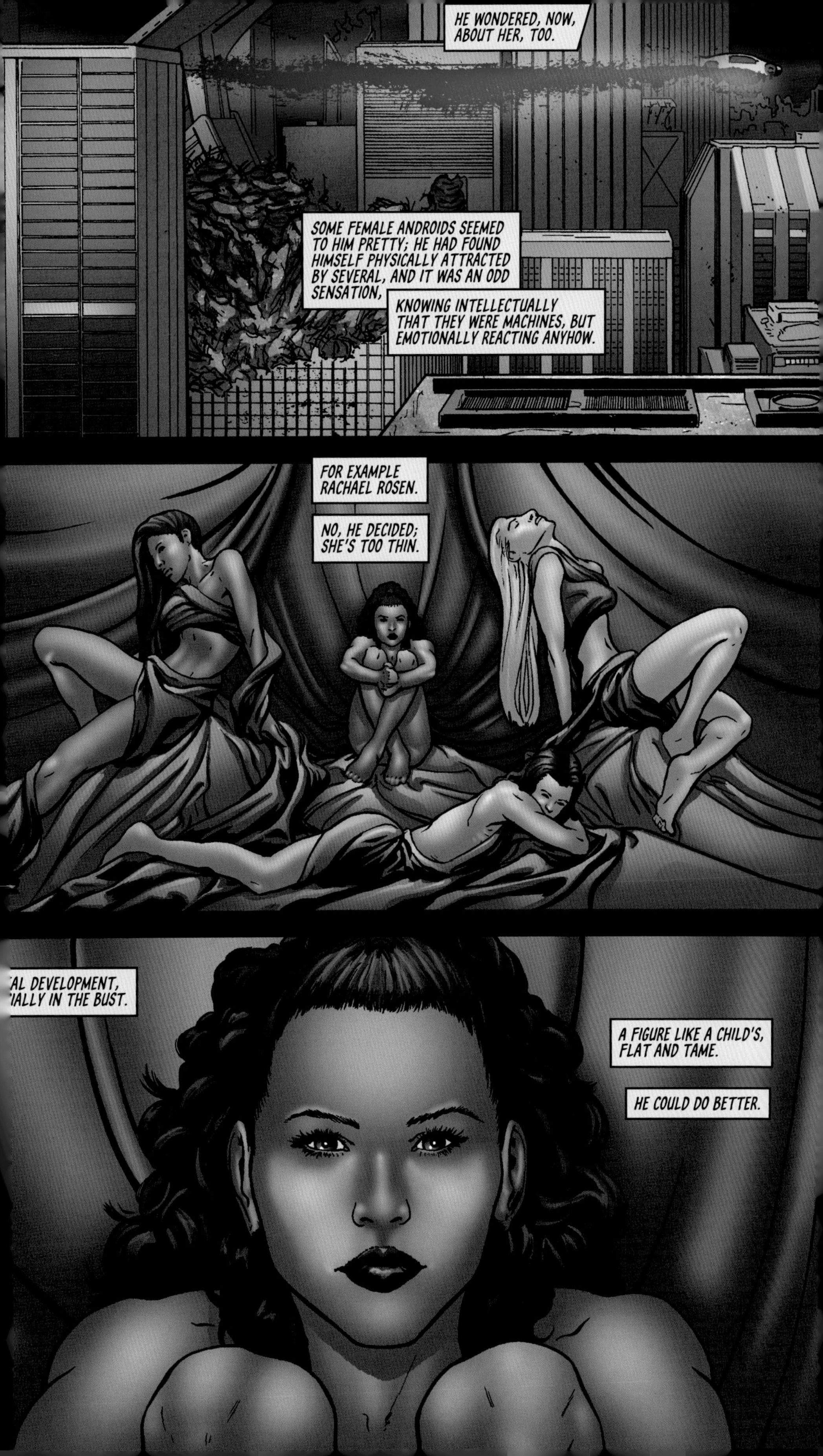
HE WONDERED, NOW, ABOUT HER, TOO.
SOME FEMALE ANDROIDS SEEMED TO HIM PRETTY; HE HAD FOUND HIMSELF PHYSICALLY ATTRACTED BY SEVERAL, AND IT WAS AN ODD SENSATION,
KNOWING INTELLECTUALLY THAT THEY WERE MACHINES, BUT EMOTIONALLY REACTING ANYHOW.
FOR EXAMPLE RACHAEL ROSEN.
NO, HE DECIDED; SHE'S TOO THIN.
AL DEVELOPMENT, IALLY IN THE BUST.
A FIGURE LIKE A CHILD'S, FLAT AND TAME.
HE COULD DO BETTER.

HOW OLD DID THE POOP SHEET SAY LUBA LUFT WAS?

AS HE DROVE HE HAULED OUT THE NOW WRINKLED NOTES, FOUND HER SO-CALLED "AGE."

TWENTY-EIGHT, THE SHEET READ.

Model: Nexus 6 Android   Company: Rosen Industries
Luft, Luba   Gender: F   Visual Age: 28
2b48-bπ–42Xα Integer Aspect: $\Omega\partial$58
Retinal Configuration: Unknown
Serial Number 908-Ω8-24
Tertiary Node: Engaged
Aspects Inc.
Design

JUDGED BY APPEARANCE, WHICH, WITH ANDYS, WAS THE ONLY USEFUL STANDARD.

IT'S A GOOD THING I KNOW SOMETHING ABOUT OPERA, RICK REFLECTED.

THAT'S ANOTHER ADVANTAGE I HAVE OVER DAVE; I'M MORE CULTURALLY ORIENTED.

I'LL TRY ONE MORE ANDY BEFORE I ASK RACHAEL FOR HELP, HE DECIDED.

IF MISS LUFT PROVES EXCEPTIONALLY HARD— BUT HE HAD AN INTUITION SHE WOULDN'T.

POLOKOV HAD BEEN THE ROUGH ONE; THE OTHERS, UNAWARE THAT ANYONE ACTIVELY HUNTED THEM, WOULD CRUMBLE IN SUCCESSION, PLUGGED LIKE A FILE OF DUCKS.

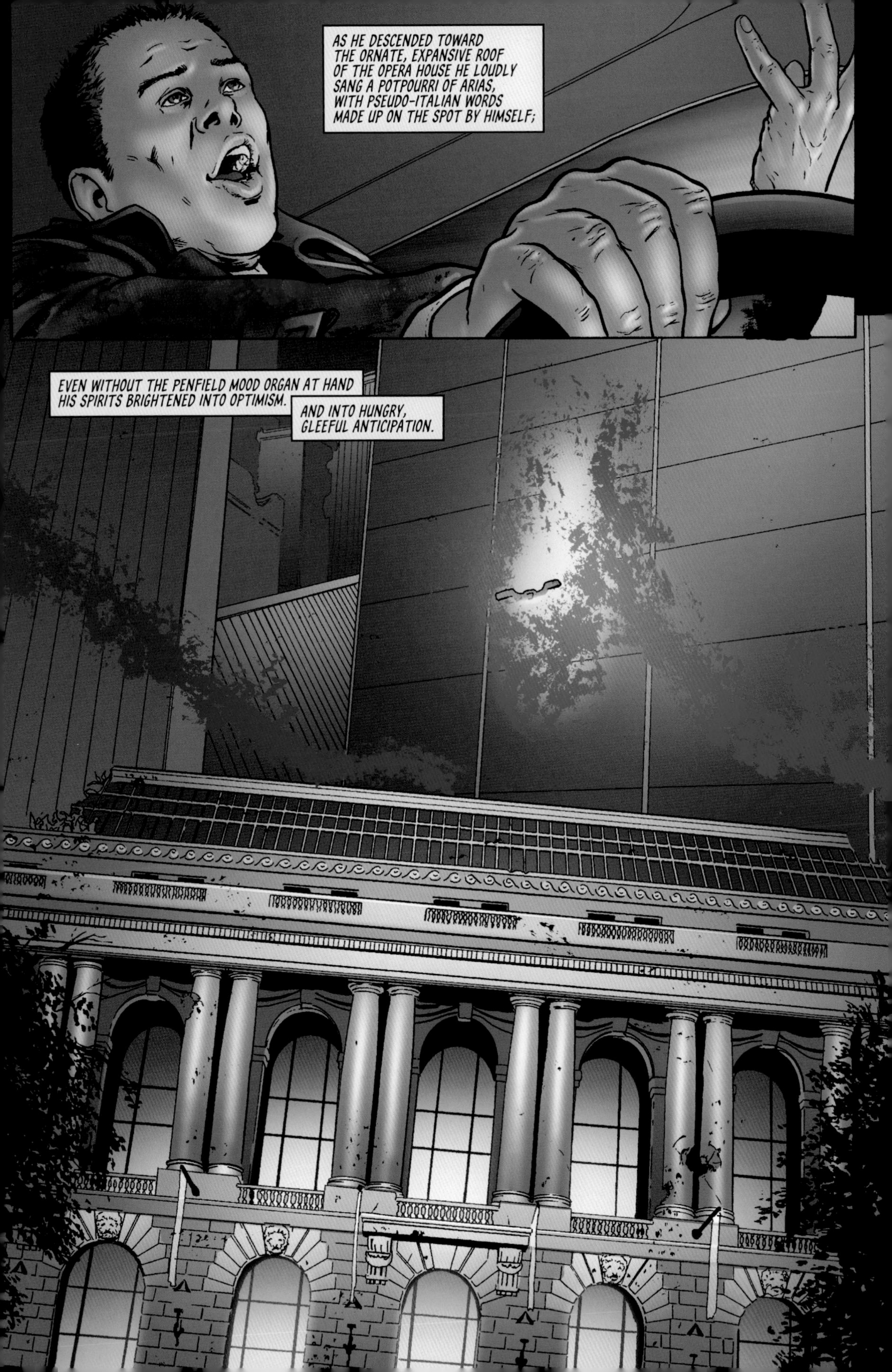
AS HE DESCENDED TOWARD THE ORNATE, EXPANSIVE ROOF OF THE OPERA HOUSE HE LOUDLY SANG A POTPOURRI OF ARIAS, WITH PSEUDO-ITALIAN WORDS MADE UP ON THE SPOT BY HIMSELF;
EVEN WITHOUT THE PENFIELD MOOD ORGAN AT HAND HIS SPIRITS BRIGHTENED INTO OPTIMISM.
AND INTO HUNGRY, GLEEFUL ANTICIPATION.

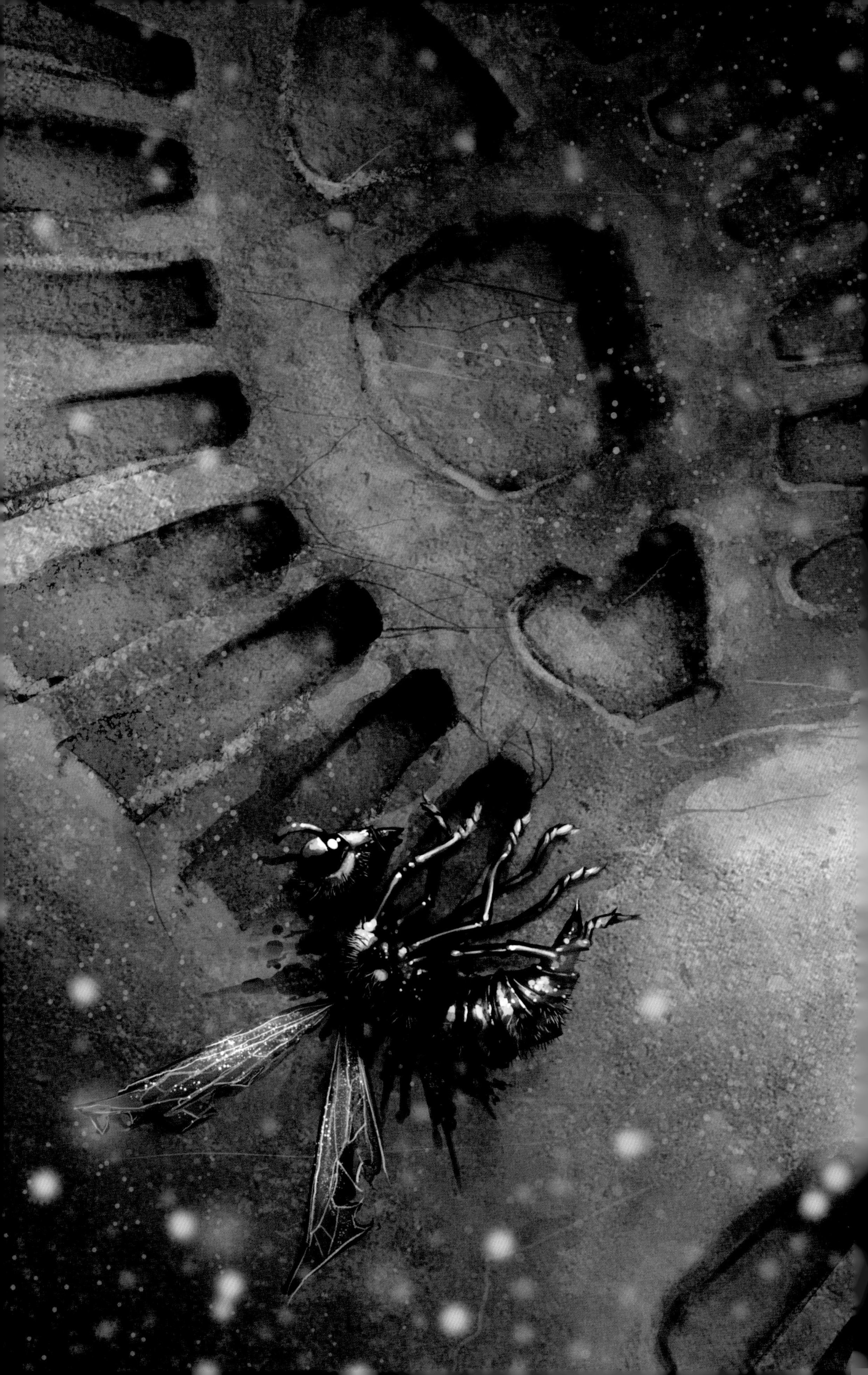

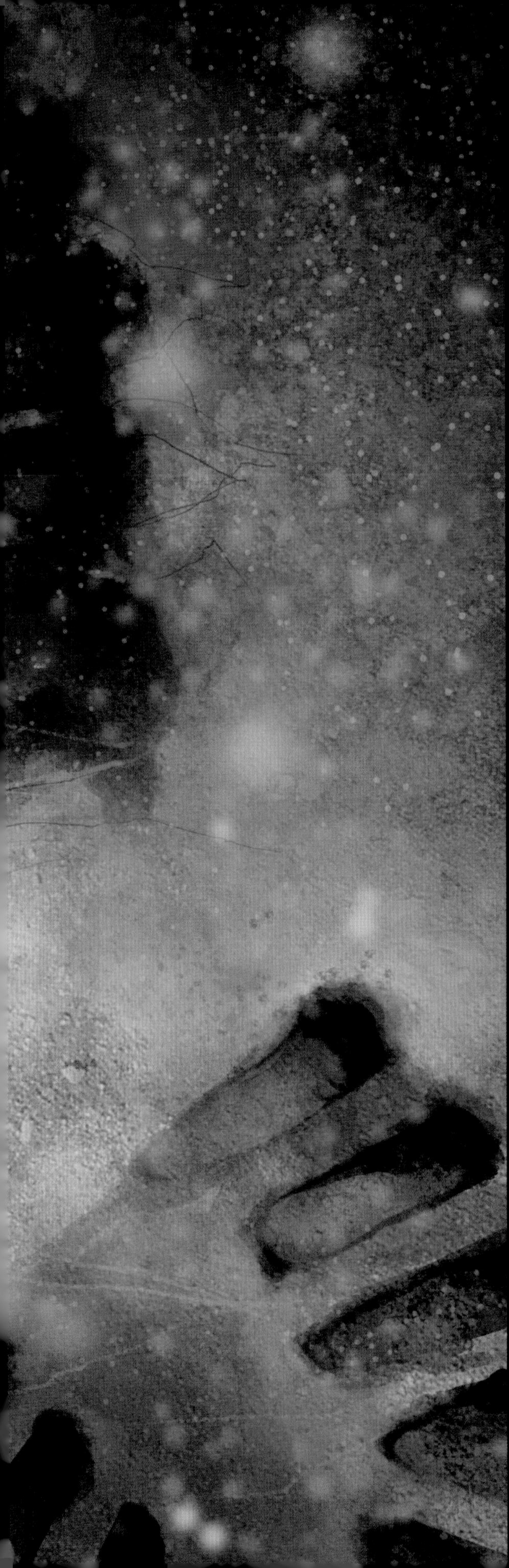

BOOK EIGHT

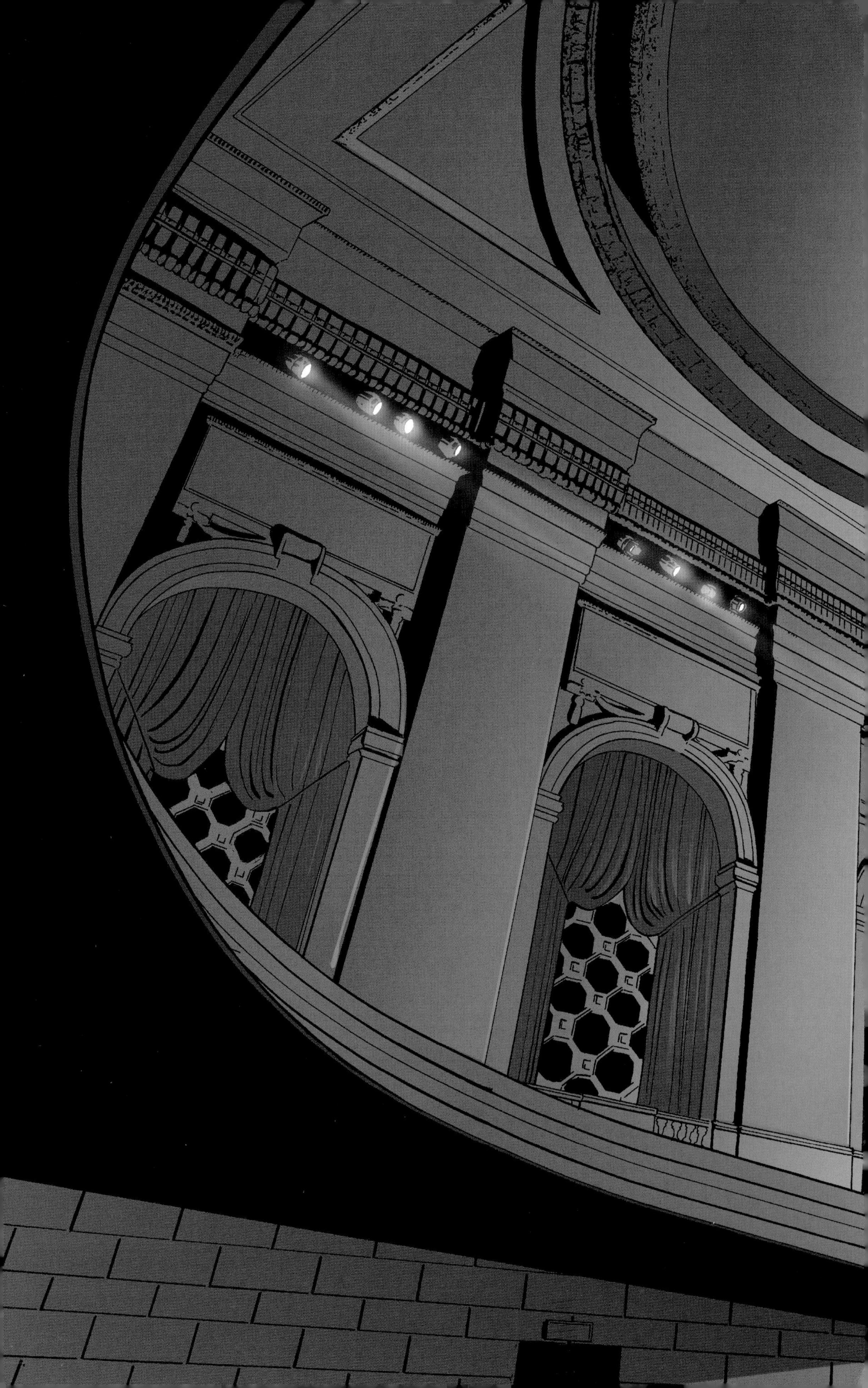

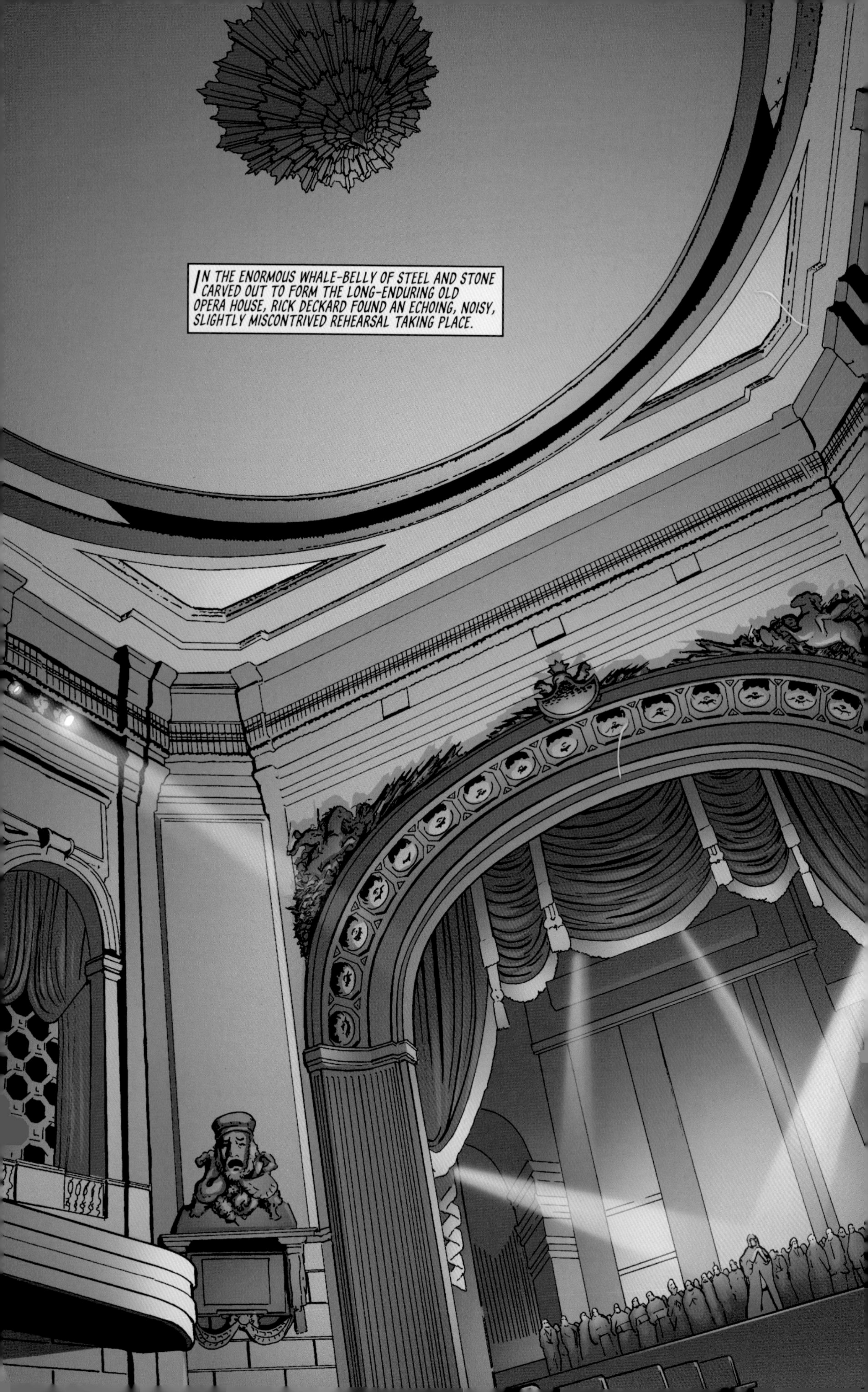
IN THE ENORMOUS WHALE-BELLY OF STEEL AND STONE CARVED OUT TO FORM THE LONG-ENDURING OLD OPERA HOUSE, RICK DECKARD FOUND AN ECHOING, NOISY, SLIGHTLY MISCONTRIVED REHEARSAL TAKING PLACE.

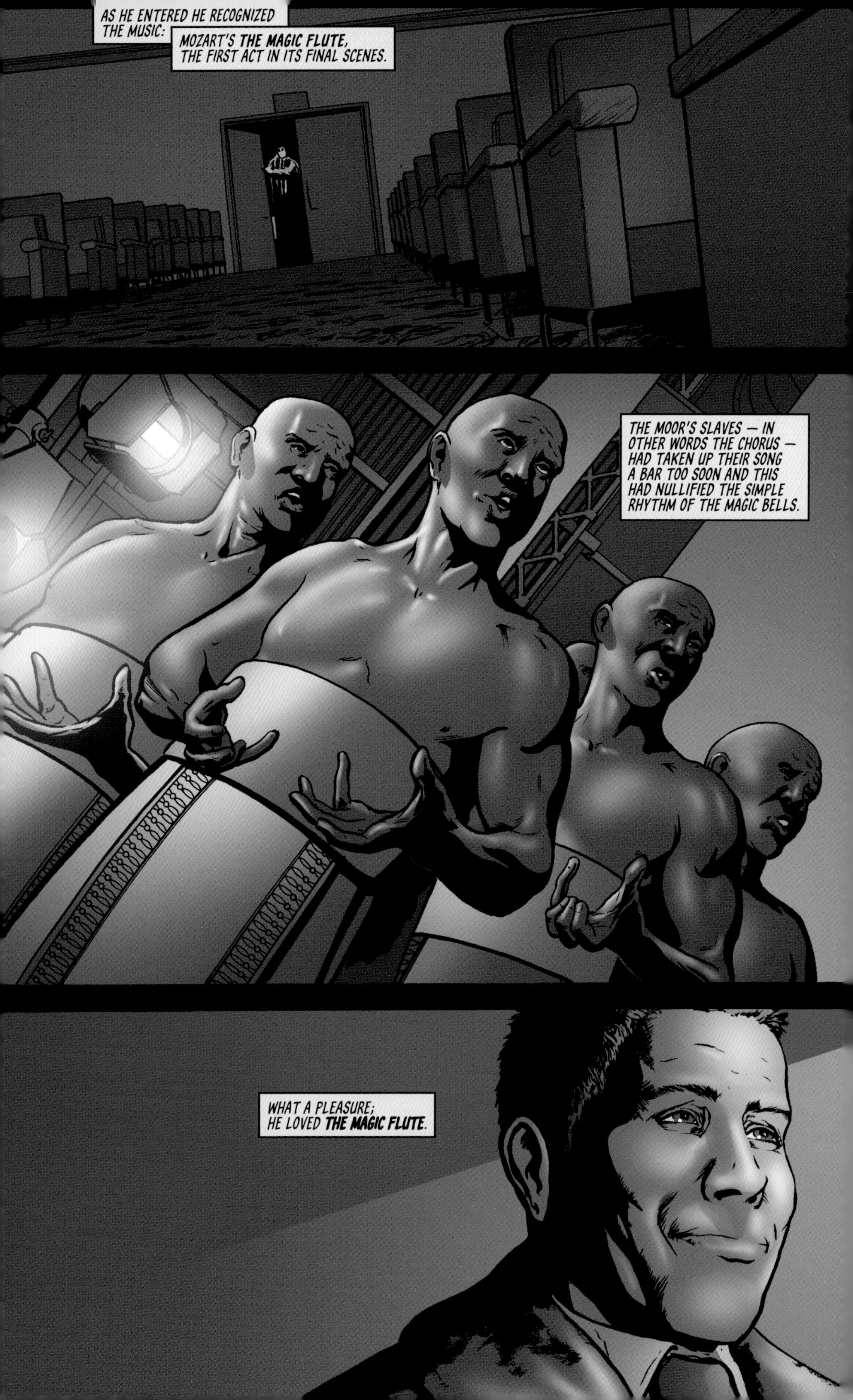
AS HE ENTERED HE RECOGNIZED THE MUSIC:
MOZART'S THE MAGIC FLUTE, THE FIRST ACT IN ITS FINAL SCENES.
THE MOOR'S SLAVES — IN OTHER WORDS THE CHORUS — HAD TAKEN UP THEIR SONG A BAR TOO SOON AND THIS HAD NULLIFIED THE SIMPLE RHYTHM OF THE MAGIC BELLS.
WHAT A PLEASURE; HE LOVED THE MAGIC FLUTE.

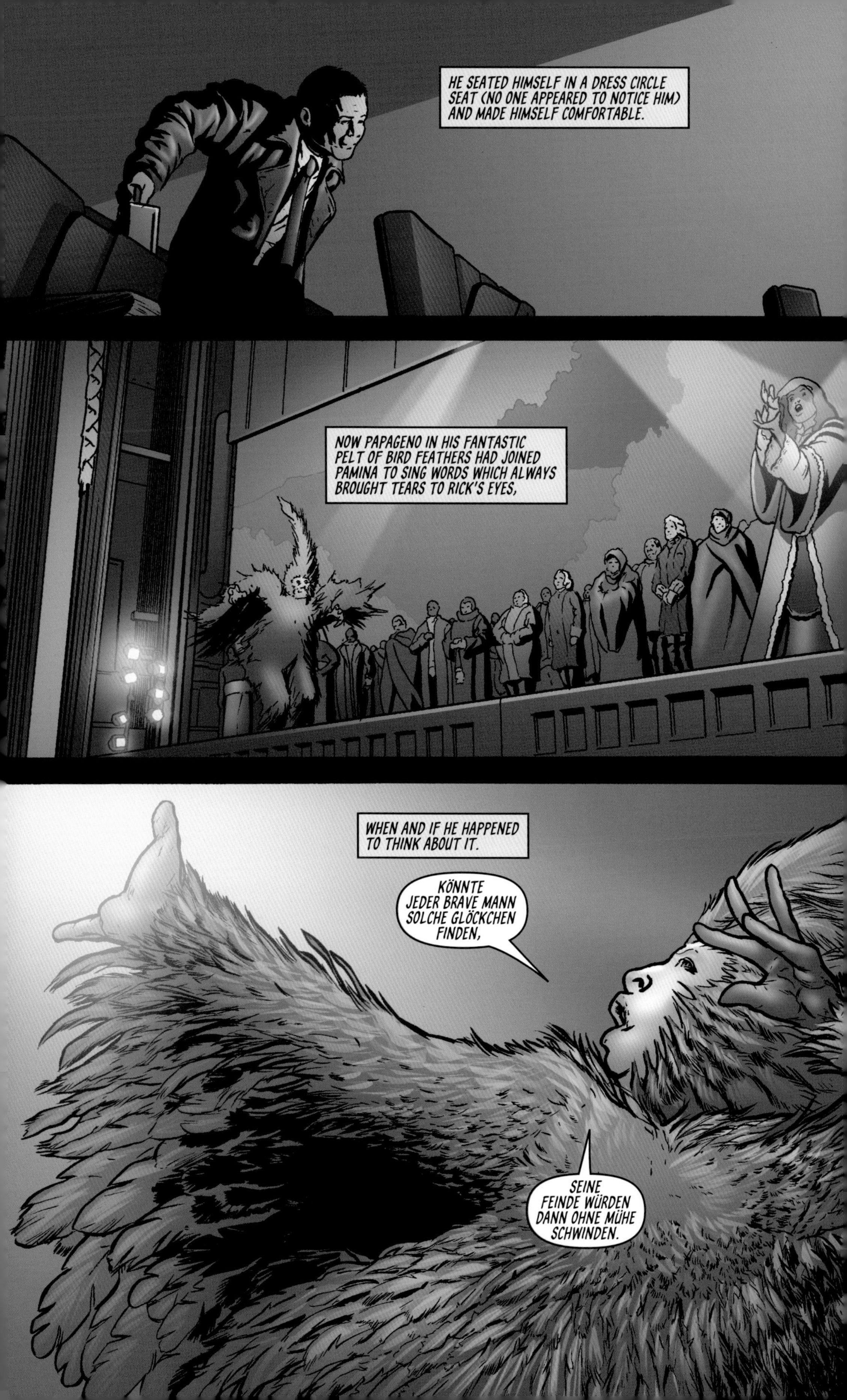
HE SEATED HIMSELF IN A DRESS CIRCLE SEAT (NO ONE APPEARED TO NOTICE HIM) AND MADE HIMSELF COMFORTABLE.
NOW PAPAGENO IN HIS FANTASTIC PELT OF BIRD FEATHERS HAD JOINED PAMINA TO SING WORDS WHICH ALWAYS BROUGHT TEARS TO RICK'S EYES,
WHEN AND IF HE HAPPENED TO THINK ABOUT IT.
KÖNNTE JEDER BRAVE MANN SOLCHE GLÖCKCHEN FINDEN,
SEINE FEINDE WÜRDEN DANN OHNE MÜHE SCHWINDEN.

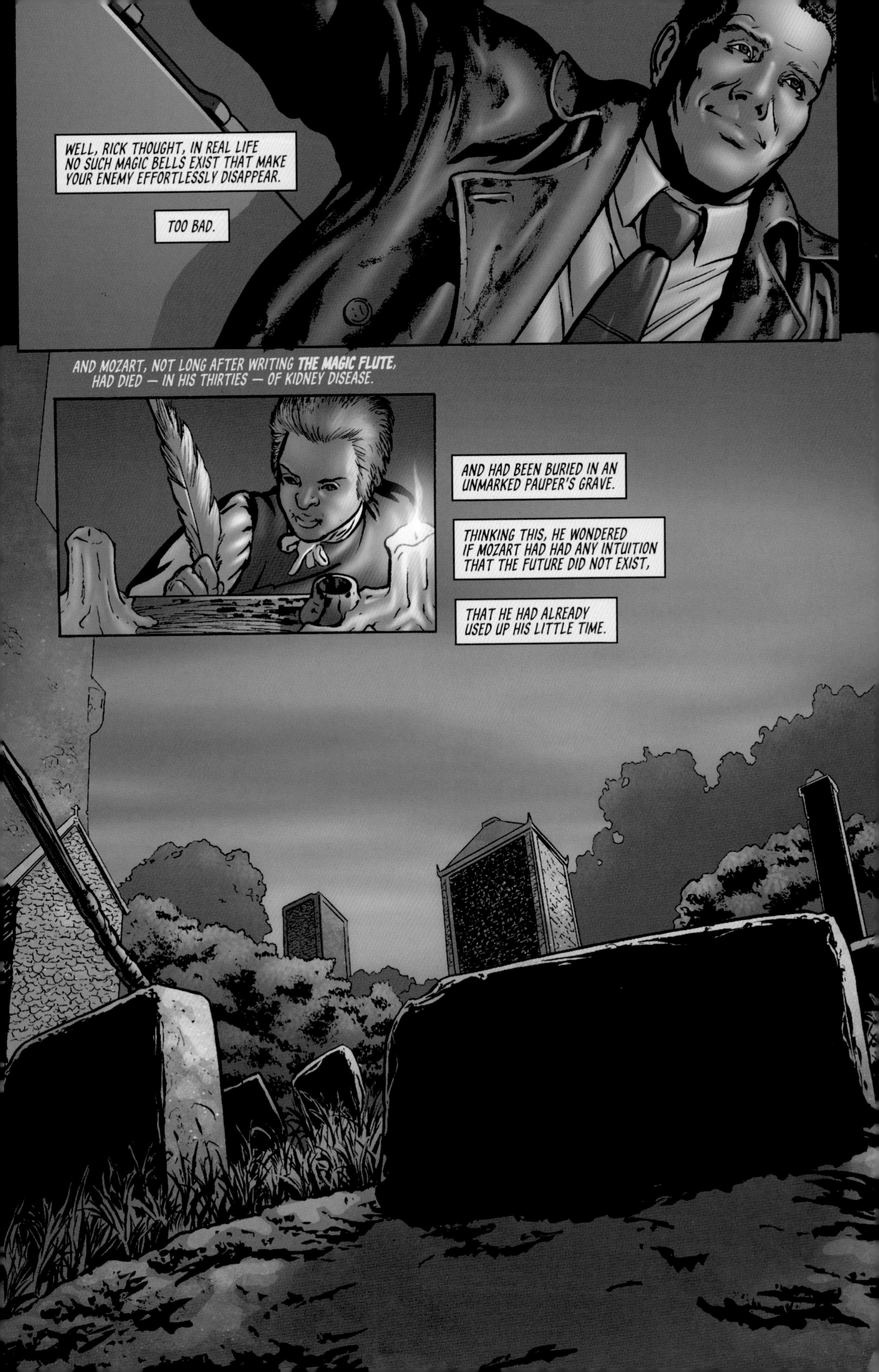
WELL, RICK THOUGHT, IN REAL LIFE NO SUCH MAGIC BELLS EXIST THAT MAKE YOUR ENEMY EFFORTLESSLY DISAPPEAR.
TOO BAD.
AND MOZART, NOT LONG AFTER WRITING THE MAGIC FLUTE, HAD DIED — IN HIS THIRTIES — OF KIDNEY DISEASE.
AND HAD BEEN BURIED IN AN UNMARKED PAUPER'S GRAVE.
THINKING THIS, HE WONDERED IF MOZART HAD HAD ANY INTUITION THAT THE FUTURE DID NOT EXIST,
THAT HE HAD ALREADY USED UP HIS LITTLE TIME.

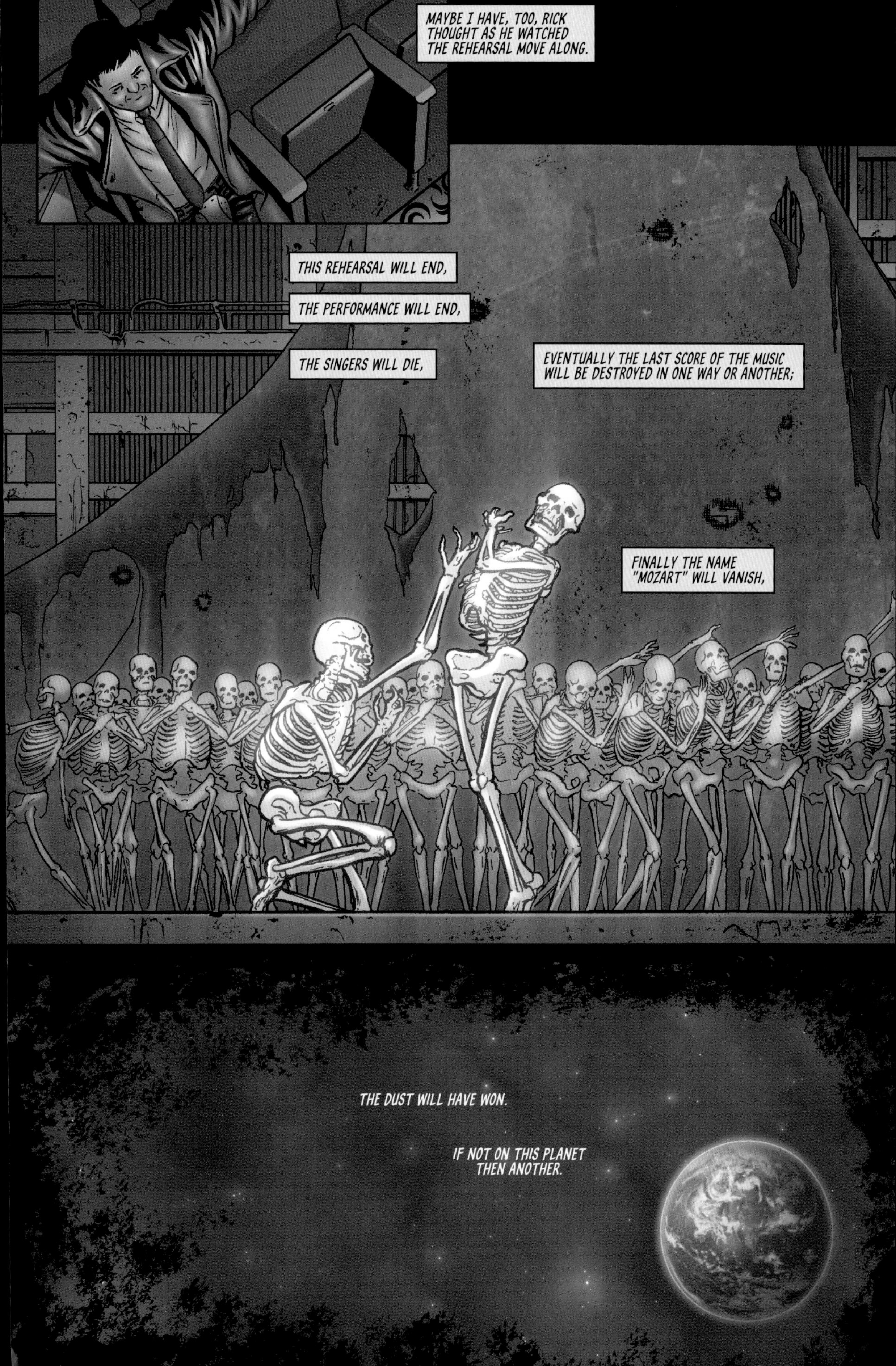
MAYBE I HAVE, TOO, RICK THOUGHT AS HE WATCHED THE REHEARSAL MOVE ALONG.
THIS REHEARSAL WILL END,
THE PERFORMANCE WILL END,
THE SINGERS WILL DIE,
EVENTUALLY THE LAST SCORE OF THE MUSIC WILL BE DESTROYED IN ONE WAY OR ANOTHER;
FINALLY THE NAME "MOZART" WILL VANISH,
THE DUST WILL HAVE WON.
IF NOT ON THIS PLANET THEN ANOTHER.

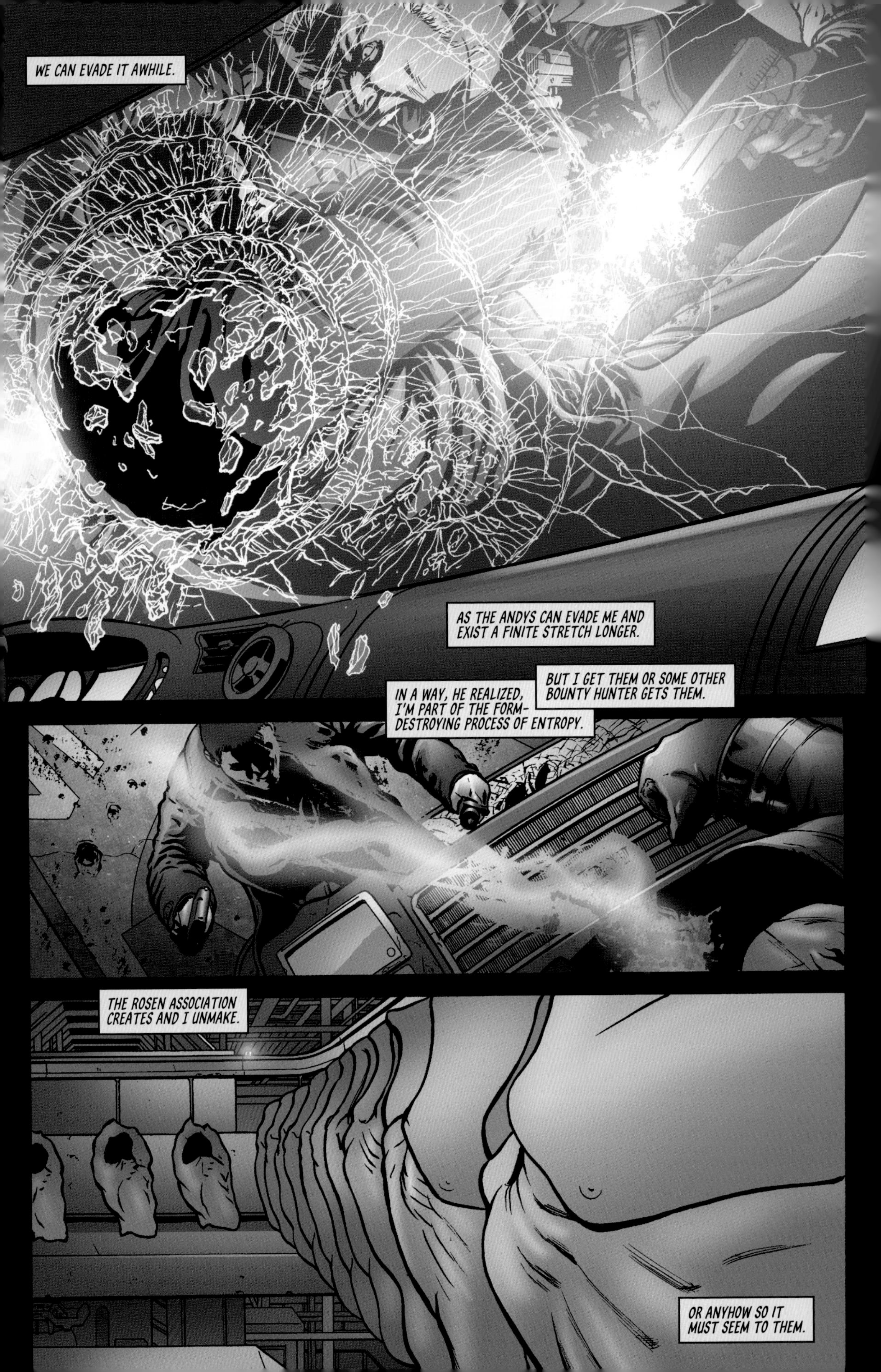
WE CAN EVADE IT AWHILE.
AS THE ANDYS CAN EVADE ME AND EXIST A FINITE STRETCH LONGER.
BUT I GET THEM OR SOME OTHER BOUNTY HUNTER GETS THEM.
IN A WAY, HE REALIZED, I'M PART OF THE FORM-DESTROYING PROCESS OF ENTROPY.
THE ROSEN ASSOCIATION CREATES AND I UNMAKE.
OR ANYHOW SO IT MUST SEEM TO THEM.

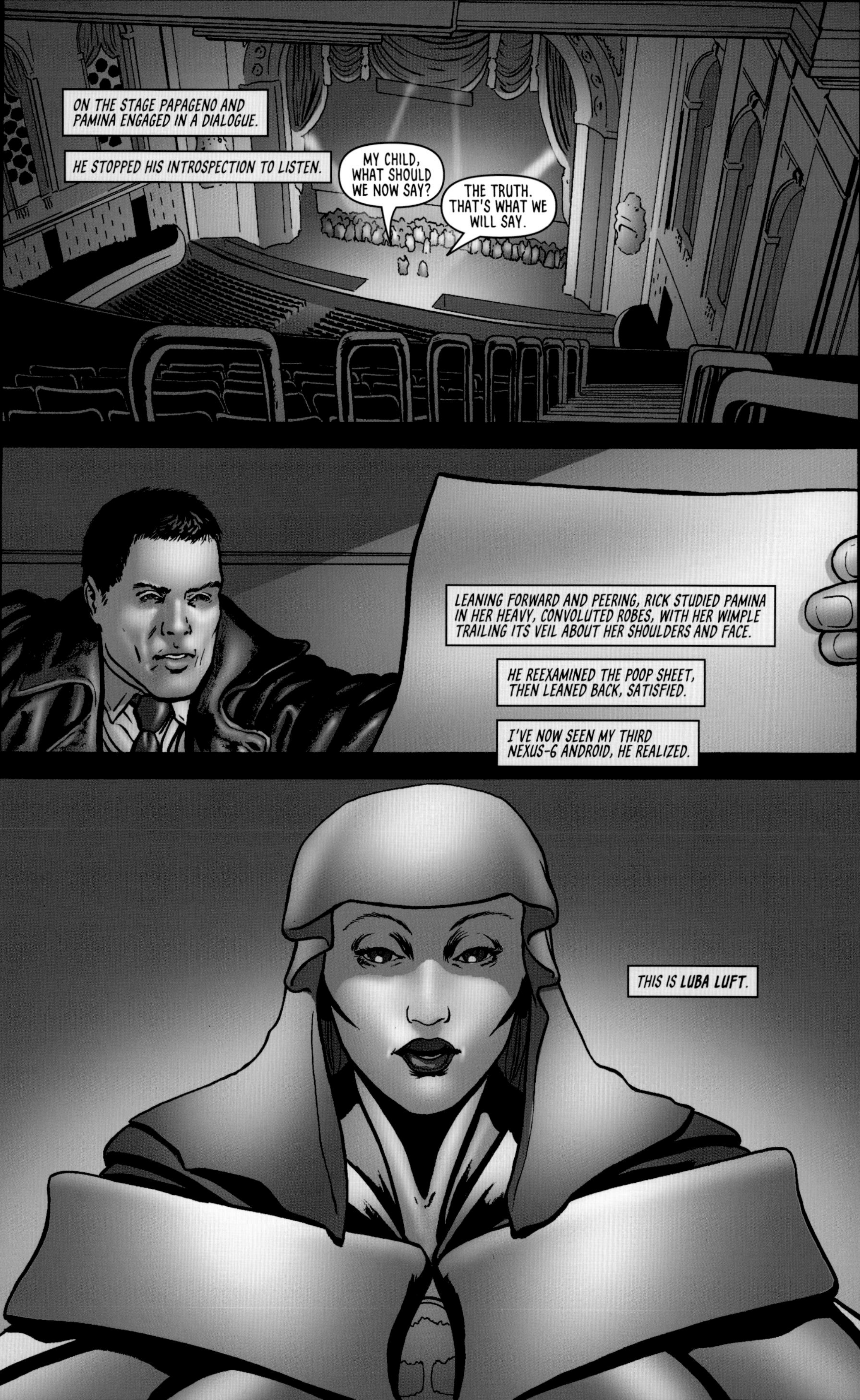

ON THE STAGE PAPAGENO AND PAMINA ENGAGED IN A DIALOGUE.
HE STOPPED HIS INTROSPECTION TO LISTEN.
MY CHILD, WHAT SHOULD WE NOW SAY?
THE TRUTH. THAT'S WHAT WE WILL SAY.
LEANING FORWARD AND PEERING, RICK STUDIED PAMINA IN HER HEAVY, CONVOLUTED ROBES, WITH HER WIMPLE TRAILING ITS VEIL ABOUT HER SHOULDERS AND FACE.
HE REEXAMINED THE POOP SHEET, THEN LEANED BACK, SATISFIED.
I'VE NOW SEEN MY THIRD NEXUS-6 ANDROID, HE REALIZED.
THIS IS LUBA LUFT.

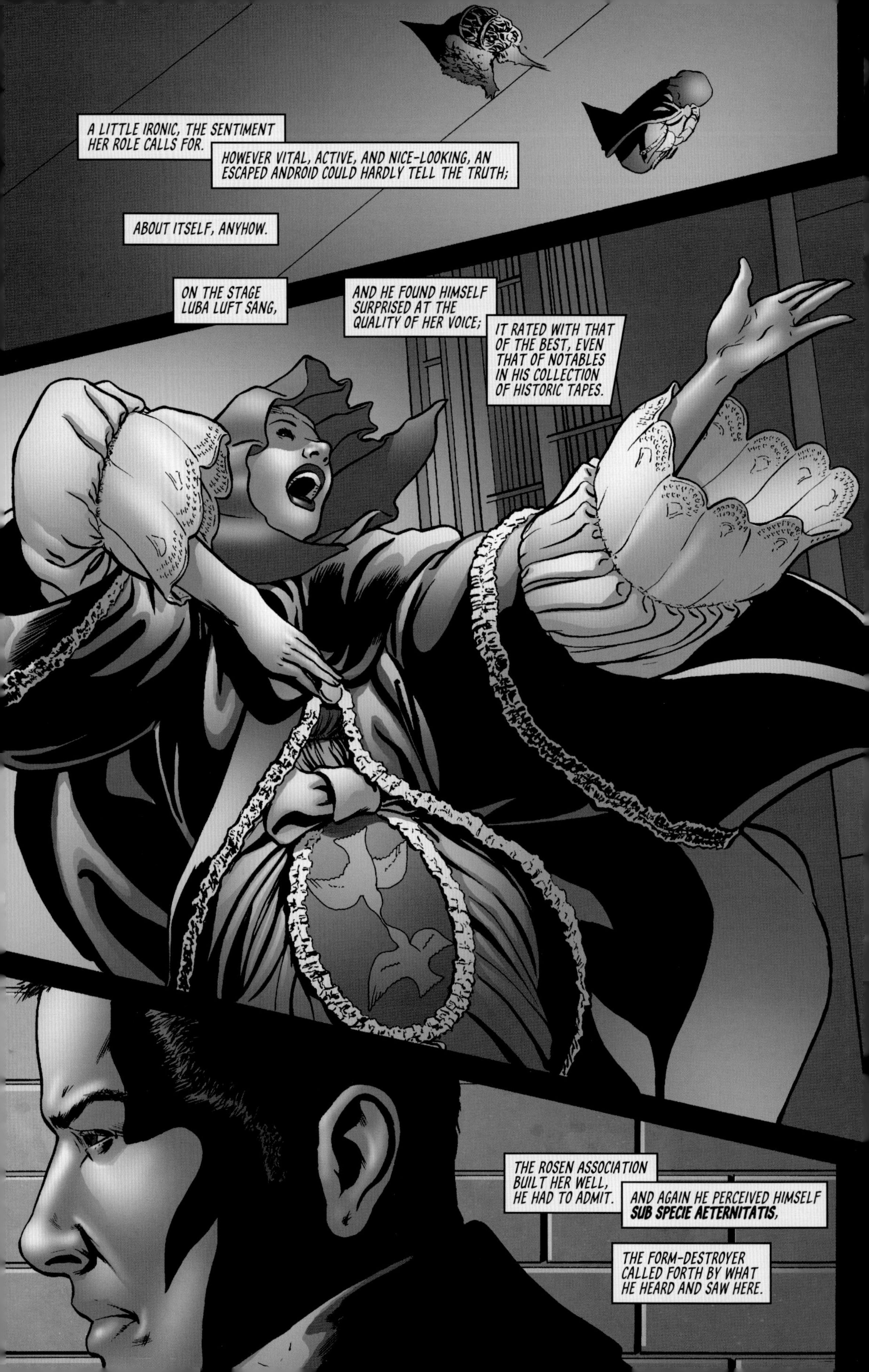
A LITTLE IRONIC, THE SENTIMENT HER ROLE CALLS FOR.
HOWEVER VITAL, ACTIVE, AND NICE-LOOKING, AN ESCAPED ANDROID COULD HARDLY TELL THE TRUTH;
ABOUT ITSELF, ANYHOW.
ON THE STAGE LUBA LUFT SANG,
AND HE FOUND HIMSELF SURPRISED AT THE QUALITY OF HER VOICE;
IT RATED WITH THAT OF THE BEST, EVEN THAT OF NOTABLES IN HIS COLLECTION OF HISTORIC TAPES.
THE ROSEN ASSOCIATION BUILT HER WELL, HE HAD TO ADMIT.
AND AGAIN HE PERCEIVED HIMSELF **SUB SPECIE AETERNITATIS**,
THE FORM-DESTROYER CALLED FORTH BY WHAT HE HEARD AND SAW HERE.

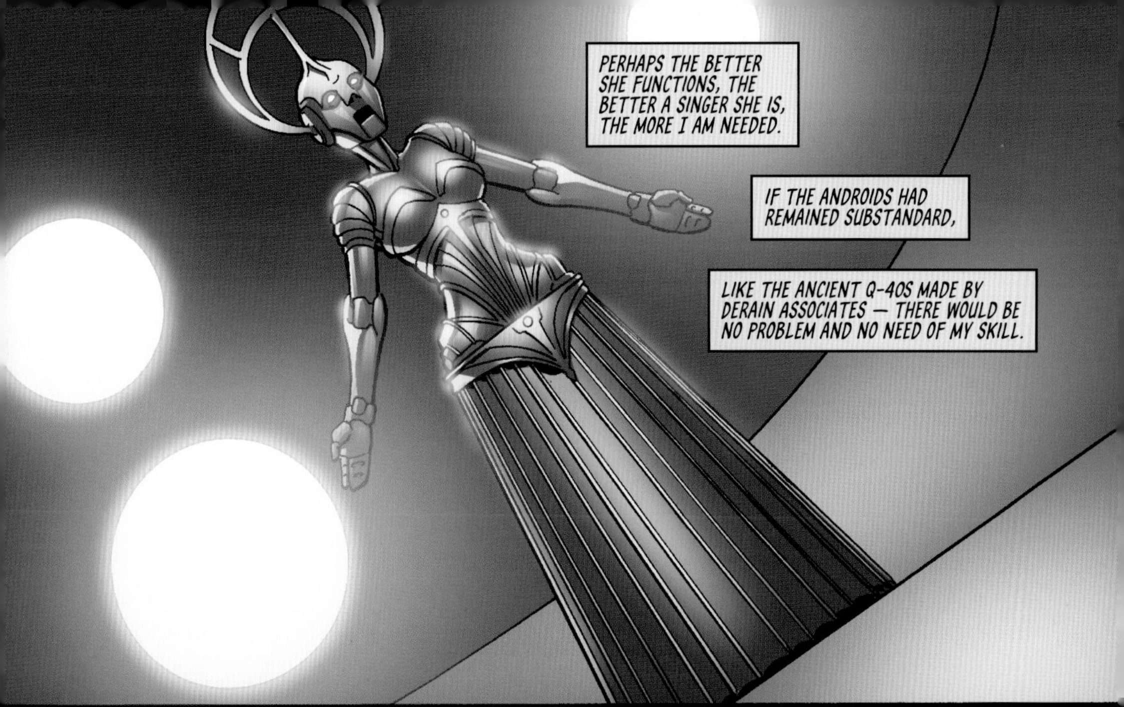
PERHAPS THE BETTER SHE FUNCTIONS, THE BETTER A SINGER SHE IS, THE MORE I AM NEEDED.
IF THE ANDROIDS HAD REMAINED SUBSTANDARD,
LIKE THE ANCIENT Q-40S MADE BY DERAIN ASSOCIATES — THERE WOULD BE NO PROBLEM AND NO NEED OF MY SKILL.

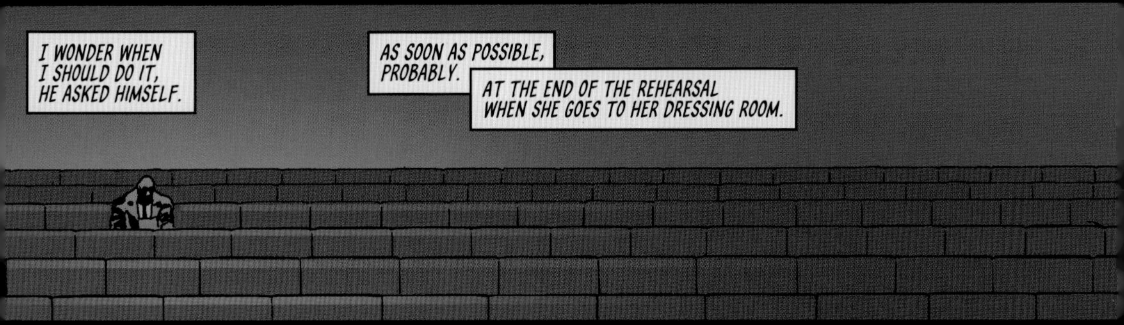
I WONDER WHEN I SHOULD DO IT, HE ASKED HIMSELF.
AS SOON AS POSSIBLE, PROBABLY.
AT THE END OF THE REHEARSAL WHEN SHE GOES TO HER DRESSING ROOM.

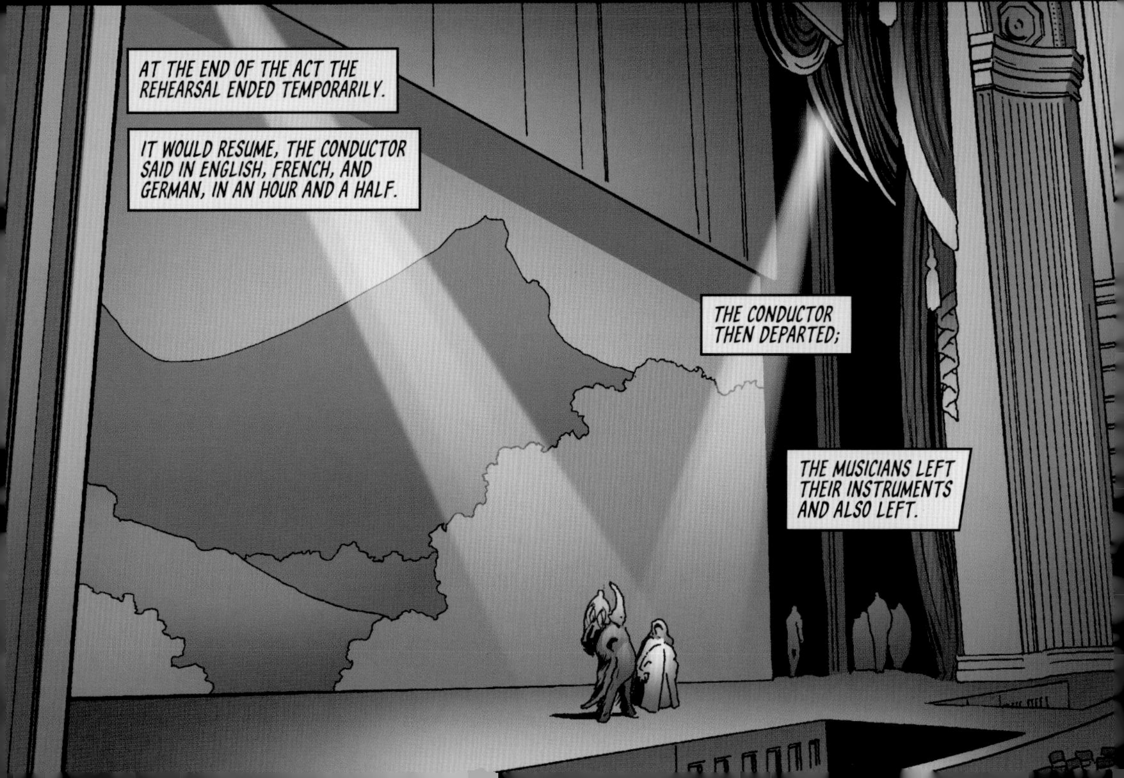
AT THE END OF THE ACT THE REHEARSAL ENDED TEMPORARILY.
IT WOULD RESUME, THE CONDUCTOR SAID IN ENGLISH, FRENCH, AND GERMAN, IN AN HOUR AND A HALF.
THE CONDUCTOR THEN DEPARTED;
THE MUSICIANS LEFT THEIR INSTRUMENTS AND ALSO LEFT.

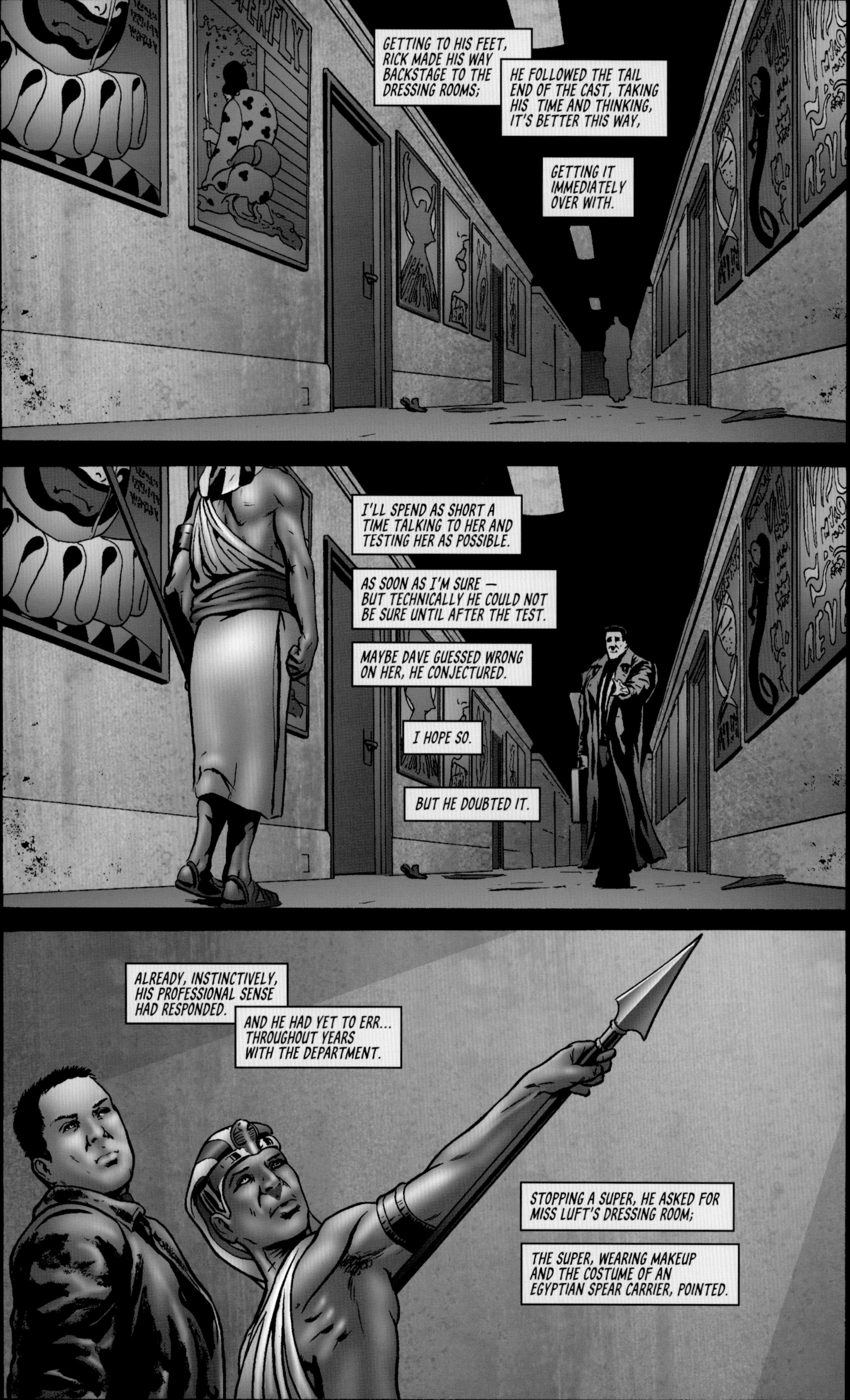
GETTING TO HIS FEET, RICK MADE HIS WAY BACKSTAGE TO THE DRESSING ROOMS;
HE FOLLOWED THE TAIL END OF THE CAST, TAKING HIS TIME AND THINKING, IT'S BETTER THIS WAY,
GETTING IT IMMEDIATELY OVER WITH.
I'LL SPEND AS SHORT A TIME TALKING TO HER AND TESTING HER AS POSSIBLE.
AS SOON AS I'M SURE — BUT TECHNICALLY HE COULD NOT BE SURE UNTIL AFTER THE TEST.
MAYBE DAVE GUESSED WRONG ON HER, HE CONJECTURED.
I HOPE SO.
BUT HE DOUBTED IT.
ALREADY, INSTINCTIVELY, HIS PROFESSIONAL SENSE HAD RESPONDED.
AND HE HAD YET TO ERR... THROUGHOUT YEARS WITH THE DEPARTMENT.
STOPPING A SUPER, HE ASKED FOR MISS LUFT'S DRESSING ROOM;
THE SUPER, WEARING MAKEUP AND THE COSTUME OF AN EGYPTIAN SPEAR CARRIER, POINTED.

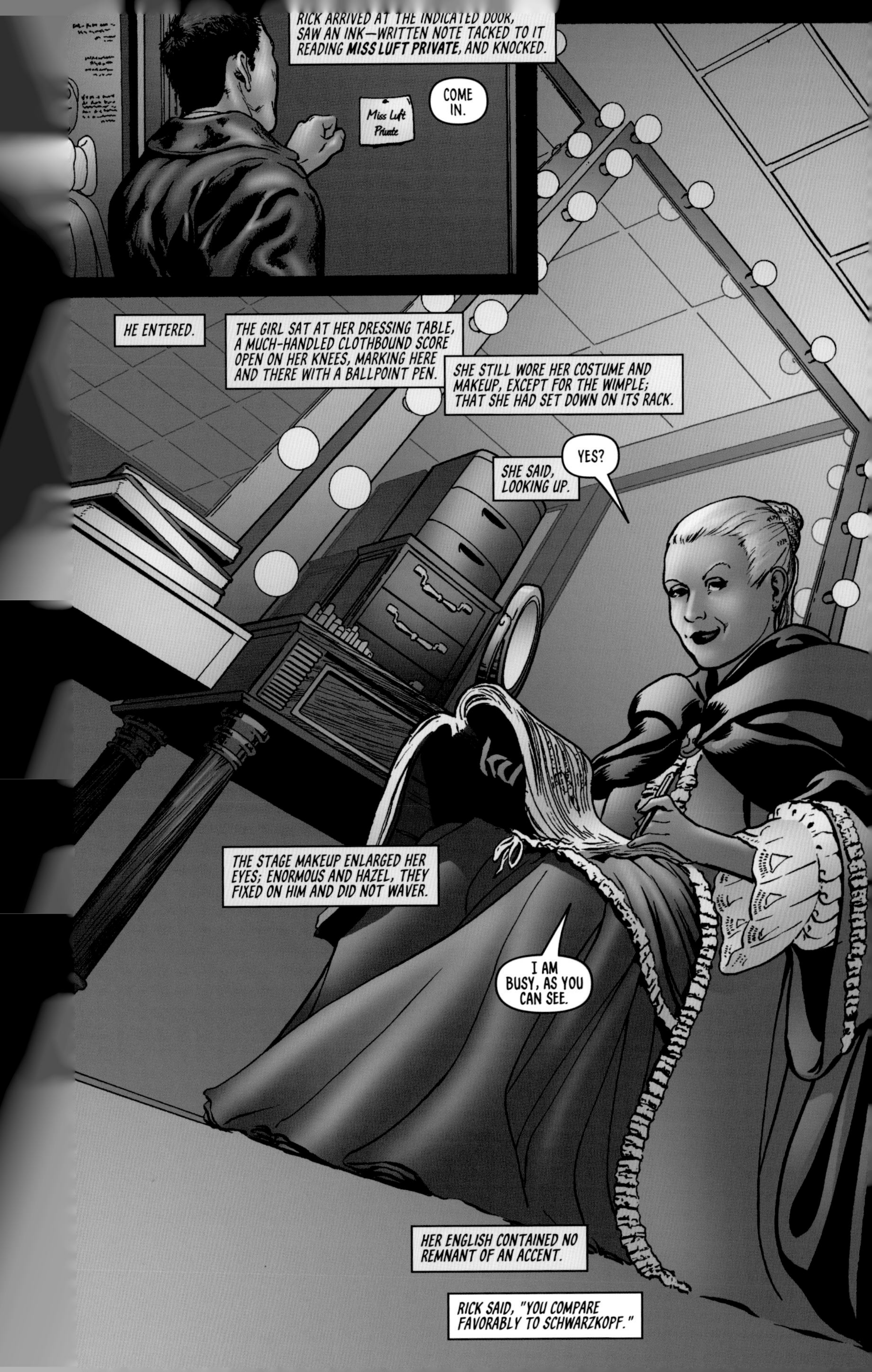
RICK ARRIVED AT THE INDICATED DOOR, SAW AN INK—WRITTEN NOTE TACKED TO IT READING MISS LUFT PRIVATE, AND KNOCKED.
Miss Luft Private
COME IN.
HE ENTERED.
THE GIRL SAT AT HER DRESSING TABLE, A MUCH-HANDLED CLOTHBOUND SCORE OPEN ON HER KNEES, MARKING HERE AND THERE WITH A BALLPOINT PEN.
SHE STILL WORE HER COSTUME AND MAKEUP, EXCEPT FOR THE WIMPLE; THAT SHE HAD SET DOWN ON ITS RACK.
SHE SAID, LOOKING UP.
YES?
THE STAGE MAKEUP ENLARGED HER EYES; ENORMOUS AND HAZEL, THEY FIXED ON HIM AND DID NOT WAVER.
I AM BUSY, AS YOU CAN SEE.
HER ENGLISH CONTAINED NO REMNANT OF AN ACCENT.
RICK SAID, "YOU COMPARE FAVORABLY TO SCHWARZKOPF."

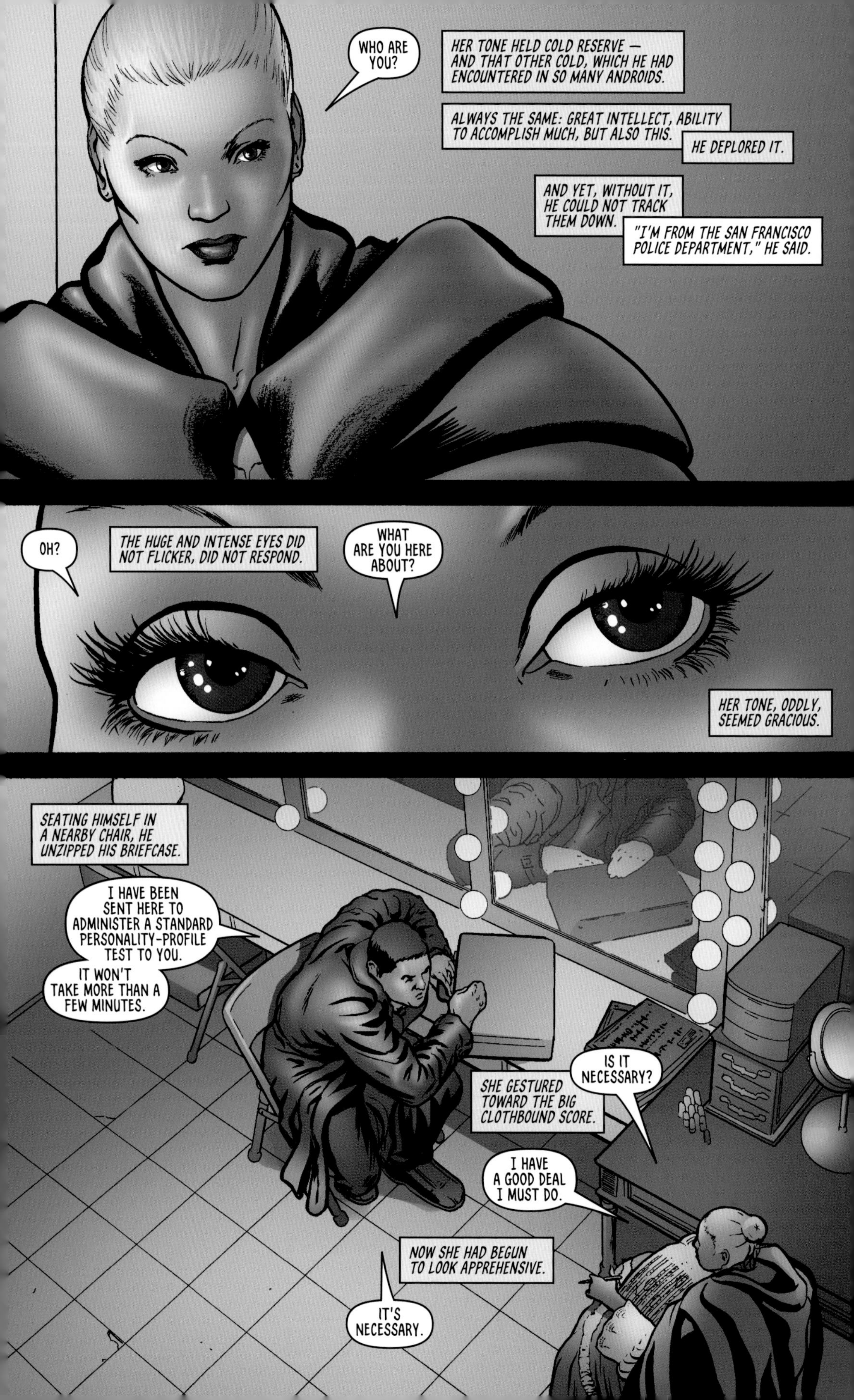
WHO ARE YOU?
HER TONE HELD COLD RESERVE — AND THAT OTHER COLD, WHICH HE HAD ENCOUNTERED IN SO MANY ANDROIDS.
ALWAYS THE SAME: GREAT INTELLECT, ABILITY TO ACCOMPLISH MUCH, BUT ALSO THIS.
HE DEPLORED IT.
AND YET, WITHOUT IT, HE COULD NOT TRACK THEM DOWN.
"I'M FROM THE SAN FRANCISCO POLICE DEPARTMENT," HE SAID.
OH?
THE HUGE AND INTENSE EYES DID NOT FLICKER, DID NOT RESPOND.
WHAT ARE YOU HERE ABOUT?
HER TONE, ODDLY, SEEMED GRACIOUS.
SEATING HIMSELF IN A NEARBY CHAIR, HE UNZIPPED HIS BRIEFCASE.
I HAVE BEEN SENT HERE TO ADMINISTER A STANDARD PERSONALITY-PROFILE TEST TO YOU.
IT WON'T TAKE MORE THAN A FEW MINUTES.
IS IT NECESSARY?
SHE GESTURED TOWARD THE BIG CLOTHBOUND SCORE.
I HAVE A GOOD DEAL I MUST DO.
NOW SHE HAD BEGUN TO LOOK APPREHENSIVE.
IT'S NECESSARY.

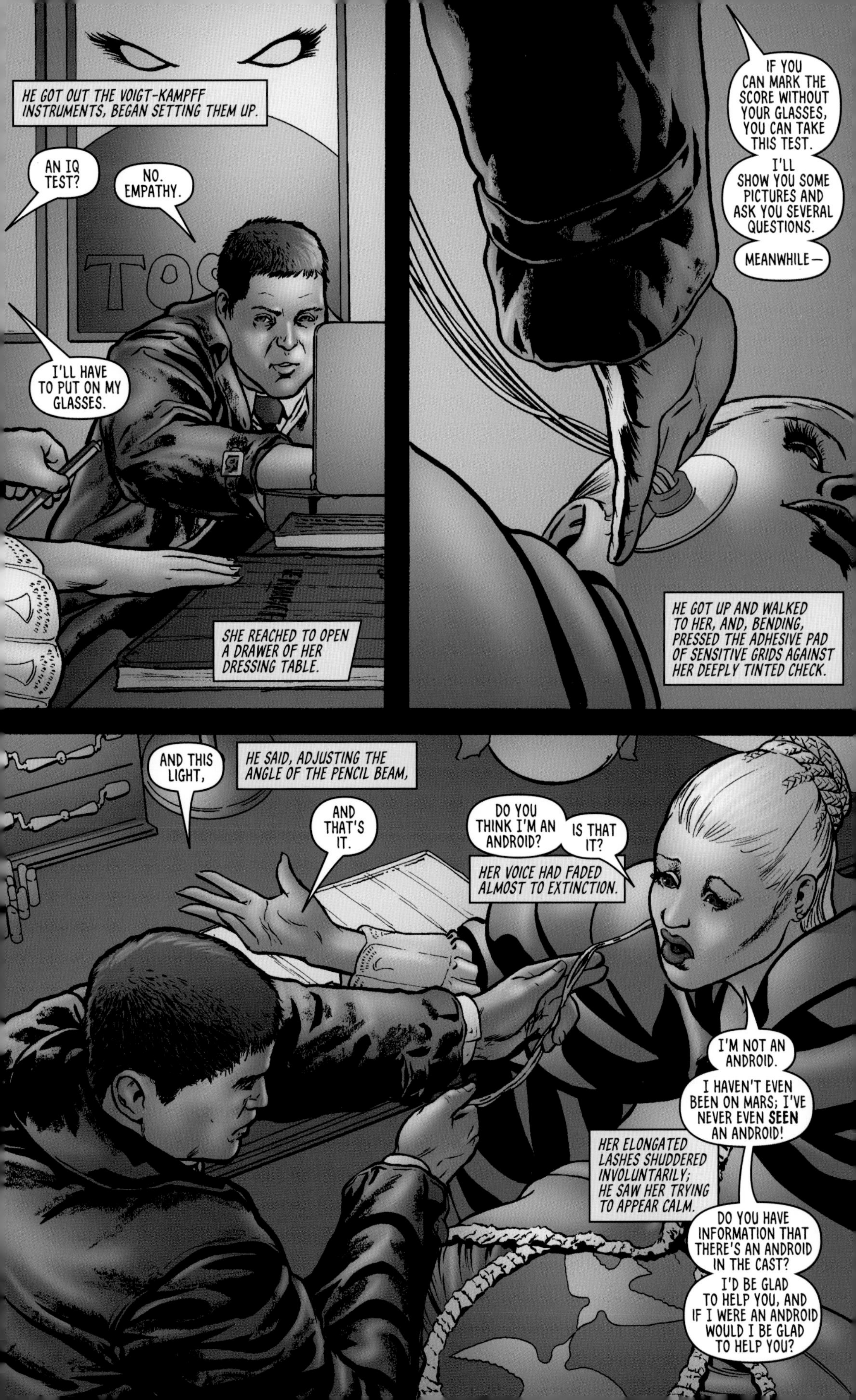
HE GOT OUT THE VOIGT-KAMPFF INSTRUMENTS, BEGAN SETTING THEM UP.
AN IQ TEST?
NO. EMPATHY.
I'LL HAVE TO PUT ON MY GLASSES.
SHE REACHED TO OPEN A DRAWER OF HER DRESSING TABLE.
IF YOU CAN MARK THE SCORE WITHOUT YOUR GLASSES, YOU CAN TAKE THIS TEST.
I'LL SHOW YOU SOME PICTURES AND ASK YOU SEVERAL QUESTIONS.
MEANWHILE—
HE GOT UP AND WALKED TO HER, AND, BENDING, PRESSED THE ADHESIVE PAD OF SENSITIVE GRIDS AGAINST HER DEEPLY TINTED CHECK.
AND THIS LIGHT,
HE SAID, ADJUSTING THE ANGLE OF THE PENCIL BEAM,
AND THAT'S IT.
DO YOU THINK I'M AN ANDROID?
IS THAT IT?
HER VOICE HAD FADED ALMOST TO EXTINCTION.
I'M NOT AN ANDROID.
I HAVEN'T EVEN BEEN ON MARS; I'VE NEVER EVEN **SEEN** AN ANDROID!
HER ELONGATED LASHES SHUDDERED INVOLUNTARILY; HE SAW HER TRYING TO APPEAR CALM.
DO YOU HAVE INFORMATION THAT THERE'S AN ANDROID IN THE CAST?
I'D BE GLAD TO HELP YOU, AND IF I WERE AN ANDROID WOULD I BE GLAD TO HELP YOU?

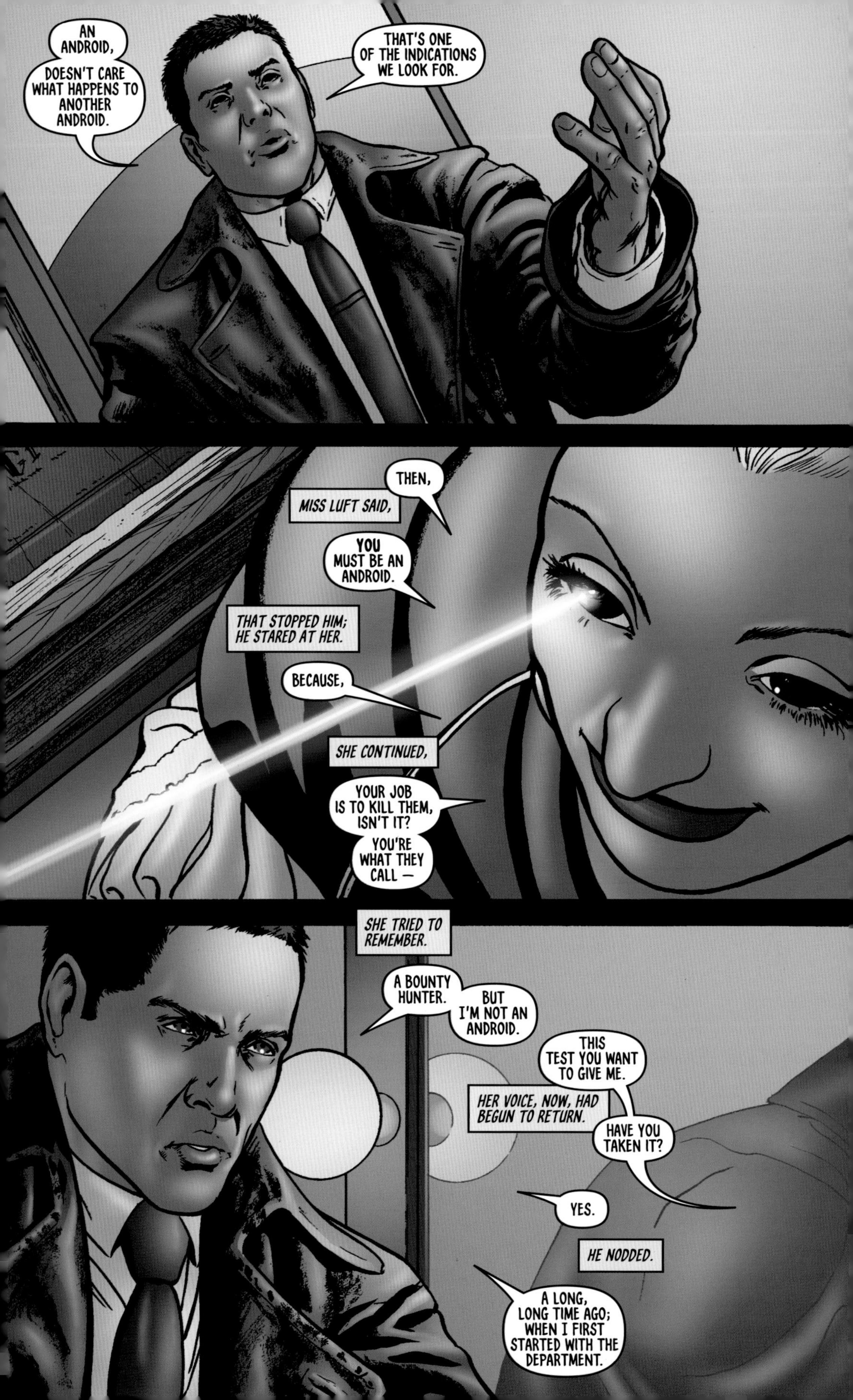
AN ANDROID,
DOESN'T CARE WHAT HAPPENS TO ANOTHER ANDROID.
THAT'S ONE OF THE INDICATIONS WE LOOK FOR.
THEN,
MISS LUFT SAID,
YOU MUST BE AN ANDROID.
THAT STOPPED HIM; HE STARED AT HER.
BECAUSE,
SHE CONTINUED,
YOUR JOB IS TO KILL THEM, ISN'T IT?
YOU'RE WHAT THEY CALL —
SHE TRIED TO REMEMBER.
A BOUNTY HUNTER.
BUT I'M NOT AN ANDROID.
THIS TEST YOU WANT TO GIVE ME.
HER VOICE, NOW, HAD BEGUN TO RETURN.
HAVE YOU TAKEN IT?
YES.
HE NODDED.
A LONG, LONG TIME AGO; WHEN I FIRST STARTED WITH THE DEPARTMENT.

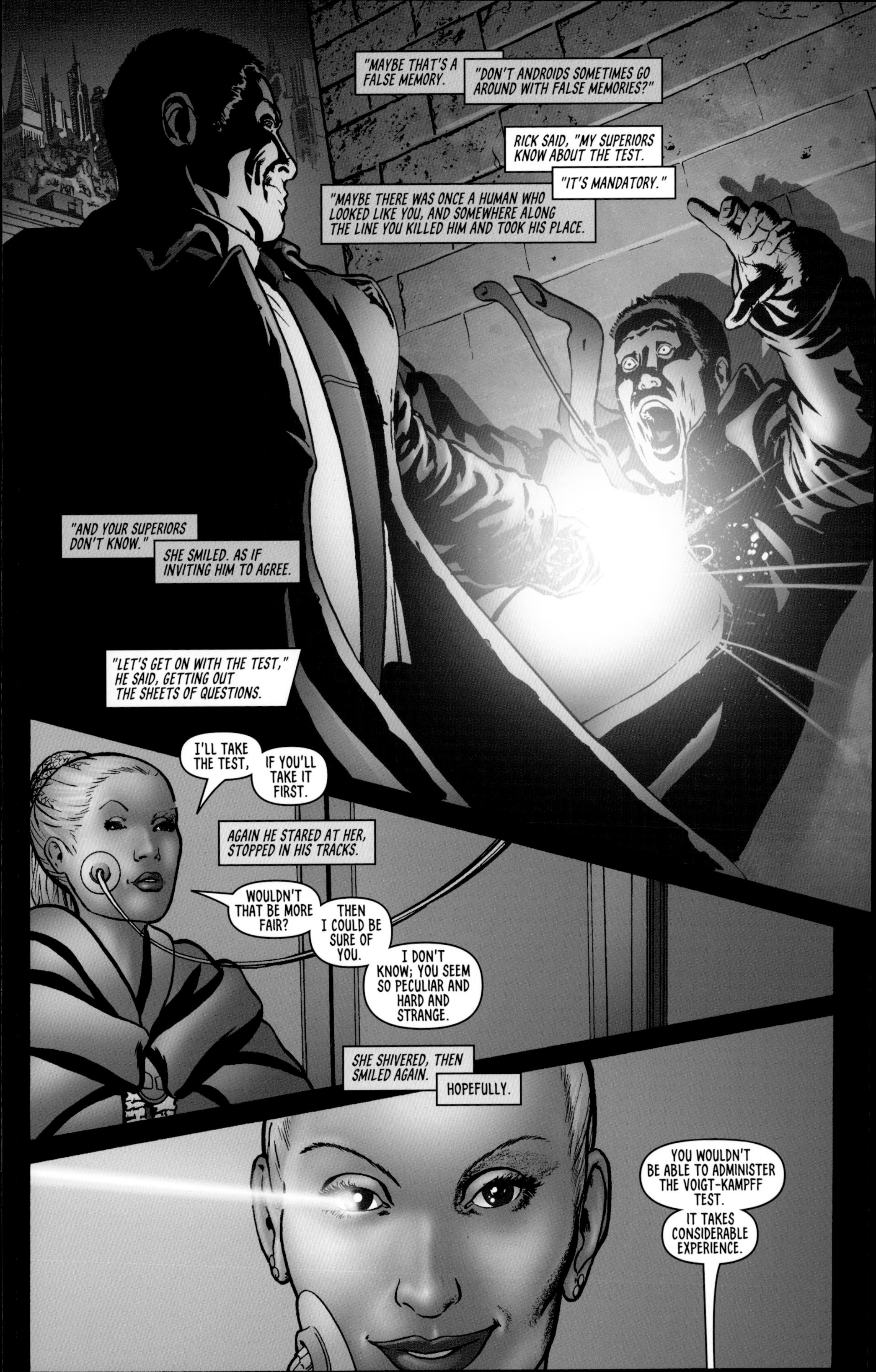
"MAYBE THAT'S A FALSE MEMORY.
"DON'T ANDROIDS SOMETIMES GO AROUND WITH FALSE MEMORIES?"
RICK SAID, "MY SUPERIORS KNOW ABOUT THE TEST.
"IT'S MANDATORY."
"MAYBE THERE WAS ONCE A HUMAN WHO LOOKED LIKE YOU, AND SOMEWHERE ALONG THE LINE YOU KILLED HIM AND TOOK HIS PLACE.
"AND YOUR SUPERIORS DON'T KNOW."
SHE SMILED. AS IF INVITING HIM TO AGREE.
"LET'S GET ON WITH THE TEST," HE SAID, GETTING OUT THE SHEETS OF QUESTIONS.
I'LL TAKE THE TEST,
IF YOU'LL TAKE IT FIRST.
AGAIN HE STARED AT HER, STOPPED IN HIS TRACKS.
WOULDN'T THAT BE MORE FAIR?
THEN I COULD BE SURE OF YOU.
I DON'T KNOW; YOU SEEM SO PECULIAR AND HARD AND STRANGE.
SHE SHIVERED, THEN SMILED AGAIN.
HOPEFULLY.
YOU WOULDN'T BE ABLE TO ADMINISTER THE VOIGT-KAMPFF TEST.
IT TAKES CONSIDERABLE EXPERIENCE.

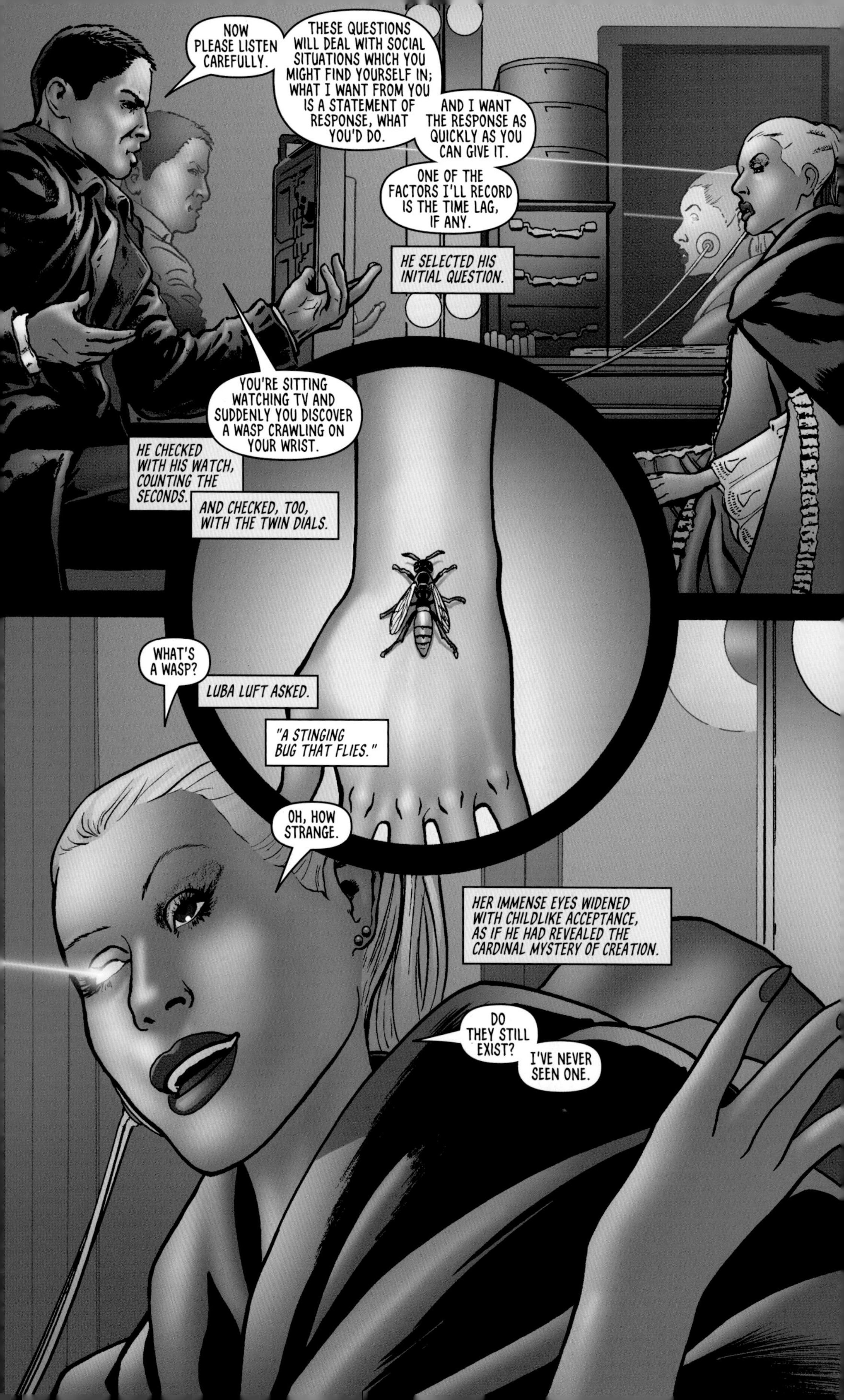
NOW PLEASE LISTEN CAREFULLY.
THESE QUESTIONS WILL DEAL WITH SOCIAL SITUATIONS WHICH YOU MIGHT FIND YOURSELF IN; WHAT I WANT FROM YOU IS A STATEMENT OF RESPONSE, WHAT YOU'D DO.
AND I WANT THE RESPONSE AS QUICKLY AS YOU CAN GIVE IT.
ONE OF THE FACTORS I'LL RECORD IS THE TIME LAG, IF ANY.
HE SELECTED HIS INITIAL QUESTION.
YOU'RE SITTING WATCHING TV AND SUDDENLY YOU DISCOVER A WASP CRAWLING ON YOUR WRIST.
HE CHECKED WITH HIS WATCH, COUNTING THE SECONDS.
AND CHECKED, TOO, WITH THE TWIN DIALS.
WHAT'S A WASP?
LUBA LUFT ASKED.
"A STINGING BUG THAT FLIES."
OH, HOW STRANGE.
HER IMMENSE EYES WIDENED WITH CHILDLIKE ACCEPTANCE, AS IF HE HAD REVEALED THE CARDINAL MYSTERY OF CREATION.
DO THEY STILL EXIST?
I'VE NEVER SEEN ONE.

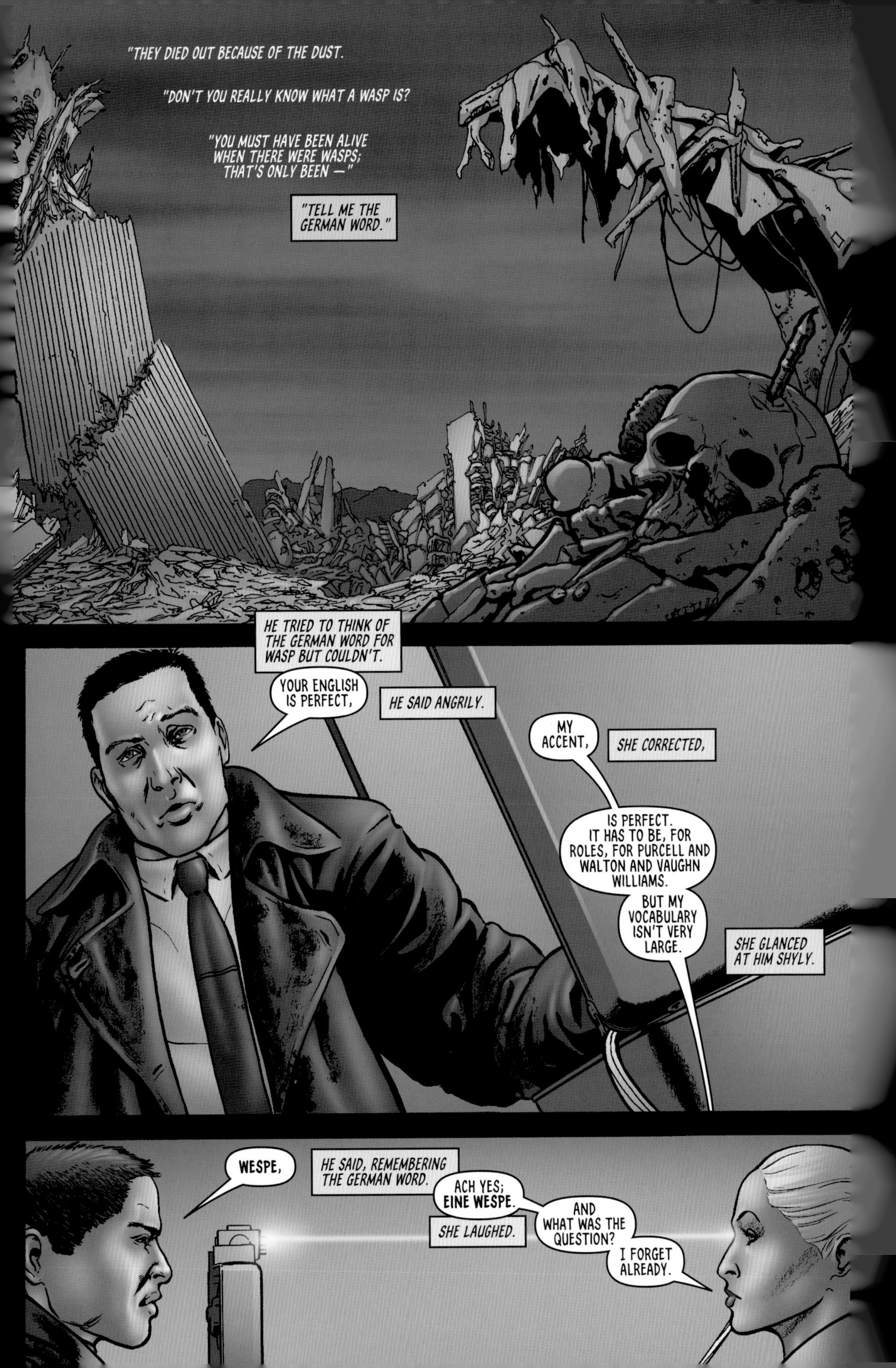
"THEY DIED OUT BECAUSE OF THE DUST.
"DON'T YOU REALLY KNOW WHAT A WASP IS?
"YOU MUST HAVE BEEN ALIVE WHEN THERE WERE WASPS; THAT'S ONLY BEEN —"
"TELL ME THE GERMAN WORD."
HE TRIED TO THINK OF THE GERMAN WORD FOR WASP BUT COULDN'T.
YOUR ENGLISH IS PERFECT,
HE SAID ANGRILY.
MY ACCENT,
SHE CORRECTED,
IS PERFECT. IT HAS TO BE, FOR ROLES, FOR PURCELL AND WALTON AND VAUGHN WILLIAMS.
BUT MY VOCABULARY ISN'T VERY LARGE.
SHE GLANCED AT HIM SHYLY.
WESPE,
HE SAID, REMEMBERING THE GERMAN WORD.
ACH YES; **EINE WESPE.**
SHE LAUGHED.
AND WHAT WAS THE QUESTION?
I FORGET ALREADY.

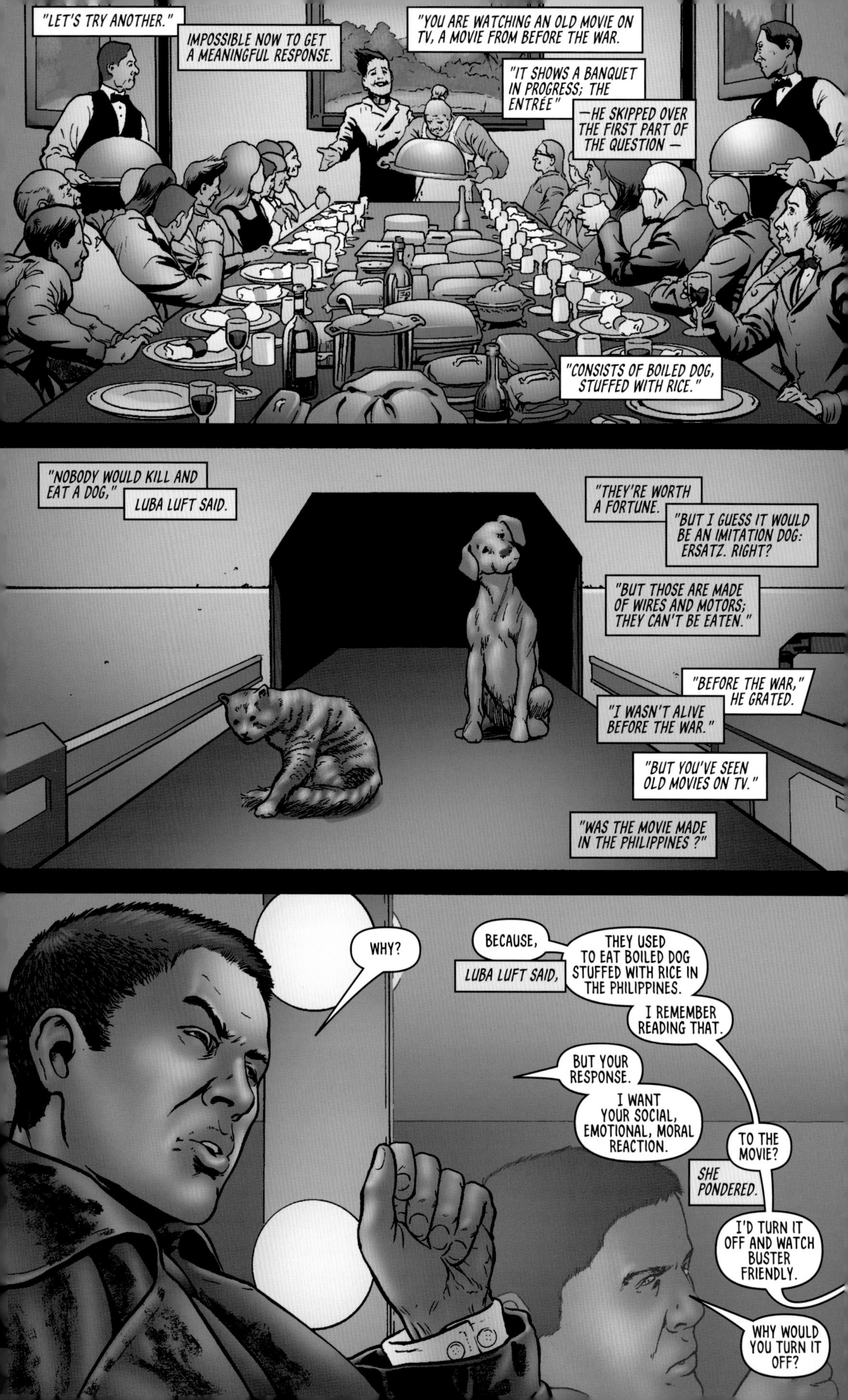
"LET'S TRY ANOTHER."
IMPOSSIBLE NOW TO GET A MEANINGFUL RESPONSE.
"YOU ARE WATCHING AN OLD MOVIE ON TV, A MOVIE FROM BEFORE THE WAR.
"IT SHOWS A BANQUET IN PROGRESS; THE ENTRÉE"
—HE SKIPPED OVER THE FIRST PART OF THE QUESTION —
"CONSISTS OF BOILED DOG, STUFFED WITH RICE."
"NOBODY WOULD KILL AND EAT A DOG,"
LUBA LUFT SAID.
"THEY'RE WORTH A FORTUNE.
"BUT I GUESS IT WOULD BE AN IMITATION DOG: ERSATZ. RIGHT?
"BUT THOSE ARE MADE OF WIRES AND MOTORS; THEY CAN'T BE EATEN."
"BEFORE THE WAR,"
HE GRATED.
"I WASN'T ALIVE BEFORE THE WAR."
"BUT YOU'VE SEEN OLD MOVIES ON TV."
"WAS THE MOVIE MADE IN THE PHILIPPINES ?"
WHY?
BECAUSE,
LUBA LUFT SAID,
THEY USED TO EAT BOILED DOG STUFFED WITH RICE IN THE PHILIPPINES.
I REMEMBER READING THAT.
BUT YOUR RESPONSE.
I WANT YOUR SOCIAL, EMOTIONAL, MORAL REACTION.
TO THE MOVIE?
SHE PONDERED.
I'D TURN IT OFF AND WATCH BUSTER FRIENDLY.
WHY WOULD YOU TURN IT OFF?

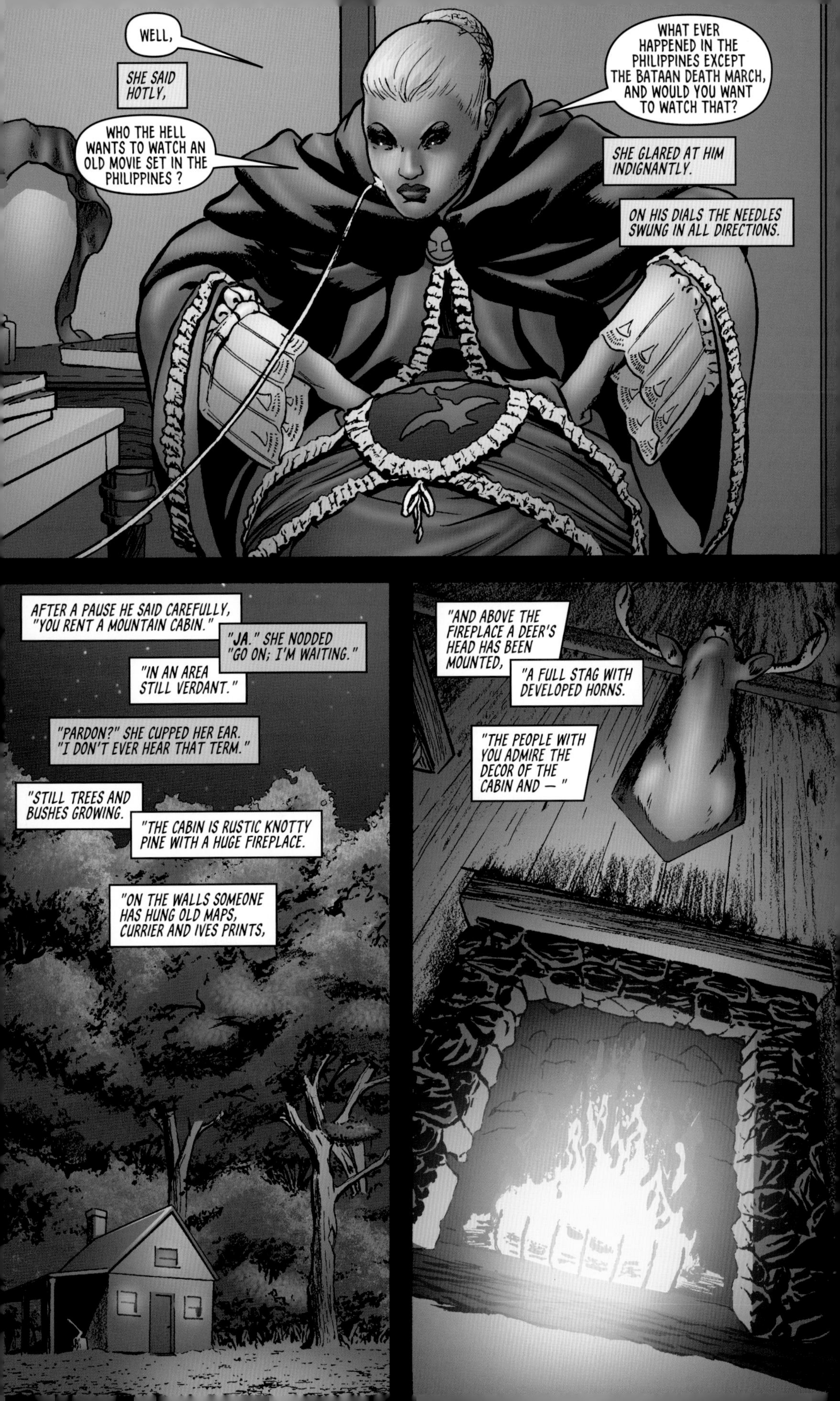
WELL,
SHE SAID HOTLY,
WHO THE HELL WANTS TO WATCH AN OLD MOVIE SET IN THE PHILIPPINES ?
WHAT EVER HAPPENED IN THE PHILIPPINES EXCEPT THE BATAAN DEATH MARCH, AND WOULD YOU WANT TO WATCH THAT?
SHE GLARED AT HIM INDIGNANTLY.
ON HIS DIALS THE NEEDLES SWUNG IN ALL DIRECTIONS.
AFTER A PAUSE HE SAID CAREFULLY, "YOU RENT A MOUNTAIN CABIN."
"JA." SHE NODDED "GO ON; I'M WAITING."
"IN AN AREA STILL VERDANT."
"PARDON?" SHE CUPPED HER EAR. "I DON'T EVER HEAR THAT TERM."
"STILL TREES AND BUSHES GROWING.
"THE CABIN IS RUSTIC KNOTTY PINE WITH A HUGE FIREPLACE.
"ON THE WALLS SOMEONE HAS HUNG OLD MAPS, CURRIER AND IVES PRINTS,
"AND ABOVE THE FIREPLACE A DEER'S HEAD HAS BEEN MOUNTED,
"A FULL STAG WITH DEVELOPED HORNS.
"THE PEOPLE WITH YOU ADMIRE THE DECOR OF THE CABIN AND — "

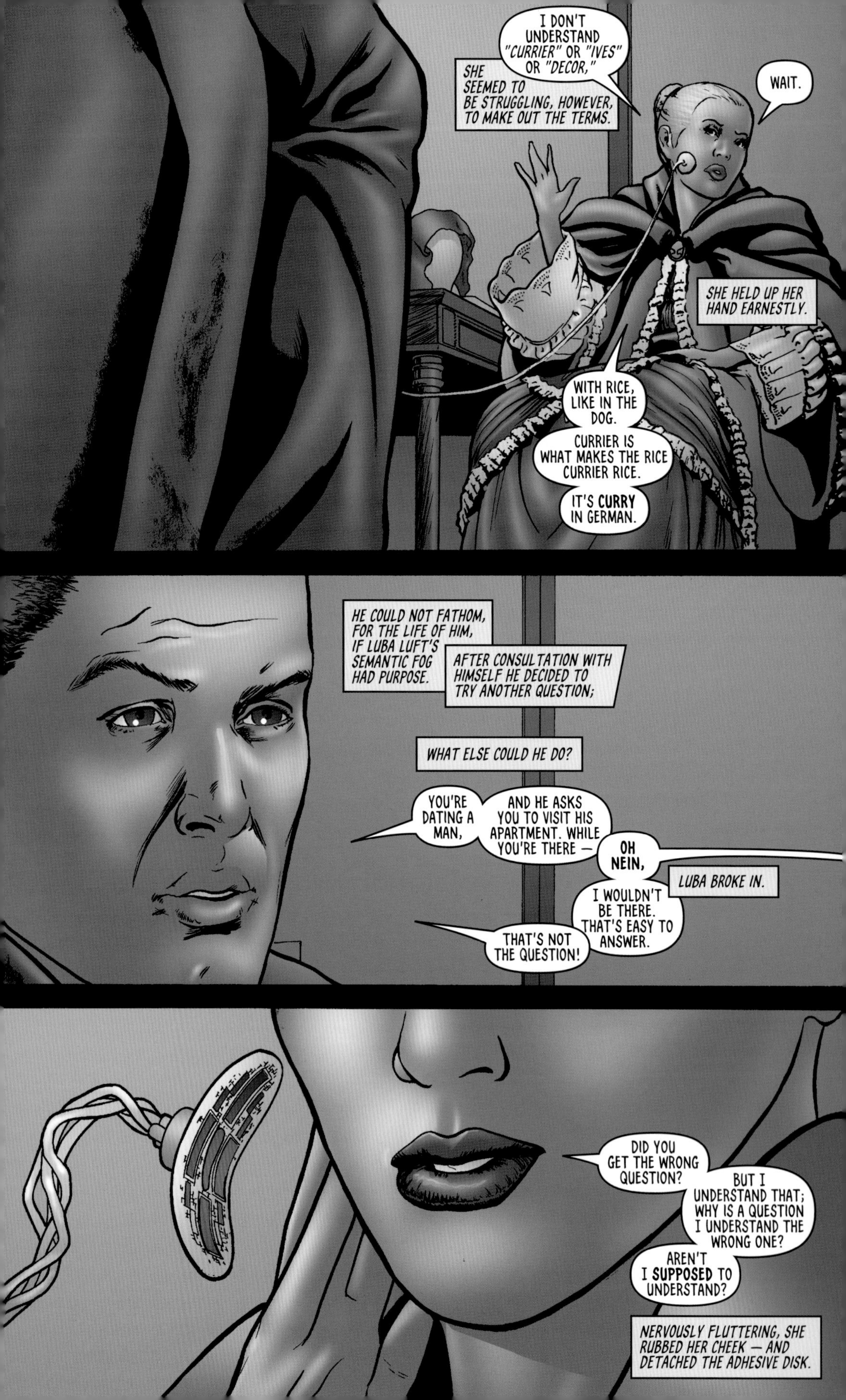

I DON'T UNDERSTAND "CURRIER" OR "IVES" OR "DECOR,"
SHE SEEMED TO BE STRUGGLING, HOWEVER, TO MAKE OUT THE TERMS.
WAIT.
SHE HELD UP HER HAND EARNESTLY.
WITH RICE, LIKE IN THE DOG.
CURRIER IS WHAT MAKES THE RICE CURRIER RICE.
IT'S CURRY IN GERMAN.
HE COULD NOT FATHOM, FOR THE LIFE OF HIM, IF LUBA LUFT'S SEMANTIC FOG HAD PURPOSE.
AFTER CONSULTATION WITH HIMSELF HE DECIDED TO TRY ANOTHER QUESTION;
WHAT ELSE COULD HE DO?
YOU'RE DATING A MAN,
AND HE ASKS YOU TO VISIT HIS APARTMENT. WHILE YOU'RE THERE —
OH NEIN,
LUBA BROKE IN.
I WOULDN'T BE THERE. THAT'S EASY TO ANSWER.
THAT'S NOT THE QUESTION!
DID YOU GET THE WRONG QUESTION?
BUT I UNDERSTAND THAT; WHY IS A QUESTION I UNDERSTAND THE WRONG ONE?
AREN'T I SUPPOSED TO UNDERSTAND?
NERVOUSLY FLUTTERING, SHE RUBBED HER CHEEK — AND DETACHED THE ADHESIVE DISK.

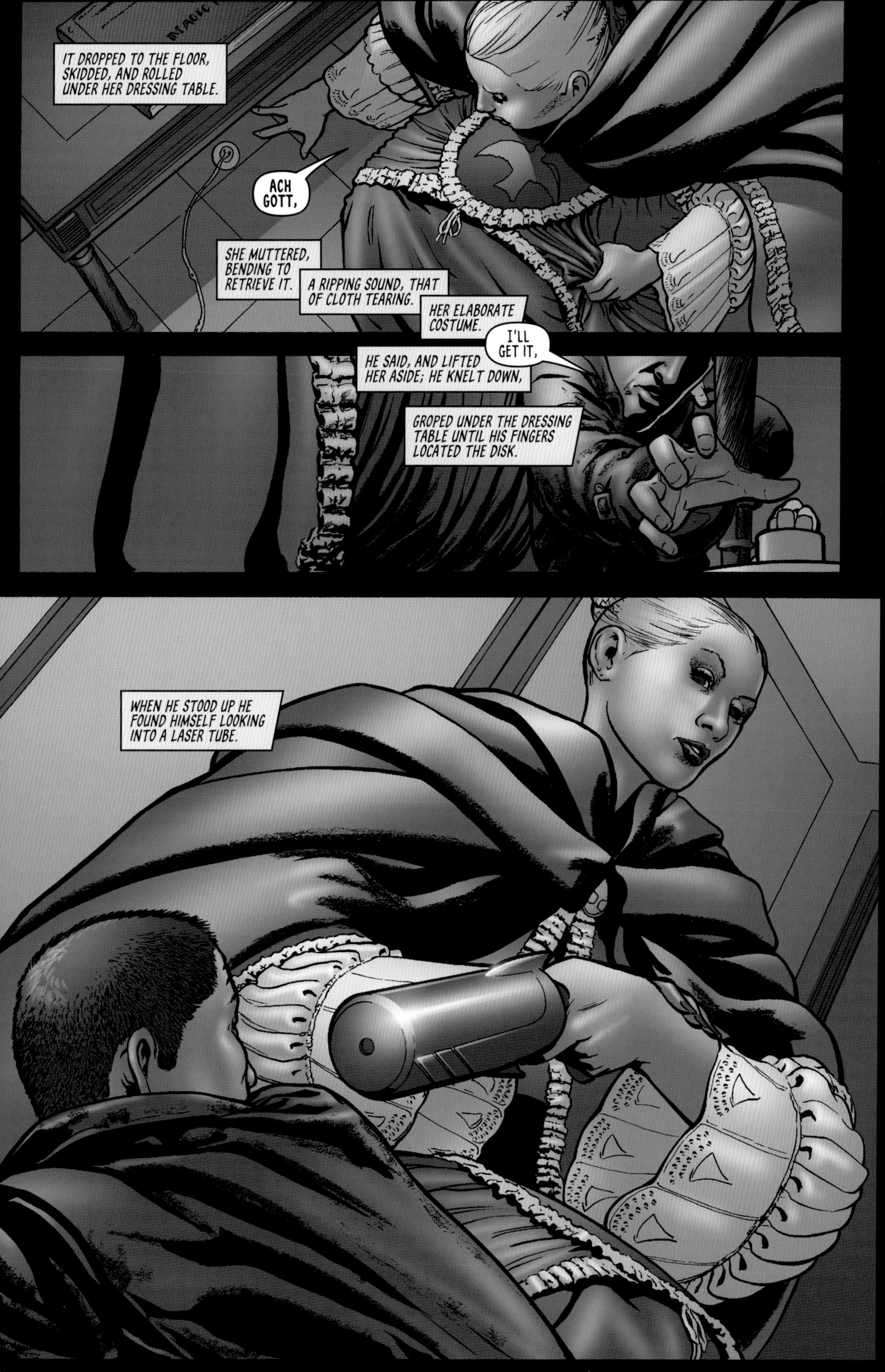
IT DROPPED TO THE FLOOR, SKIDDED, AND ROLLED UNDER HER DRESSING TABLE.
ACH GOTT,
SHE MUTTERED, BENDING TO RETRIEVE IT.
A RIPPING SOUND, THAT OF CLOTH TEARING.
HER ELABORATE COSTUME.
HE SAID, AND LIFTED HER ASIDE; HE KNELT DOWN,
I'LL GET IT,
GROPED UNDER THE DRESSING TABLE UNTIL HIS FINGERS LOCATED THE DISK.
WHEN HE STOOD UP HE FOUND HIMSELF LOOKING INTO A LASER TUBE.

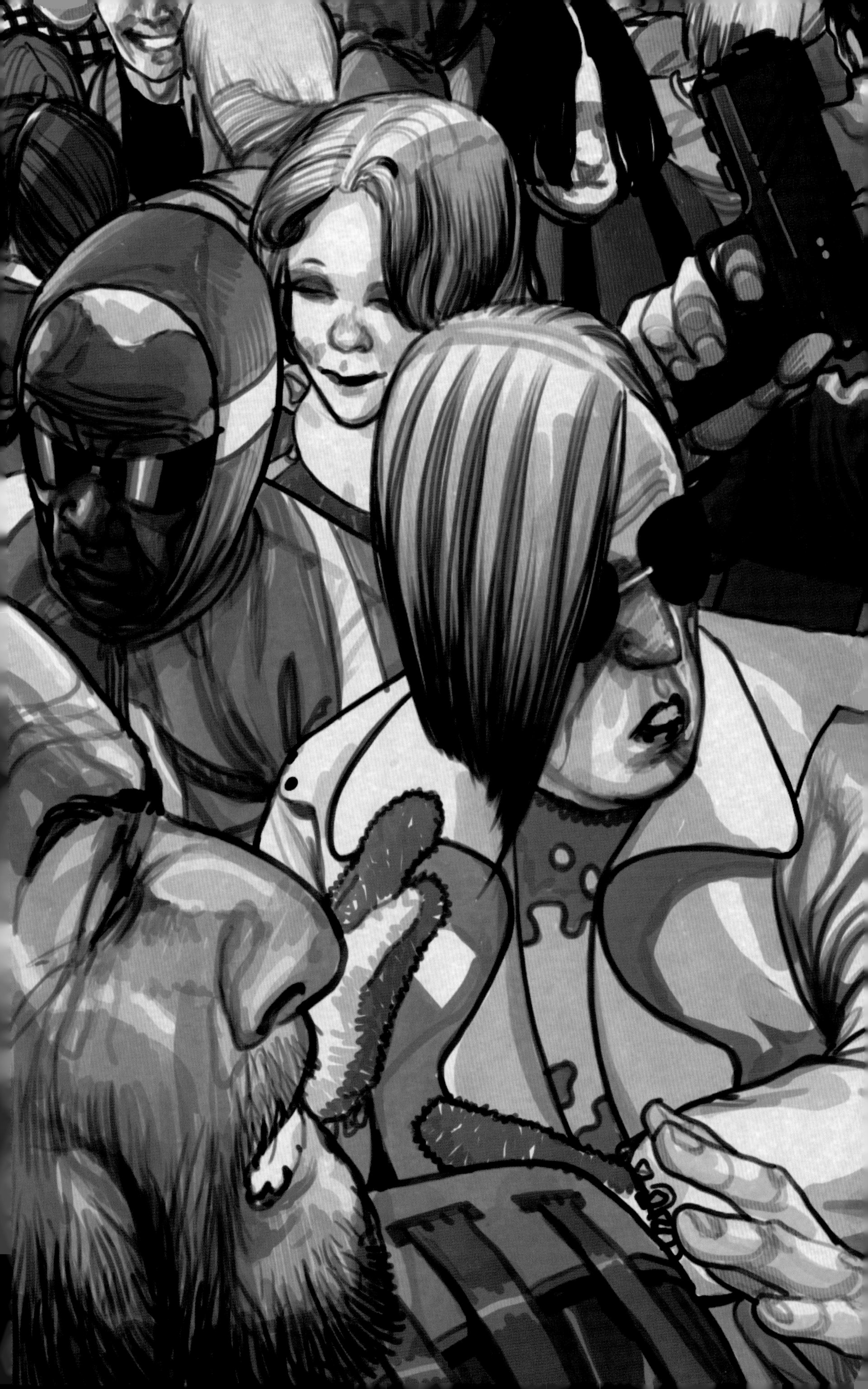

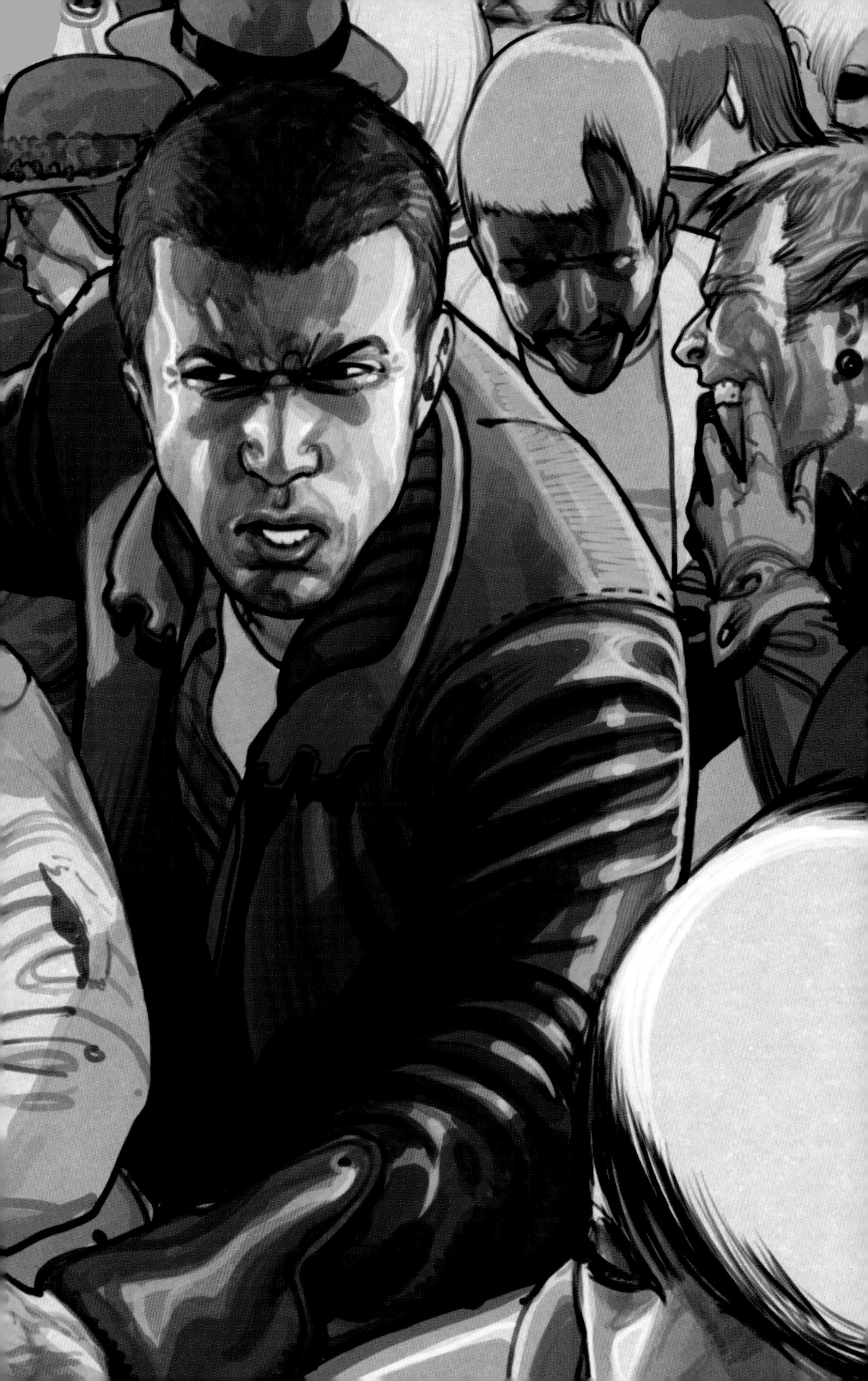

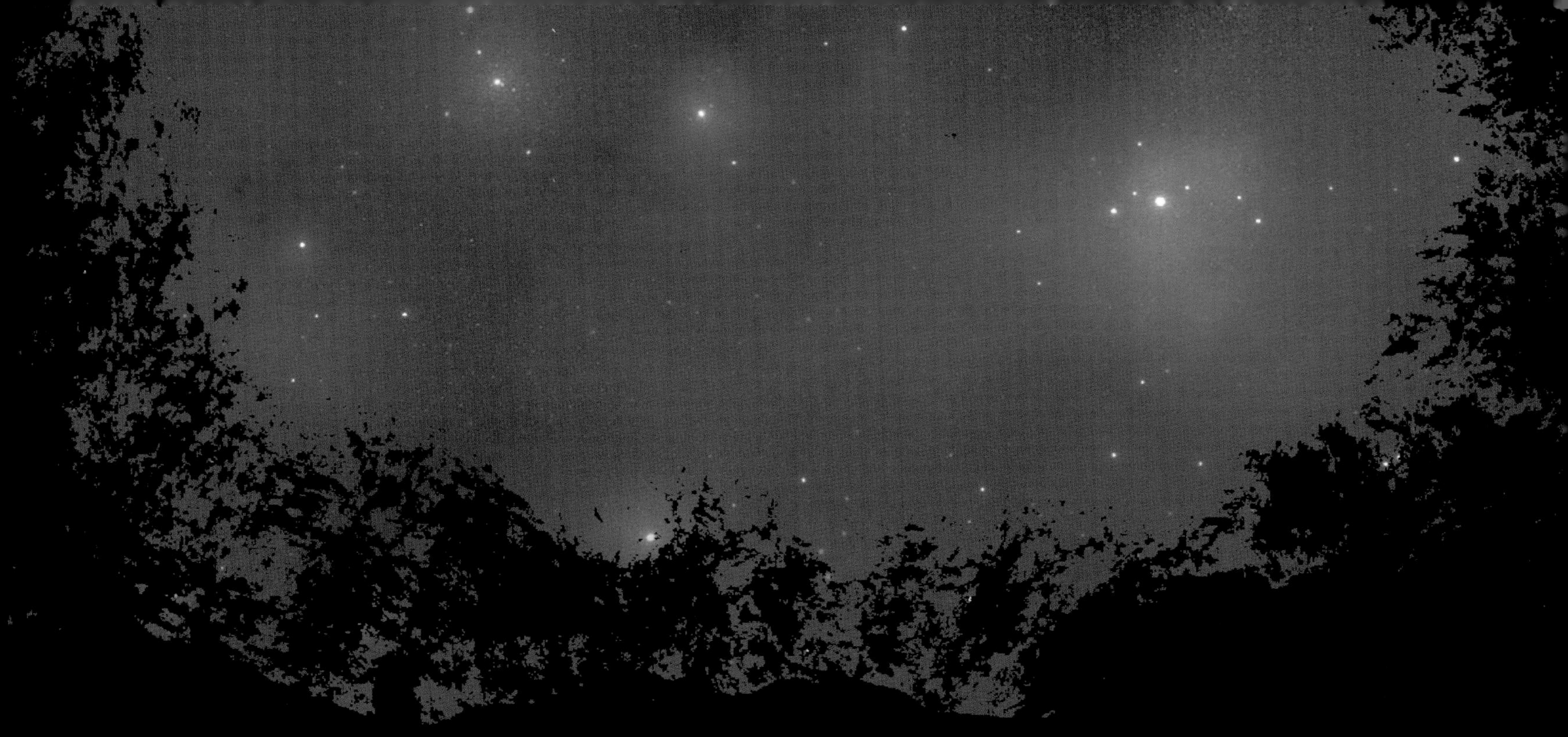

ON
PHILIP K. DICK

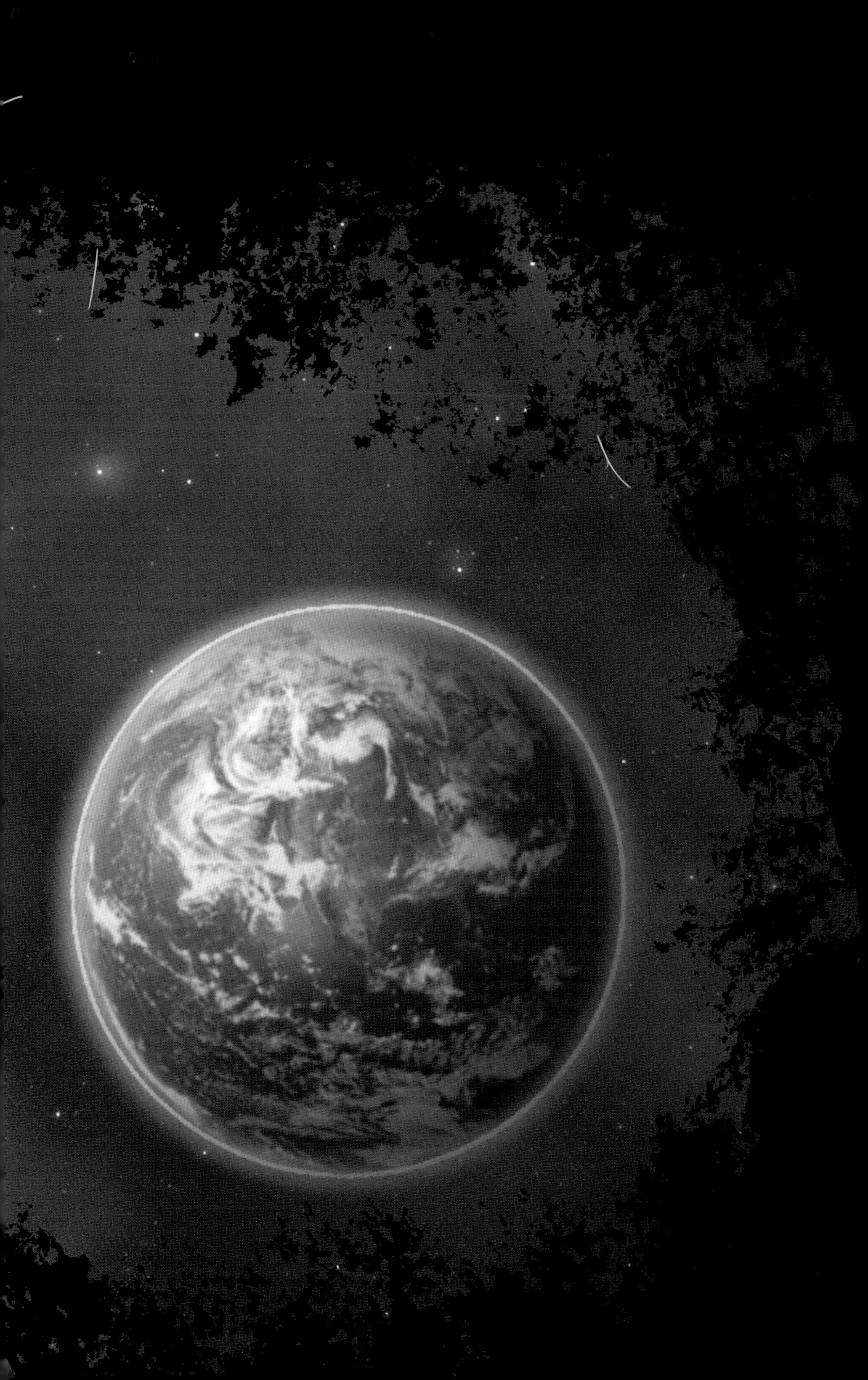

GRAEME MCMILLAN

It was only when I sat down to write this that I realized that my relationship with Philip K. Dick was pretty much a Philip K. Dick story. I was convinced, you see, that the first time I met Dick was the last time that the world was supposed to end.

Of course, when I say "met," I really mean "found his books and started reading them voraciously, convinced on some level that they had some deeper meaning about life in general and my life in particular," but I'm sure that he'd have understood what I mean, and also appreciated the way in which I came to regard each of the books I read as some kind of mystical, meaningful text beyond just an entertaining sci-fi novel.

(Like the works of Kurt Vonnegut, another writer who started writing around the middle of the 20th century, it almost feels like an insult to call any of Dick's novels "entertaining sci-fi," for some reason. Don't get me wrong, they're all both entertaining and science fiction, but they're also more than that, somehow, asking questions and addressing subjects that the stuff that we've come to consider sci-fi now, whether it's BATTLESTAR GALACTICA or TRANSFORMERS or even DISTRICT 9 or MOON, tend to stay away from for fear of being called pretentious or trying-too-hard. Dick - and Vonnegut, for that matter - were neither, however; they just had a lot of questions about the way everything is, and discovered that science fiction was one of the better outlets in which to ask them. But I think I've gotten away from what I was meaning to say.)

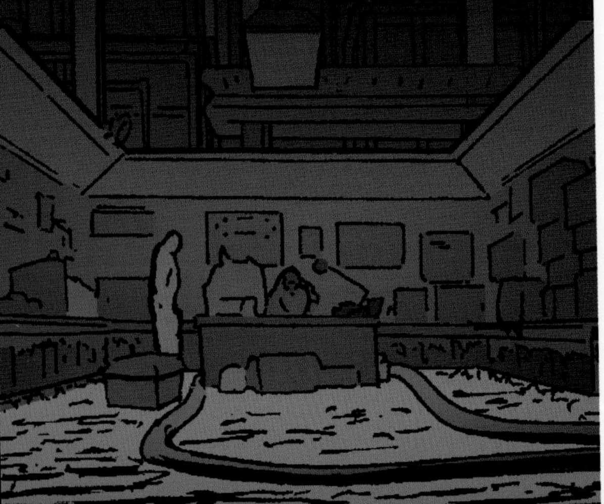

This was in 1999, when I first discovered

Philip K. Dick for the second time. Back when we were all worried about abstract concepts like the loss of all data or a worldwide computer crash bringing down international information infrastructure with names like "Y2K" and "The Millennium Doomsday Bug." It was a strange moment (year) in time when real life seemed to actually become science fiction and it felt as if we really were living in the future. We were finally leaving the 20th Century, after all, and what else could that mean if not *some* kind of sci-fi real world crossover, and a science fiction closer to dystopian disaster novels than anything George Lucas or Gene Roddenberry had dreamt up?

In the middle of all of this, there I was, having my own metaphysical crisis; certain things that I'd believed and relied upon for the majority of my life were slowly unraveling around me, and it felt more often than not that reality itself might not have been exactly what I thought it was (There was a girl involved, of course, but despite what the previous sentences made it sound like, no drugs. This was a purely straight-edge, involuntary, redefinition of reality). And while all of this was going on, I was reading books like VALIS and THE DIVINE INVASION and THE TRANSMOGRIFICATION OF TIMOTHY ARCHER. Here were books that make sense of this strange time, I thought to myself as I eagerly devoured each one. *Here* were stories about the nature of reality and religion and faith and spirituality, just as I was questioning all of those very things, and at a time when the world seemed to be vaguely wondering, in between replaying old Prince songs, about the same things.

(For those who haven't read any of these novels - which are very different in tone and subject to DO ANDROIDS DREAM OF ELECTRIC SHEEP?, different enough that I almost feel guilty for bringing them up here - they're a thematic trilogy written in response to a series of experiences that Dick had that led him to believe that he had been contacted by some kind of transcendental quasi-deity that Dick ended up calling VALIS, which stood for Vast Active Living Intelligence System; think Grant Morrison's Barbelith in THE INVISIBLES, if you're looking for some comic-centric point of reference, as well as my entry point into the novels.)

Each of the three books, although I read them out of publication order and unaware that they were theoretically part of any trilogy, was exactly what I needed to read when I read it. Whether it was coincidence or divine invasions of the literary kind, Philip K. Dick had arrived in my life at exactly the right time, and was telling me exactly what I needed to hear, in a way that not only made sense, but felt as if it was written entirely for me. It was the greatest introduction to any author I could've imagined.

Only problem is, it wasn't the first time I'd been introduced to Philip K. Dick.

Rewind almost ten years, and look at me in the final year of high school: Nervous, awkward and convinced that there was something more to life, even if I didn't know what it was just yet (Also given to astonishingly bad personal hygiene habits, but we don't need to go into that right now, I don't think). For one of my English classes, we had to write what was worryingly called a dissertation - although it would end up being shorter than this essay - about a topic of our choice, and I had chosen to write about the English novelist Martin Amis' then-just-released, critically-acclaimed novel TIME'S ARROW.

It was, in some way, some teenage way of showing my teachers that there was more to me than the pulpy science fiction that had formed my reading up until that point, much to their displeasure, and also a way to show them that there was more to science fiction than their prejudices allowed them to believe (It had been shortlisted for the prestigious Booker Prize for Fiction, after all, I'd tell people defensively). But the more that I looked into where Amis' conceit of a man living his life backwards came from, the more I realized he was simply telling a story that had been told before.

At first, I thought the idea came from Kurt Vonnegut's SLAUGHTERHOUSE FIVE, where Billy Pilgrim famously became unstuck in time and inspired LOST and Captain America's high-selling rebirth, but a local comic book store owner at the time knew the truth. "Dick did it first," he said, in a mix of smug knowing and attempt to be helpful.

For years, I didn't remember any of this at all; I'd apparently been surprisingly successful in some subconscious attempt to block out as much of high school as possible that I didn't even know about, but suddenly I remembered everything about it in a jumble of images and information: The way that the comic store owner told me about Dick's COUNTER-CLOCK WORLD, which predated SLAUGHTERHOUSE FIVE by two years as if the book, and Philip K. Dick in general, was contraband, some kind of dangerous secret that wasn't supposed to be known by anyone, least of all he or I. That he didn't have the book in stock, but that in order to tell me that, he took me into the back of the store, which looked like the kind of place you'd see serial killers live in in movies and reeked of pot, all of which was a strange and slightly terrifying new world to me at the time.

He ended up lending me his copy, and telling me not to let anyone know where it had come from; I took it away from the store wrapped in a brown paper bag, and feeling slightly convinced that I had just learned something - or a few somethings - that I wasn't supposed to know. All the way home, I kept the bag closed, clutched close, as if to open it and look at the book would've meant something very bad indeed.

I can't help but feel as if that whole experience - Not just the secretive paranoia of actually finding out about Philip K. Dick and getting the book in the first place, but also somehow completely forgetting about it and then, years later, (re)discovering Dick's work at a completely different time of my life when it felt like there was some level of predestination or higher power involved - is something that should've come from one of Philip K. Dick's novels. For all that he's most well-known for - coming up with the stories that were turned

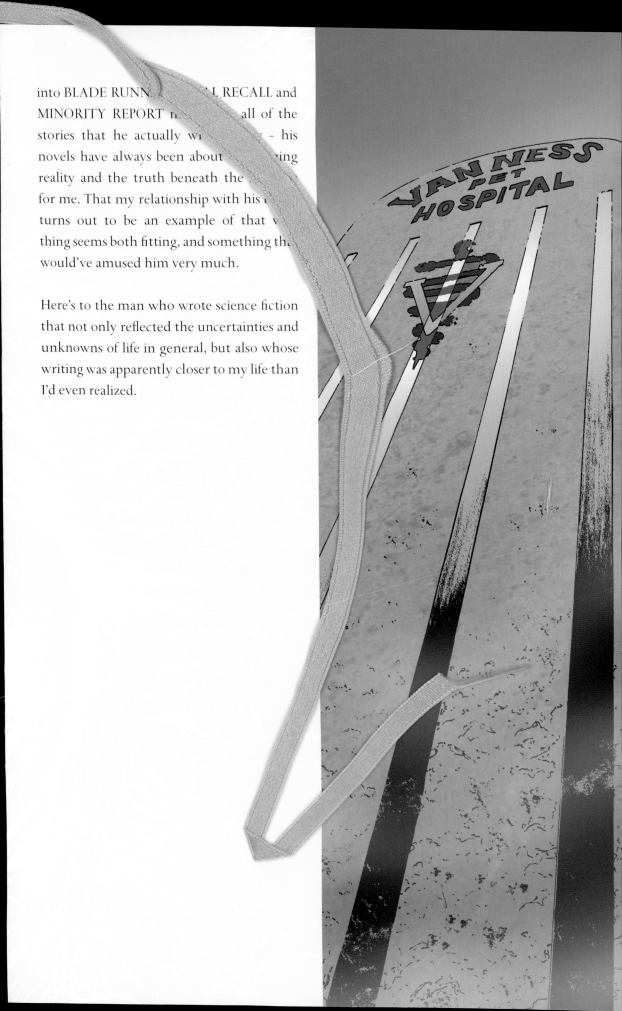

into BLADE RUNN[illegible]L RECALL and MINORITY REPORT n[illegible] all of the stories that he actually wr[illegible] - his novels have always been about [illegible]ing reality and the truth beneath the [illegible] for me. That my relationship with his [illegible] turns out to be an example of that [illegible] thing seems both fitting, and something th[illegible] would've amused him very much.

Here's to the man who wrote science fiction that not only reflected the uncertainties and unknowns of life in general, but also whose writing was apparently closer to my life than I'd even realized.

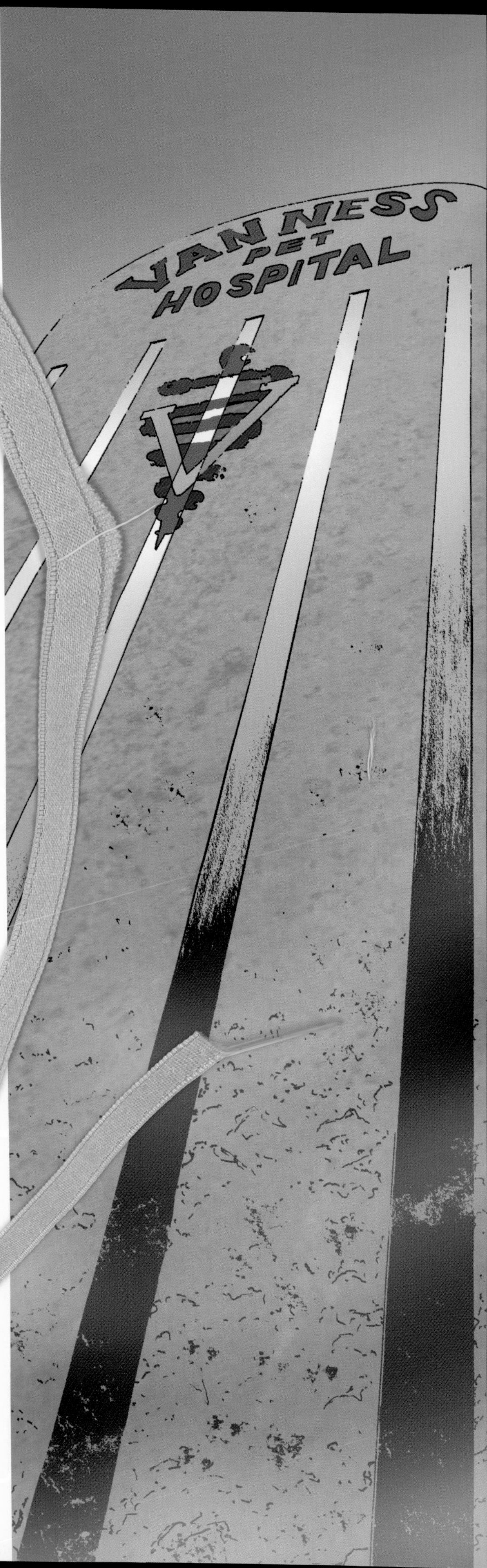
VAN NESS
PET
HOSPITAL

TONY
PARKER
& BLOND

BOOK
SIX

PARKER -- I generally try to avoid the breaking of the panel with the subject, but this one screamed it for me. I also wanted something that also causes a delay in visual flow, so that there is a greater pause in revealing the empty room.

BLOND -- The scene here is in a big, dark, empty building. The cool color scheme of these pages is in stark contrast to the warm, rich colors of the opulent building in the last scene.

PAGE FORTY-NINE
PANEL ONE

Using an infinity key, which analyzed and opened all forms of locks known, he entered Polokov's apartment, laser beam in hand.

-- Chapter 8

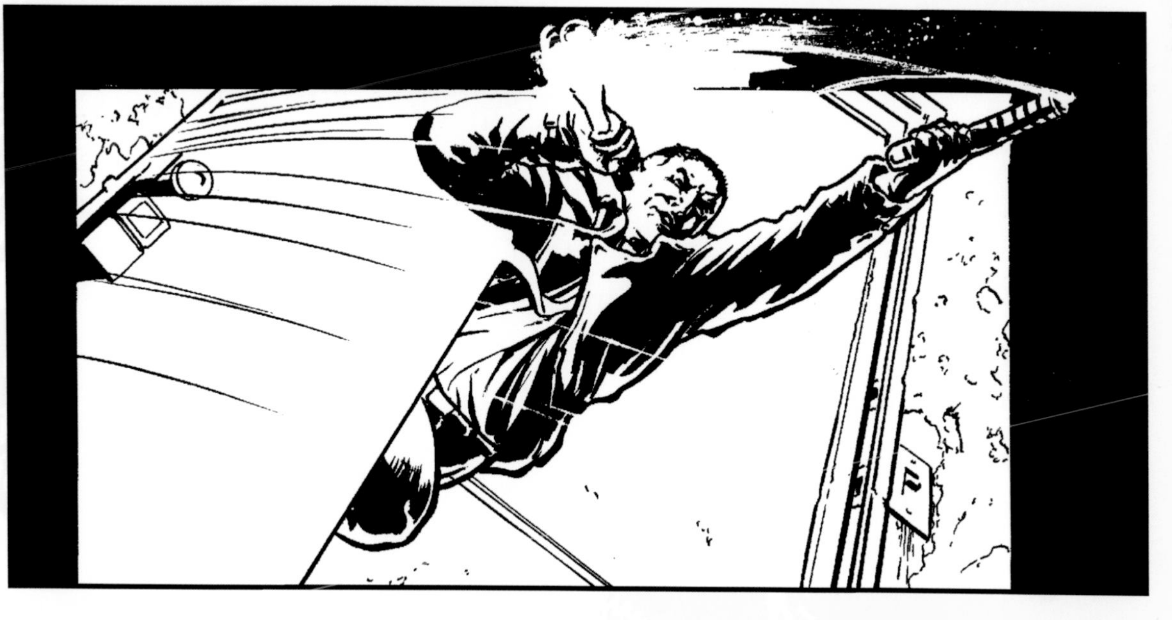

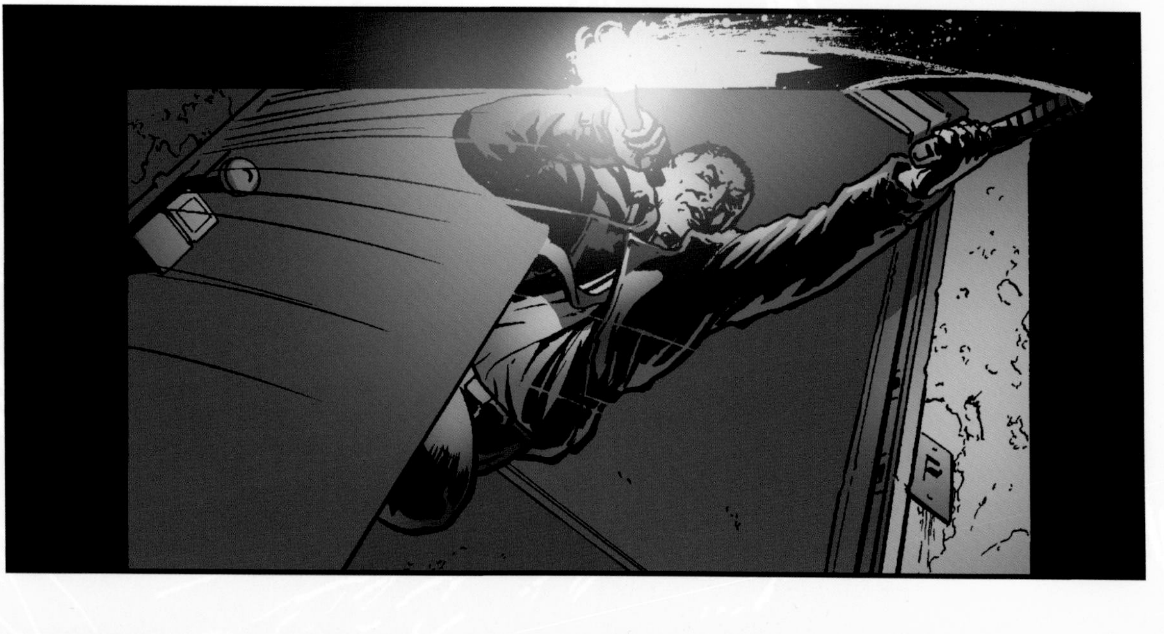

PAGE FORTY-NINE
PANEL TWO

No Polokov. Only semi-ruined furniture, a place of kipple and decay. In fact no personal articles: what greeted him consisted of unclaimed debris which Polokov had inherited when he took the apartment and which in leaving he had abandoned to the next — if any — tenant.

-- Chapter 8

PARKER -- This was one of my favorite panels that I've done in a while. How dilapidated and war torn would a room have to be to stand out from the standard "kipple" filled room? Polokov also struck me as a massive packrat, so nothing would be thrown out. Visually, the eyes stop and get lost in the clutter, holding the power of the image (and its isolation and destitute desperation and anxiety). By the way, Blond knocked it out of the park with this one.

BLOND -- Keeping the building dark highlights the danger as Deckard hunts a murderous android to his lair, as well as emphasizing the emptiness and loneliness of his surroundings, which is a recurring theme throughout the story.

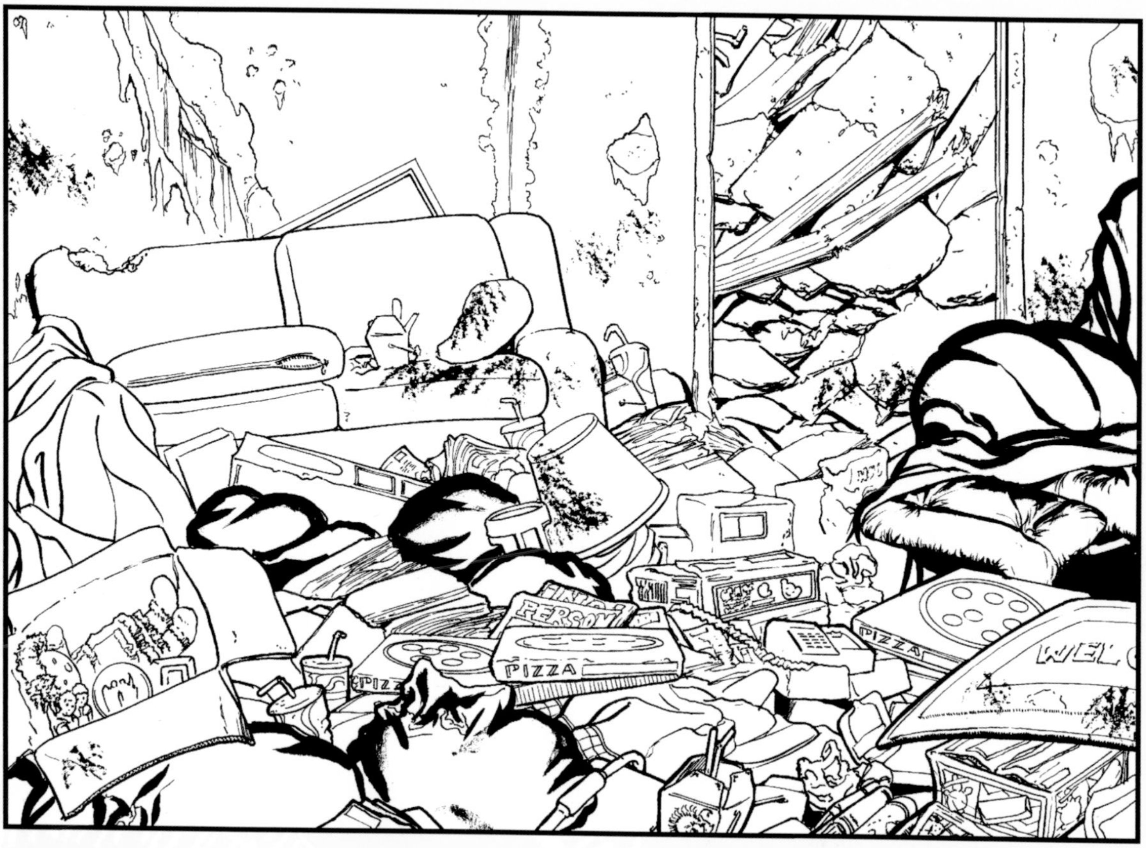
PERSON
PIZZA
PIZZA
PIZZA
WEL

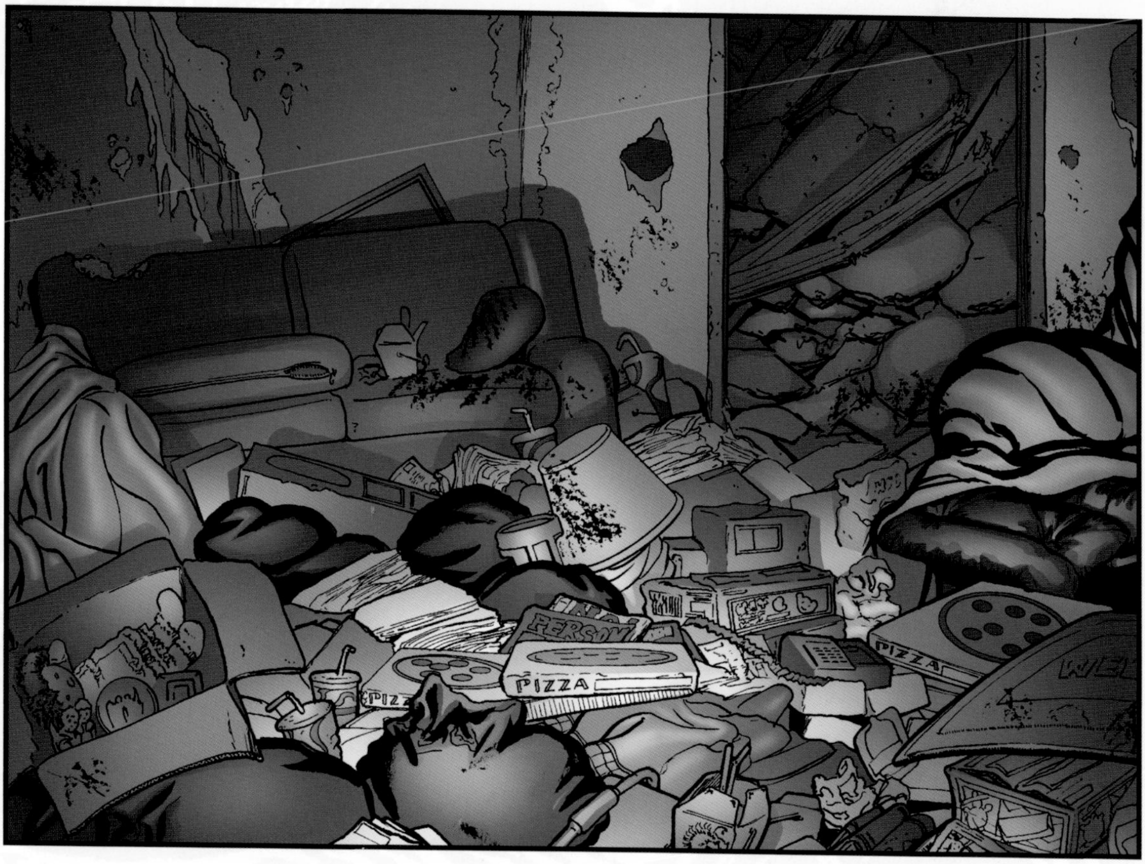
PERSON
PIZZA
PIZZA
WEL

PAGE FORTY-NINE
PANEL THREE

I knew it, he said to himself. Well, there goes the first thousand dollars' bounty; probably skipped all the way to the Antarctic Circle. Out of my jurisdiction; another bounty hunter from another police department will retire Polokov and claim the money. On, I suppose, to the andys who haven't been warned, as was Polokov. On to Luba Luft.

-- Chapter 8

PARKER -- Dark, gritty, noir, or in other words, pure fun.

BLOND -- Thankfully Deckard has a powerful flashlight so we can actually see in the darkness, as his search comes up... empty.

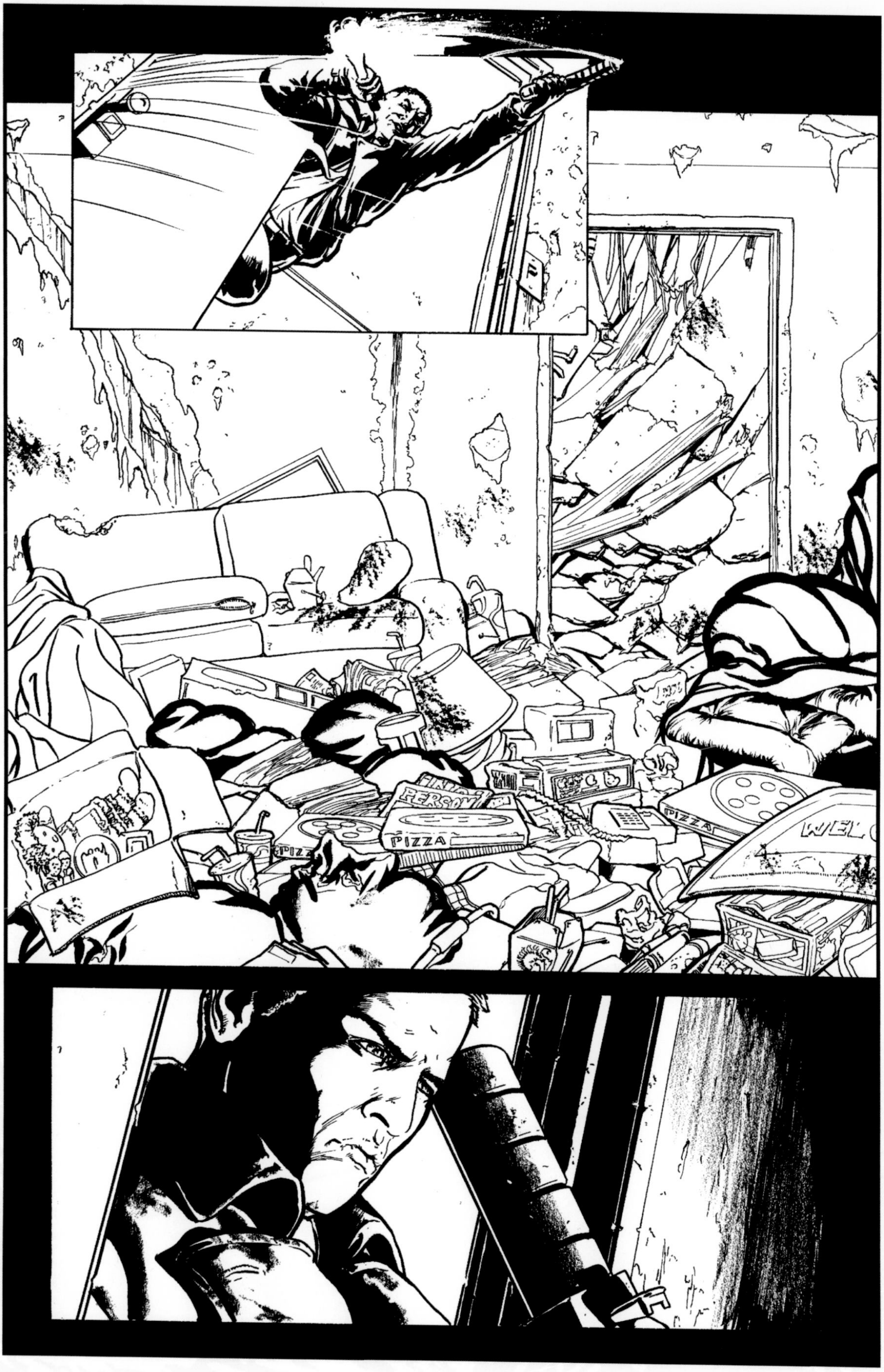
PIZZA
PIZZA
PIZZA
WEL

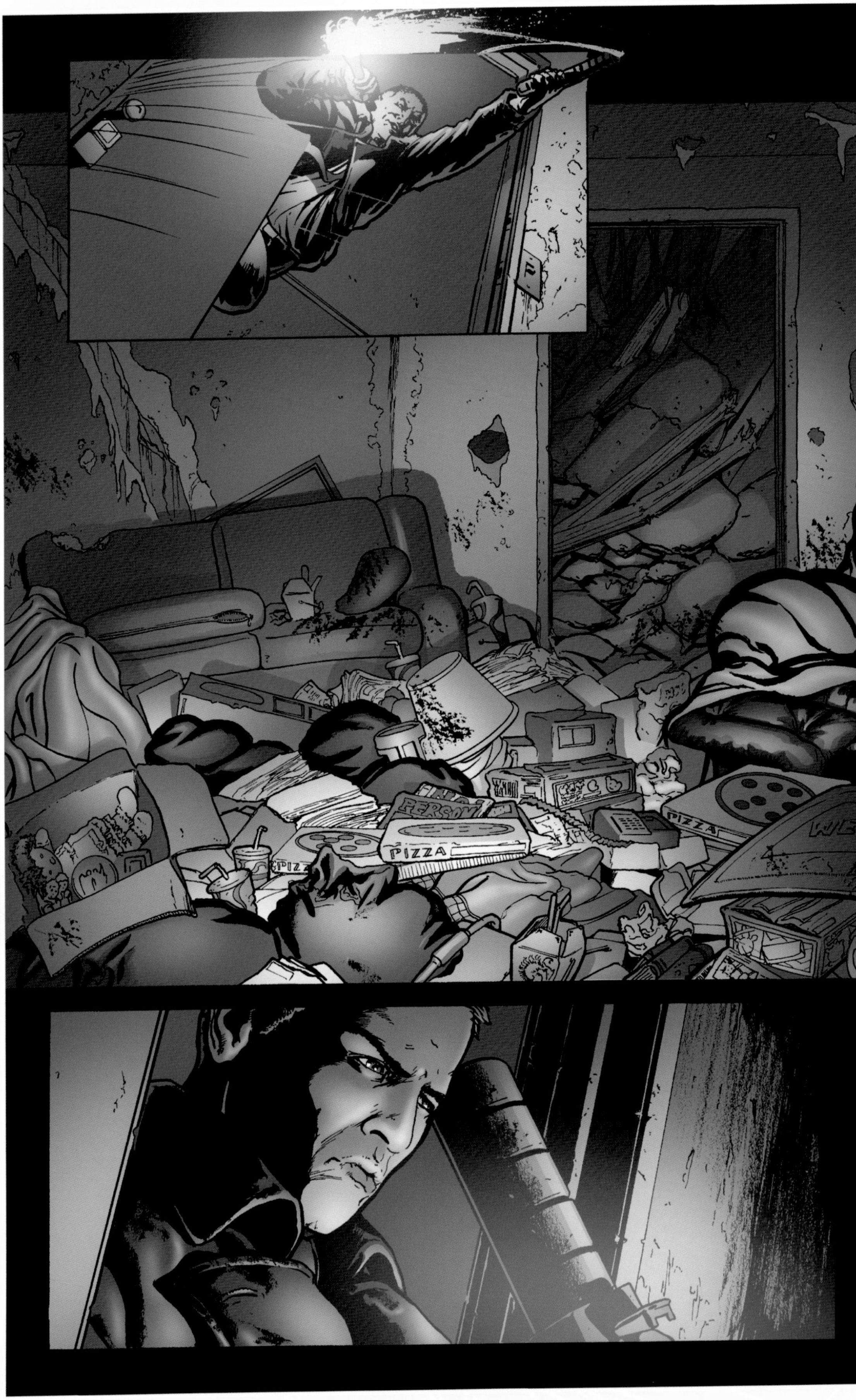
PIZZA
PIZZA
PIZZA

BOOK SIX
PAGE
FORTY-NINE

Using an infinity key, which analyzed and opened all forms of locks known, he entered Polokov's apartment, laser beam in hand.

No Polokov. Only semi-ruined furniture, a place of kipple and decay. In fact no personal articles: what greeted him consisted of unclaimed debris which Polokov had inherited when he took the apartment and which in leaving he had abandoned to the next — if any — tenant.

I knew it, he said to himself. Well, there goes the first thousand dollars' bounty; probably skipped all the way to the Antarctic Circle. Out of my jurisdiction; another bounty hunter from another police department will retire Polokov and claim the money. On, I suppose, to the andys who haven't been warned, as was Polokov. On to Luba Luft.

-- Chapter 8

GREGG RICKMAN

The following is the address I composed for the March 4, 2007 memorial service in Berkeley, California, on the occasion of the twenty-fifth anniversary of Philip K. Dick's death. This is its first publication – in a graphic adaptation of one of Phil's most famous novels, a fact which I think would have amused him. This is the address' first publication.

– Gregg Rickman

Phil Dick's reputation as a major writer is I think secure. Ursula LeGuin once spoke of him as "America's home-grown Borges." I prefer to think of him as our Dostoyevsky. When I read Dostoyevsky, the excitability of all of his characters – the way that they seem ready to fly apart – reminds me of Phil Dick's fiction. That and the breadth and depth of his characters, which parallels in their way Dostoyevsky's cross-section of Russian life in the 19th Century. THE THREE STIGMATA is THE BROTHERS KARAMAZOV in deep space. MARTIAN TIME SLIP is CRIME AND PUNISHMENT on Mars. A lot of his Bay Area-set novels could be retitled PRINCE MYSHKIN IN CALIFORNIA. Dick's story of the dead come to life – UBIK – parallels Dostoyevsky's story of the dead come to life – BOBOK. I think the echo is deliberate. Phil Dick was a well-read man.

We're here today to remember the man, more than the writer, but the two sides of Phil can't be separated. He was a writer – that's how he saw the world. When I think of Phil Dick I think of him sitting in his apartment, surrounded by books and his tins of snuff. I met him there a few times, in our brief acquaintance, and it was usually daylight, but when I think of Phil Dick I think of him at night. A writer's life is a lonely one, but his I think was lonelier than most, because I think he was at the furthest frontiers of thought, and was going there alone.

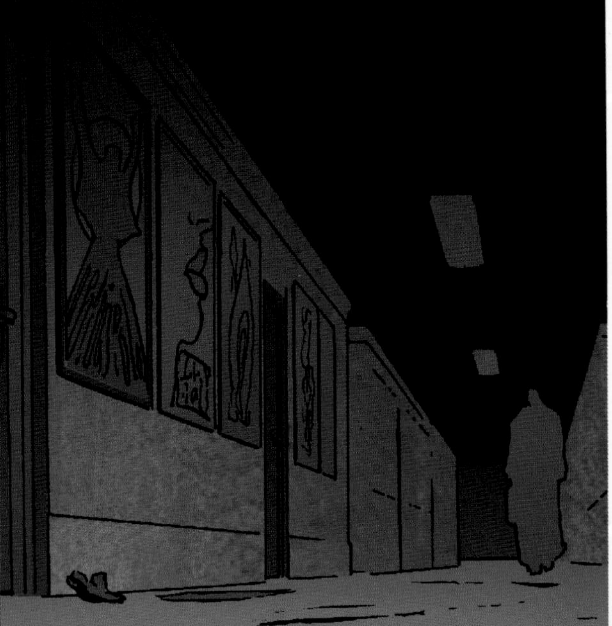

I recently rewatched Ken Burns' documentary on jazz. It mentioned that Duke Ellington had had many brilliant ideas about music, but had no one to communicate with about them until he met and began his long collaboration with Billy Strayhorn. They hit it off instantly. They understood each other perfectly.

Phil Dick never met his Billy Strayhorn. Of necessity he worked alone. I'm one of the few people to have been privileged to read thru the hundreds of pages of notes he took on his Dostoyevskian spiritual experience of 1974, in what he called his EXEGESIS. What struck me above all in reading through those hand-scrawled pages were their lucidity, and their honesty. He intelligently explored every path that might explain his experiences. I have a mental picture of Phil Dick in his tiny apartment, bending over yet another sheet of typewriter paper, pursuing another theory, at 1 or 2 or 3 o'clock in the morning. He wrote by hand, and the penmanship flies up the paper. It goes uphill, like Mercer the martyr in DO ANDROIDS DREAM OF ELECTRIC SHEEP?.

It was the same all-night writing method, albeit on a typewriter keyboard, he had followed to write his novels. He was past that now, and he only occasionally wrote fiction in his final years, although when he did write a short story like THE EXIT DOOR LEADS IN, he effortlessly operated at the top of his field. We tend to forget that Phil was only 53 when he died, and in my view had his finest work to come.

I don't think of Phil Dick as, particularly, a science fiction writer — I think of him as a writer. The written word is how he apprehended the world, how he processed his experiences. The written word was always very important to him, from his early novel EYE IN THE SKY (which takes place just a couple of miles from here, in the Berkeley Bevatron), when words of fire fall from the sky — through to his EXEGESIS, and his hundreds of pages of talk about the Logos, the Word of God.

I also think of Phil as something of a moral example. Critics of Dick, or critics of Dick's fans, have sometimes accused him or them as planning to start a new religion. Nothing could be further than the truth. There are no celebrities in this building. As I know very well from talking to people who knew him much better than I, Philip K. Dick was no saint, but I think of him when I occasionally try to rise above myself and do something good. In one of his novels Phil wrote about the "beside helper" who tries to aid people in need. Mercer, the martyr figure in DO ANDROIDS DREAM OF ELECTRIC SHEEP?, is one of those figures. I think of Phil that way. I think of the way he took care of his cats. I think of the way he raged, in our final conversations, about the mistreatment of the innocent. There are worse moral examples out there than Phil Dick's "beside helper." I know that there are times when we could all use one.

Finally, I think of Phil Dick as a martyr to his own empathy. In my last conversation with him he could talk of little else but Maitreya the Christ with the burns on his legs. Those of us who spoke with him in his last month or so of life will remember I think similar conversations. He was expecting the Maitreya's imminent return — that, and the end of the world. I only knew Phil Dick the last year of his life. Photos of him in the 1970s show a burly man, with a big chest, who looked like (he once said) a bouncer in a Mexican bar. But when I knew him he was thin — thin, and in our last conversation burning with urgency. I think his moral and his ethical concerns had burned away his burliness, worn through what remained of his health. It was the first year of the Reagan Administration, and for an old Berkeley resident, as someone who had celebrated the fall of Richard Nixon as divinely inspired, the new Republican dispensation was a hard blow to handle. "The Empire," he wrote in his EXEGESIS, "never ended." 25 years later, in the seventh year of the second Bush Administration, we see how true that is.

One of the concepts Phil Dick liked to wrestle with was that of false time. 2000 years of history would dissolve away, and we would be back in the time of the Roman Empire — the year 70 C.E. He devoted many pages of his EXEGESIS to exploring this concept, and was already wrestling with it when he wrote THE MAN IN THE HIGH CASTLE in 1962. "What if the Nazis hadn't won the war?" people in Japanese-occupied San Francisco wonder. What if we're living in a false, dreadful history, where the wrong people won, and the wrong people died? What if we could suddenly wipe away the occlusion and see life as it really is? What if we could dissolve the last 25 years, and arrive back in the time of Philip K. Dick? What would he say? "How are the cats?" he might ask. "Are the children safe? Are the children well?"

Postscript, 2010: The chapters of DO ANDROIDS DREAM OF ELECTRIC SHEEP? illustrated in this volume don't illustrate this side of our author that I have discussed above. Other chapters — the Mercer passages — do. But it's nonetheless true that one of Philip Dick's major themes, both in his life and writing, was the need for empathy, and how the ability to feel it separated one from what he called the "android" personality. "Within the universe there exist fierce cold things," he wrote in his 1972 essay MAN, ANDROID AND MACHINE, "which I have given the name 'machines' to."

> *Their behavior frightens me, especially when it imitates human behavior so well that I get the uncomfortable sense that these things are trying to pass themselves off as humans but are not. I call them "androids," which is my own way of using that word. (...) I mean a thing somehow generated to deceive us in a cruel way, to cause us to think it to be one of ourselves. (...) In my science fiction I write about them constantly.*

Dick wrote often of this android personality, building several of his key fictions around the war between this android and the "authentically human" soul. DO ANDROIDS DREAM OF ELECTRIC SHEEP? (1968) is perhaps the novel that foregrounds that struggle most successfully.

It is thanks to Ridley Scott's brilliantly visualized version of this novel, BLADE RUNNER, that DO ANDROIDS DREAM OF ELECTRIC SHEEP? is perhaps the author's best-known work. But the film only suggests the vital struggle Dick wrote about — another reason to be glad this graphic visualization of what Philip Dick actually wrote now exists. Scott's suggestions in his various re-edited versions of BLADE RUNNER over the years that Rick Deckard is really an android ("replicant") himself directs our attention away from what mattered to Dick, making nonsense of the author's intention. It's important to Dick that it's a frail, human Rick Deckard who takes on the androids – the android Polokov calls him a "pencil neck" in a chapter from the novel serialized here. Polokov then tries to kill him, in an exciting action scene.

Dick's greatest philosophical concern, the struggle for empathy, is represented in this novel by the martyr figure Mercer – a character absent from the film. One feels empathy with Mercer by grasping an attachment to a television – Dick here anticipates a total immersion mass media technology that's still, as of 2010, in our future.

Empathy was important to Philip Dick. Set against the non-human androids are Deckard's hostile, sullenly depressed wife Iran, the "chickenhead" J. R. Isidore, and his harsh and violent police colleagues. How fully human are they? Which of them have empathy? "Most androids I've known have more vitality and desire to live" than Iran, he muses. As he "retires" one escaped android after another Rick Deckard begins to wonder about the souls of these machines. His encounter with the opera singer Luba Luft, prefigured in this installment, will cause him to truly doubt himself and his mission.

Of Deckard and his war with the androids there is much more to say, but it's best to let his struggle with them here speak for Philip K. Dick for now.

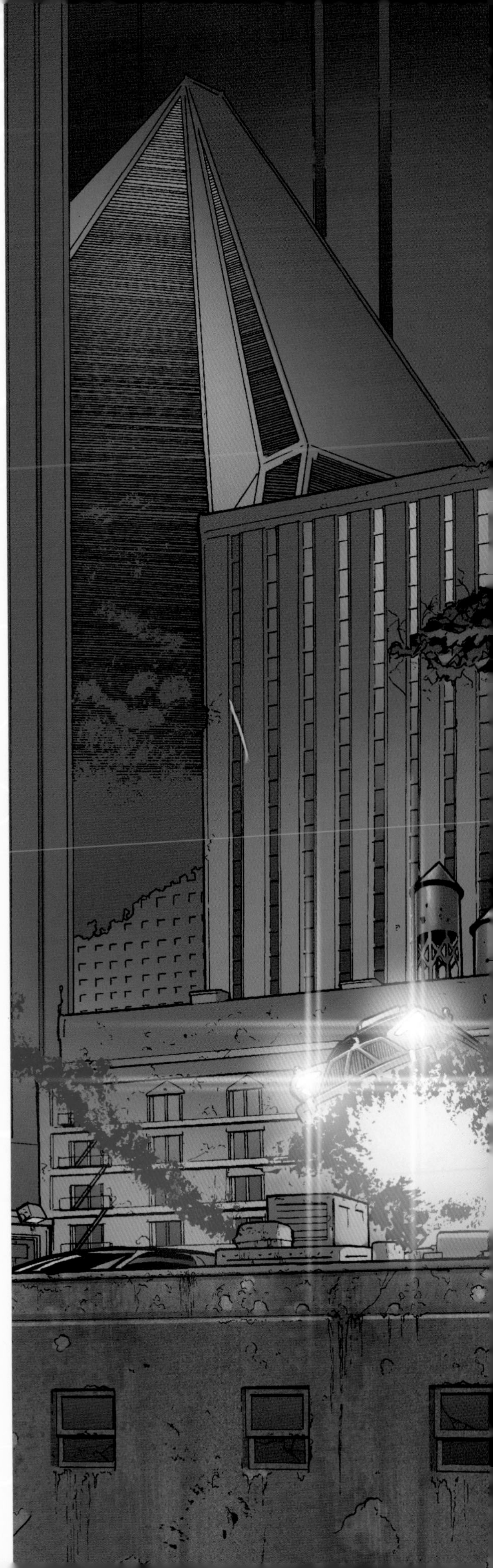

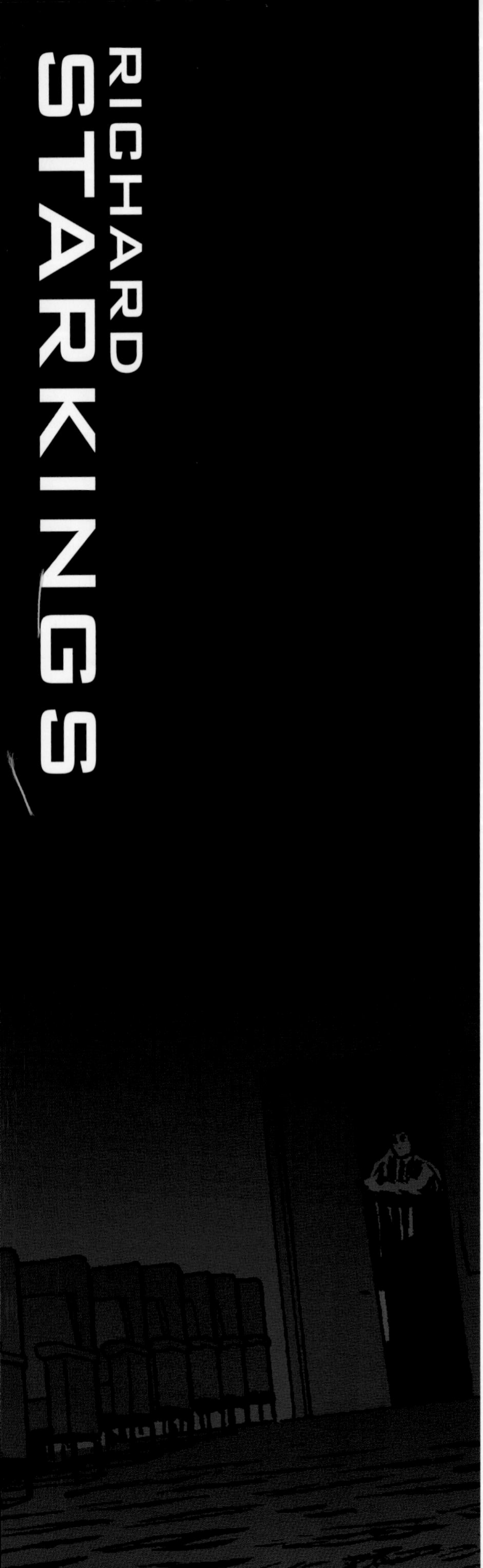
RICHARD
STARKINGS

"Human and animal suffering make me mad; whenever one of my cats dies I curse God and I mean it; I feel fury at him. I'd like to get him here where I could interrogate him, tell him that I think the world is screwed up, that man didn't sin and fall but was pushed — which is bad enough — but was then sold the lie that he is basically sinful, which I know he is not. I have known all kinds of people (I turned fifty a while ago and I'm angry about that; I've lived a long time), and those were by and large good people. I model the characters in my novels and stories on them. Now and again one of these people dies, and that makes me mad — really mad, as mad as I can get. 'You took my cat,' I want to say to God, 'and then you took my girlfriend. What are you doing? Listen to me; listen! It's wrong what you're doing.'"

Introduction to THE GOLDEN MAN
by Philip K. Dick

I was relieved to discover recently that, years ago, BLADE RUNNER director Ridley Scott had confessed to OMNI magazine that he had found DO ANDROIDS DREAM OF ELECTRIC SHEEP? *"too difficult to read."* I was relieved because I had felt the same way about DADOES? as a teenager, and even though I struggled valiantly through to the end of the book some time after watching BLADE RUNNER, and even though I later eyed my college roommate's copies of VALIS and FLOW MY TEARS, THE POLICEMAN SAID, it seemed to me that the very titles of Dick's books steadfastly refused to adequately describe his stories to me in short, easily digestible phrases.

BLADE RUNNER somehow made sense to me as a title, it was visceral and it satisfactorily suggested the urgent hunt depicted in the movie -- but the title of DADOES? annoyed me -- like most of Dick's titles it asked me to think -- and it urged my eyes to auto-correct the title to DO ANDROIDS COUNT ELECTRIC SHEEP?. That's what Dick really meant, right? Didn't he?

Like most people I was drawn to DADOES? *because* it was the source material for BLADE RUNNER and I am personally of the mind that there are two kinds of Science Fiction -- Science Fiction before BLADE RUNNER and Science Fiction after BLADE RUNNER. In the same way that DO ANDROIDS DREAM OF ELECTRIC SHEEP? is a gateway into the work of Philip K. Dick for people who are only aware of his work because of BLADE RUNNER, BLADE RUNNER is a gateway into Science Fiction for people who don't dig Science Fiction. I wasn't aware of this until I happened to watch BLADE RUNNER with a friend almost twenty years ago. She had shuffled through the videotapes in my collection looking for something to pass a Saturday evening and came across BLADE RUNNER and exclaimed with glee, "Oh, my favourite!" This was the late 80's, and it was not yet chic to be geek, and my friend was strikingly beautiful and into Jazz and clothes and all other kinds of trendy stuff, but not comics or SF or anything remotely nerdish. As the movie came to a close and Rutger Hauer delivered his famous "Tears in rain," soliloquy, my friend turned to me and told me, "Chicks dig that."

Really? Chicks dig that?

From that point on I started watching BLADE RUNNER with a different perspective. When it opened in 1981 in the UK, I had watched it in Leeds, my hometown in Northern England. It was cold and pouring with rain that night, and when I emerged from the Odeon, it was as if the movie had spilled out into the streets; car brake lights and neon store signs were tracing multicoloured patterns in the water that covered the roads, and those of us that emerged from the theater huddled up inside our long coats as drops of rainwater trickled down our faces, and we quickly made our way to the bus stations and home. We didn't need to see BLADE RUNNER's future, we were *living* it!

My renewed interest in BLADE RUNNER's appeal to the fairer sex led me to the Nuart Theater in Los Angeles in 1991; the screening which sparked the resurgence of interest in the movie nationwide. This was the first cut that ran without Deckard's voiceover, the one that led to the rerelease of the movie as THE DIRECTOR'S CUT. I much prefer my BLADE RUNNER voiceoverless, and the girls who happily escorted me to screenings in '91 and '92 seemed to concur. Wow, my friend had been right, BLADE RUNNER was a perfect date movie . . . chicks really did dig BLADE RUNNER -- but, beyond Rutger Hauer's stylish replicant delivering poetry, why was that?

I think the answer lies at the heart of Dick's work, in the issues that compelled him to write science fiction in general and DO ANDROIDS DREAM OF ELECTRIC SHEEP? in particular. The concept of Mercerism, which is referred to extensively in DADOES?, but never mentioned in BLADE RUNNER, is essentially a belief system stressing the value of empathy between living beings. Deckard reasons that androids are incapable of empathizing with human beings, or animals for that matter. Deckard's obsession with acquiring a real animal -- a sheep, a goat or a toad -- is his way of demonstrating to his wife -- a stay-at-home, good-for-nothing who would rather dial up an attitude on her mood organ than actually risk feeling something by experiencing life outside her apartment -- that he has feelings, that he has value in the world.

Chicks dig that.

Mercerism allows Deckard to kill the killers -- to justify the deaths of androids because they lack the ability to care for others, animals included. Deckard, like Dick, is motivated by fear, and the anticipation of pain, qualities he believes that the androids lack, qualities that develop in us empathy and compassion.

It's not long before Deckard himself realizes "*Most androids I've known have more vitality and desire to live than my wife.*" Fear of those who do not feel fear, or pain or compassion is the theme that Ridley Scott successfully carries over from DADOES? into BLADE RUNNER, a theme that transforms the movie from a straightforward action adventure into a science fiction romance.

Chicks dig that.

The significance of DADOES? having been written, and set, in California was lost on me when I read it 30 years ago. Growing up in the North of England meant that I was never far from a pig, or a cow, a horse . . . or a sheep. I went to a school next door to a farm, so we took animals for granted. Not until I lived in cities like London and New York, and then Los Angeles -- in fact, not until I was actually raising children in Los Angeles -- did I become aware that the sight of a cow anywhere other than on TV or in a reference book was a remarkable occasion that would provoke excitement amongst my kids. In the neighborhood I live in, close to LAX, we were shocked quite recently to see a lean and hungry looking coyote walking down the center of Lincoln Boulevard near Loyola University. What was it doing there? Was it not aware of the unspoken agreement between man and coyotes -- we would tolerate and fear them in the desert, but they should never dare to be seen on the city streets of civilized towns? We stayed in the car, frozen like tourists on safari, until the coyote made its way across the traffic light and out of sight.

Deckard's role in DADOES? is to visibly demonstrate his compassion -- to his wife, to his neighbors -- by buying and nurturing an animal, originally in the shape of an electric sheep. The real question asked by the book's title asks us if androids yearn to demonstrate compassion too. It is made clear in the course of the novel that androids are considered to be incapable of empathy, whereas humans demonstrate their ability to feel for others by communing with Mercer through the empathy box, or by seeking out and acquiring animals to nurture and raise. Roy Baty and the androids resent the empathy box, regarding it as another human machine designed to prove that andys are less than human.

> *"Standing there, he realized, all at once, that he had acquired an overt incontestable fear directed toward the principal android."*

DO ANDROIDS DREAM OF ELECTRIC SHEEP?

Even after Mercer's origins are exposed in DADOES?, *"the principal android,"* Roy Baty, is disposed of quickly and easily. After Isidore's naive attempts to befriend the androids are betrayed, it is left to Deckard to ponder the sham exposed by Buster Friendly and yet still reach the conclusion that *"electric things have their lives too."* In BLADE RUNNER there's no question that the androids, the replicants, have just as much, if not more, vitality and desire to live than the humans, but it is Roy Batty that truly struggles to demonstrate compassion, not Deckard. When he lets Deckard live in the final battle at the end of the film, he demonstrates the compassion he was not able to extend to Tyrell just a few scenes earlier.

Chicks dig that.

> *"Quite an experience to live in fear, isn't it?"*

BLADE RUNNER

When Batty asks this question, he finally becomes more human than human, as promised by Tyrell, because at this point we're aware that Deckard would have killed him had he had the chance. Like Deckard in DADOES?, he believes that killing the killers is justified.

In the movie's climax, Mercer's Sisyphean climb in the book is serendipitously preserved in the ascent of the Bradbury Building and when they reach the top, the two men share an intimate moment. Batty has overcome his fear of death and welcomes it, and Deckard empathizes.

Before Dick saw footage from BLADE RUNNER he suggested that the movie would be "*one titanic collision of androids being blown up, androids killing humans, general confusion and murder . . .*" and went on to say "*you wouldn't want to see my novel on screen because it is full of people conversing, plus the personal problems of the protagonist . . .*" Later he admitted that "*the book and the movie do not fight each other. They reinforce each other . . . this movie will stimulate the brain . . .*" Somehow the interpersonal issues featured in the book refused to leave the screenplay and were translated into a romance that underscored the action adventure storyline sought by the movie's producers.

As BLADE RUNNER's Deckard considers Roy Batty's final poetic words and watches him die, something has changed inside him. Rachael will eventually die, but he doesn't have to be the one who kills her. Batty's compassion for Deckard becomes Deckard's compassion for Rachael and when he discovers the possibility that he may be a replicant too, he has compassion for himself.

Yeah, Chicks dig that.

"I want to write about people I love, and put them into a fictional world spun out of my own mind, not the world we actually have, because the world we actually have does not meet my standards. Okay, so I should revise my standards; I'm out of step. I should yield to reality. I have never yielded to reality . . ."

Introduction to THE GOLDEN MAN
by Philip K. Dick

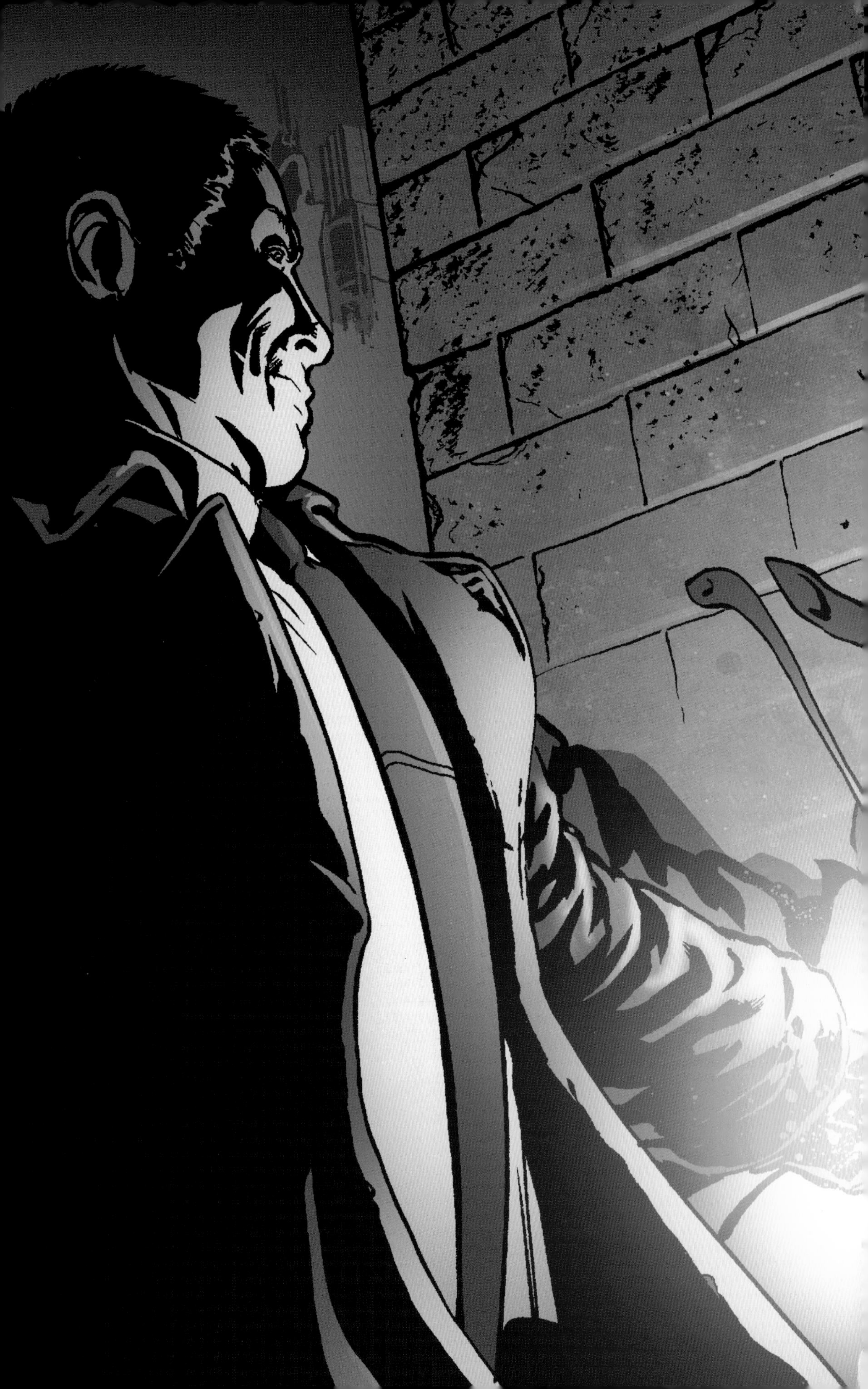

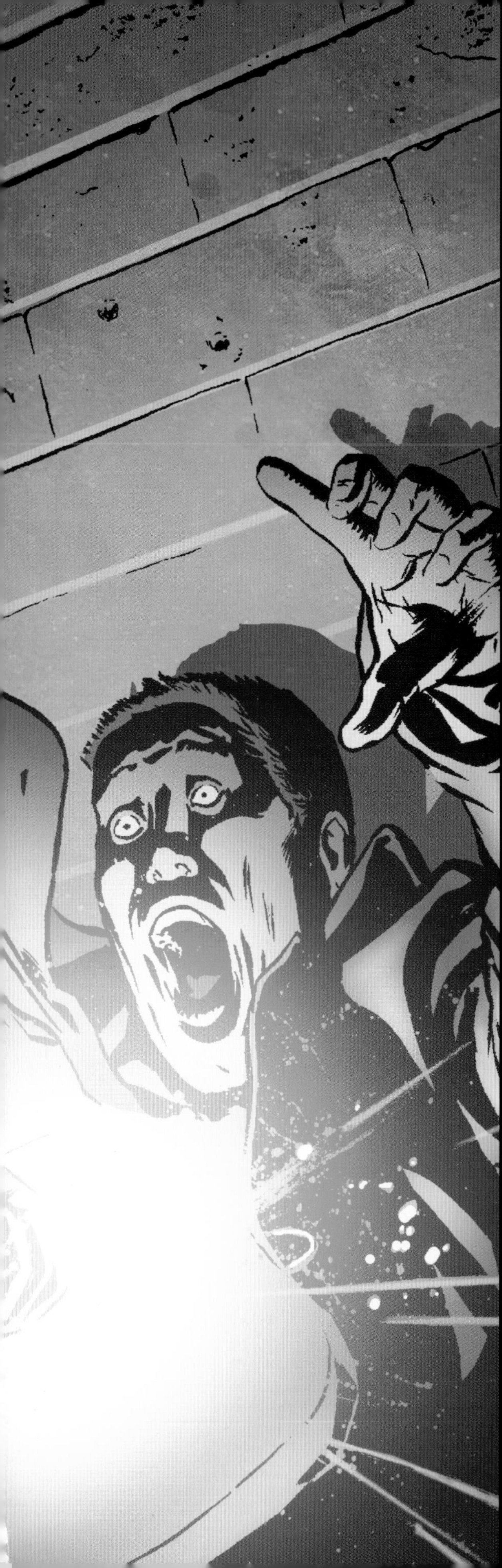

COVER GALLERY

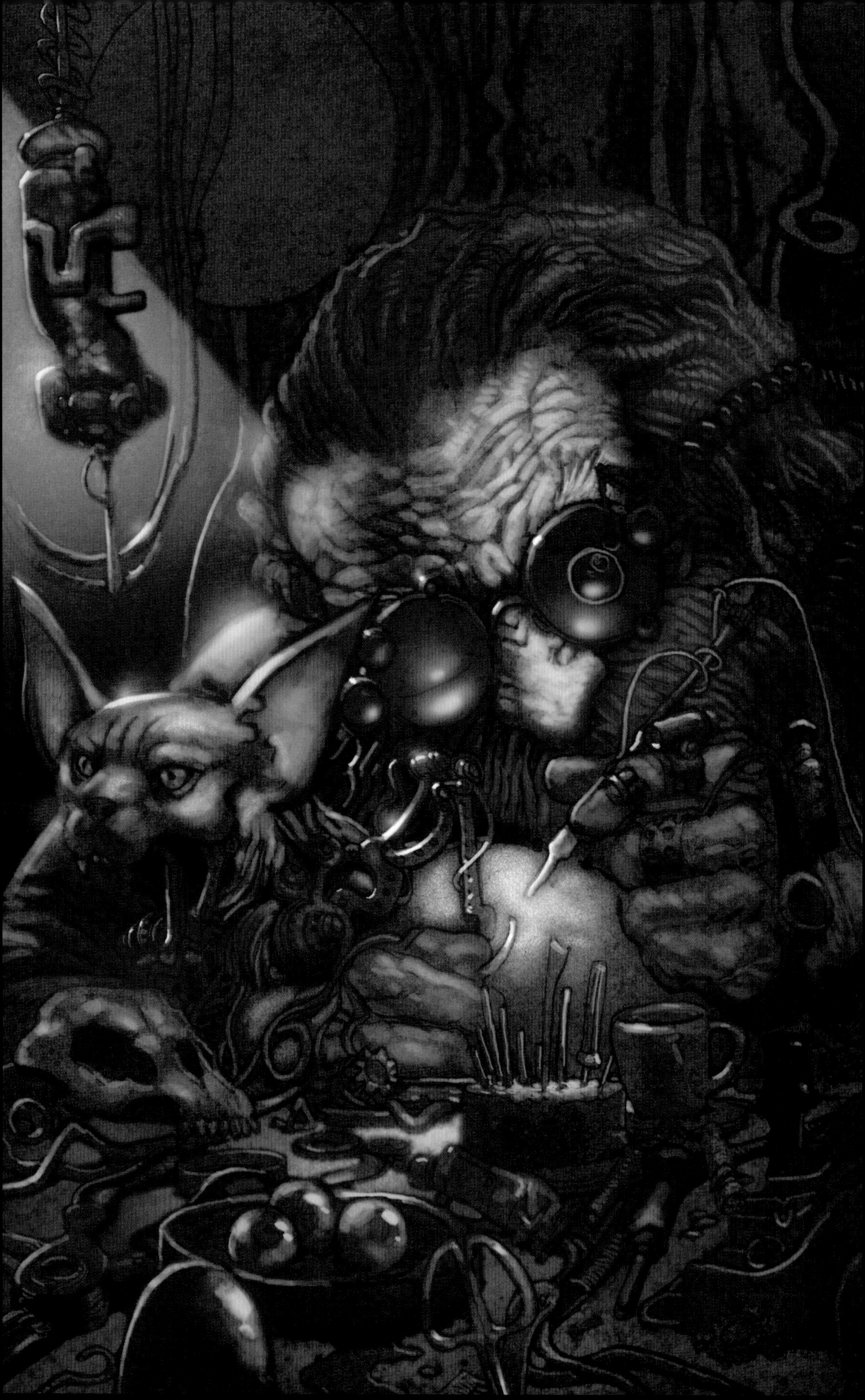

COVER 5A
MORITAT

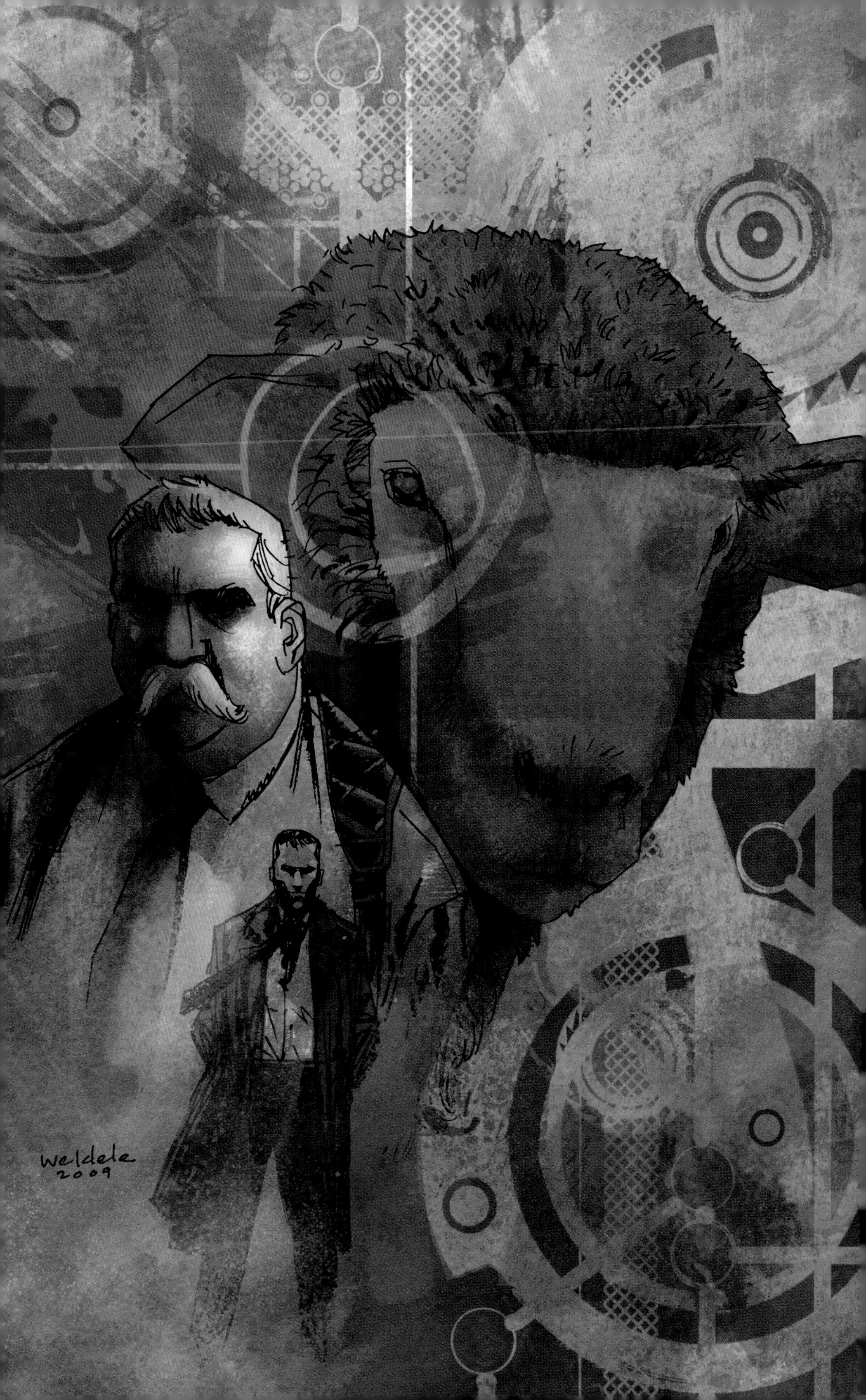
Weldele
2009

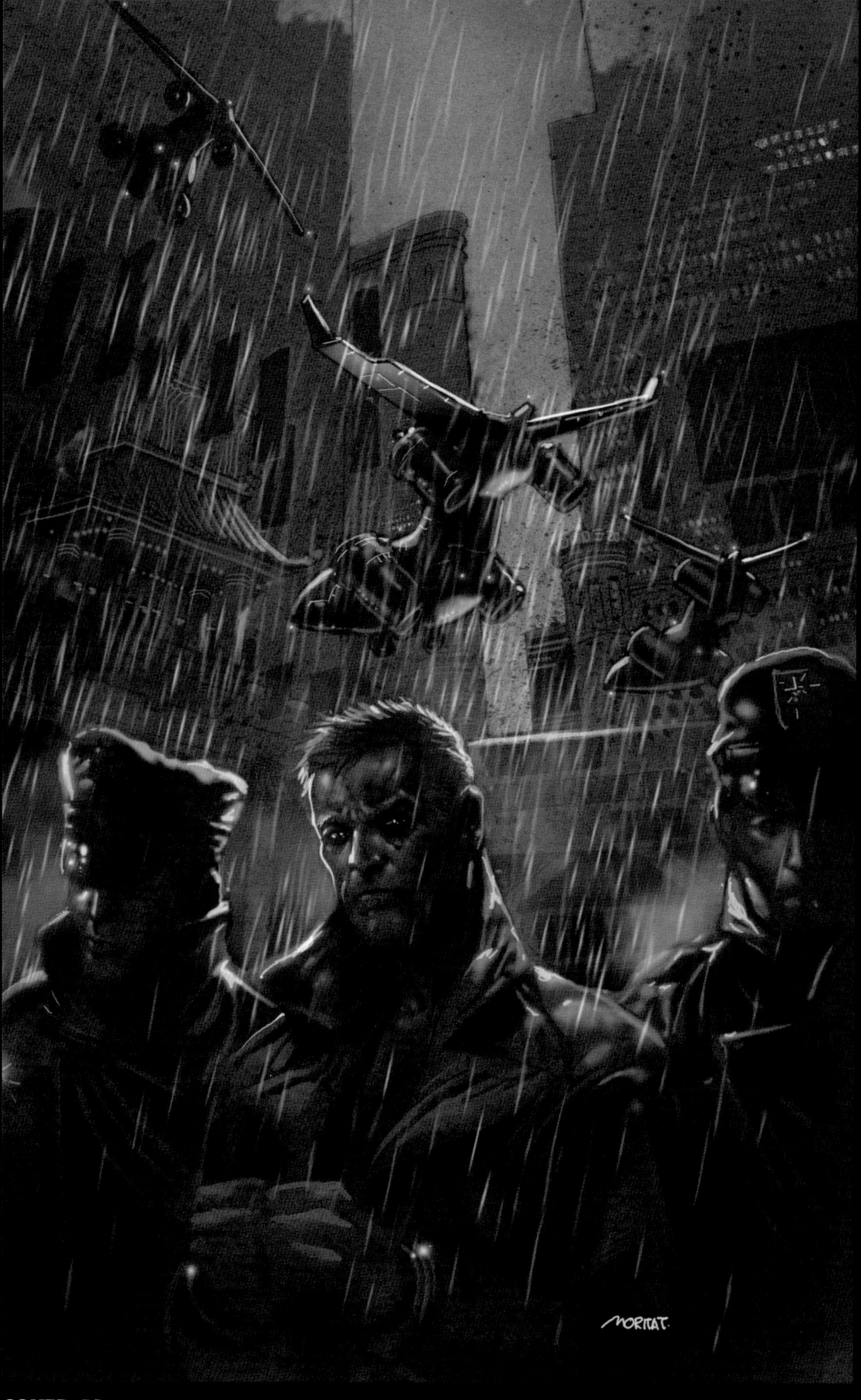
MORITAT.

COVER 6A

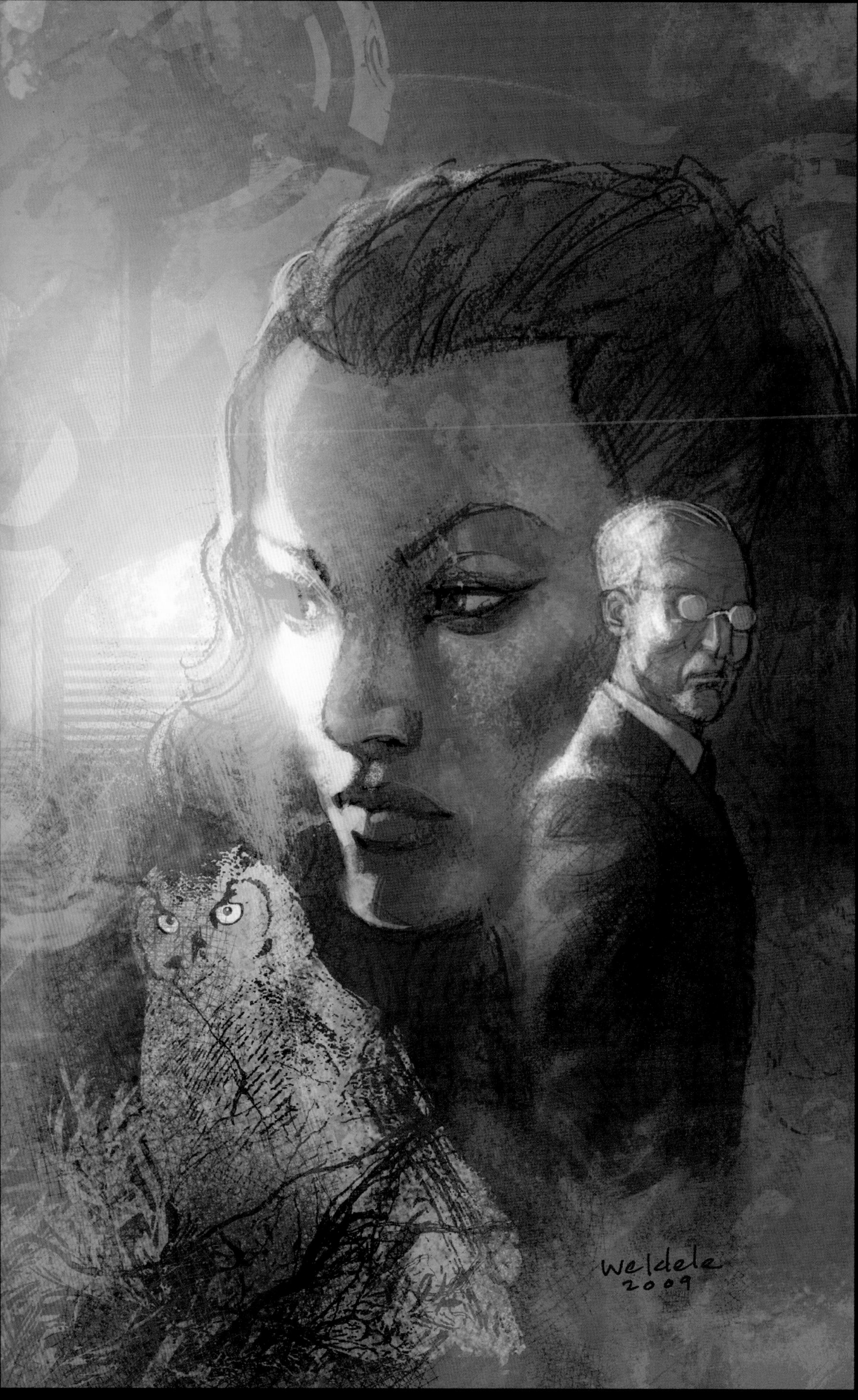
weldele
2009

COVER 6B

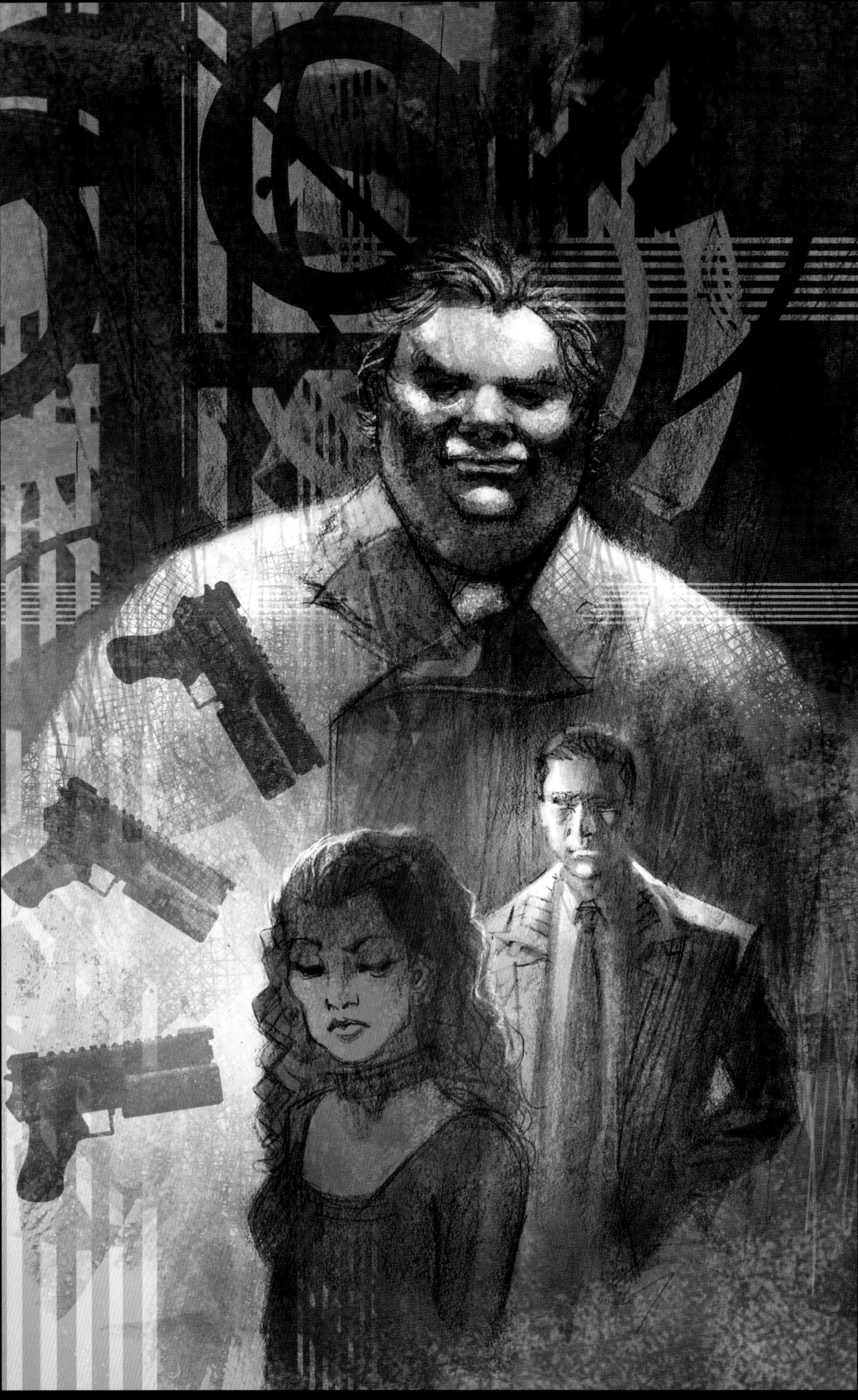

COVER 7A

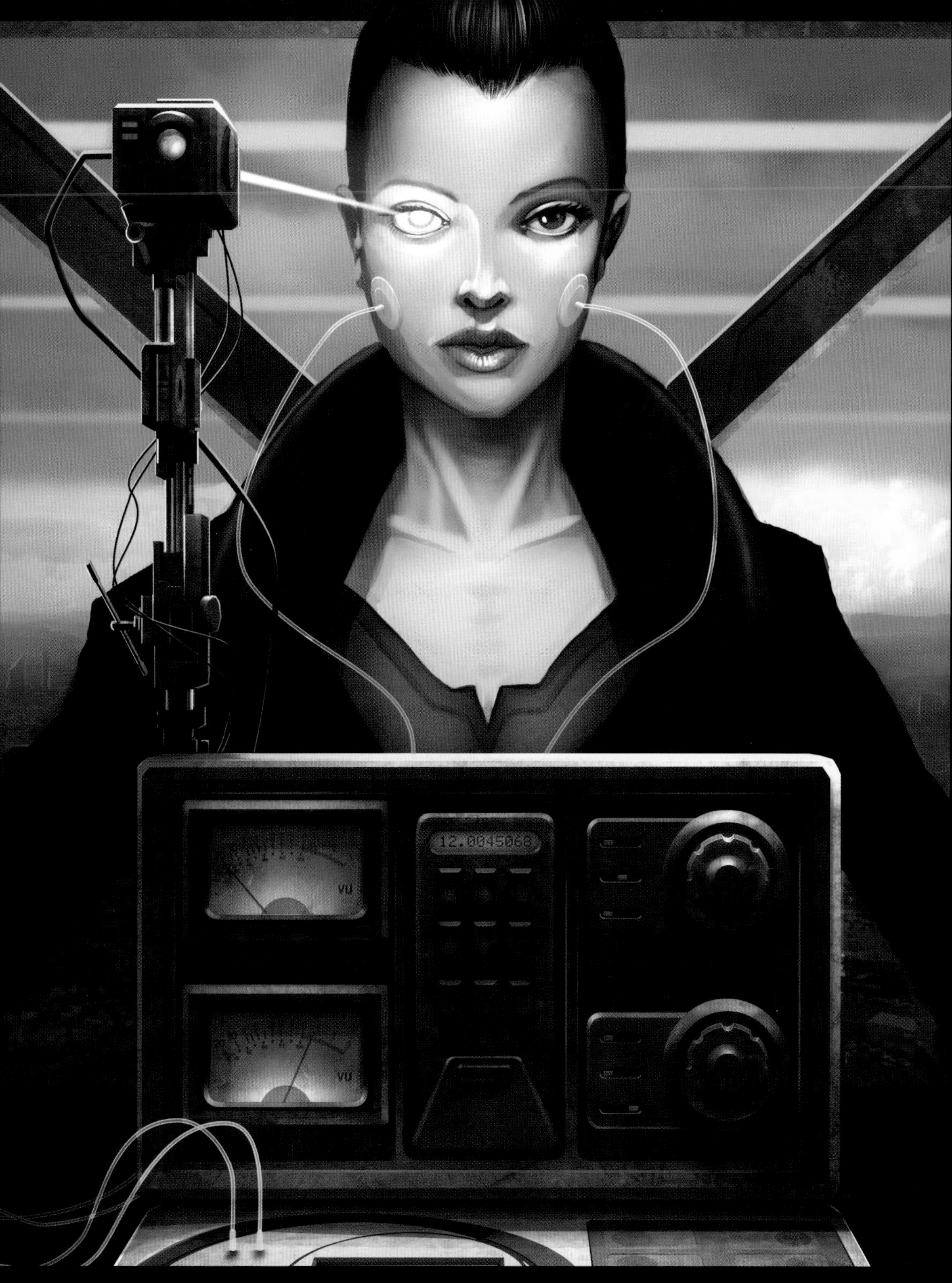
12.0045068
VU
VU

COVER 7B
SCOTT KEATING

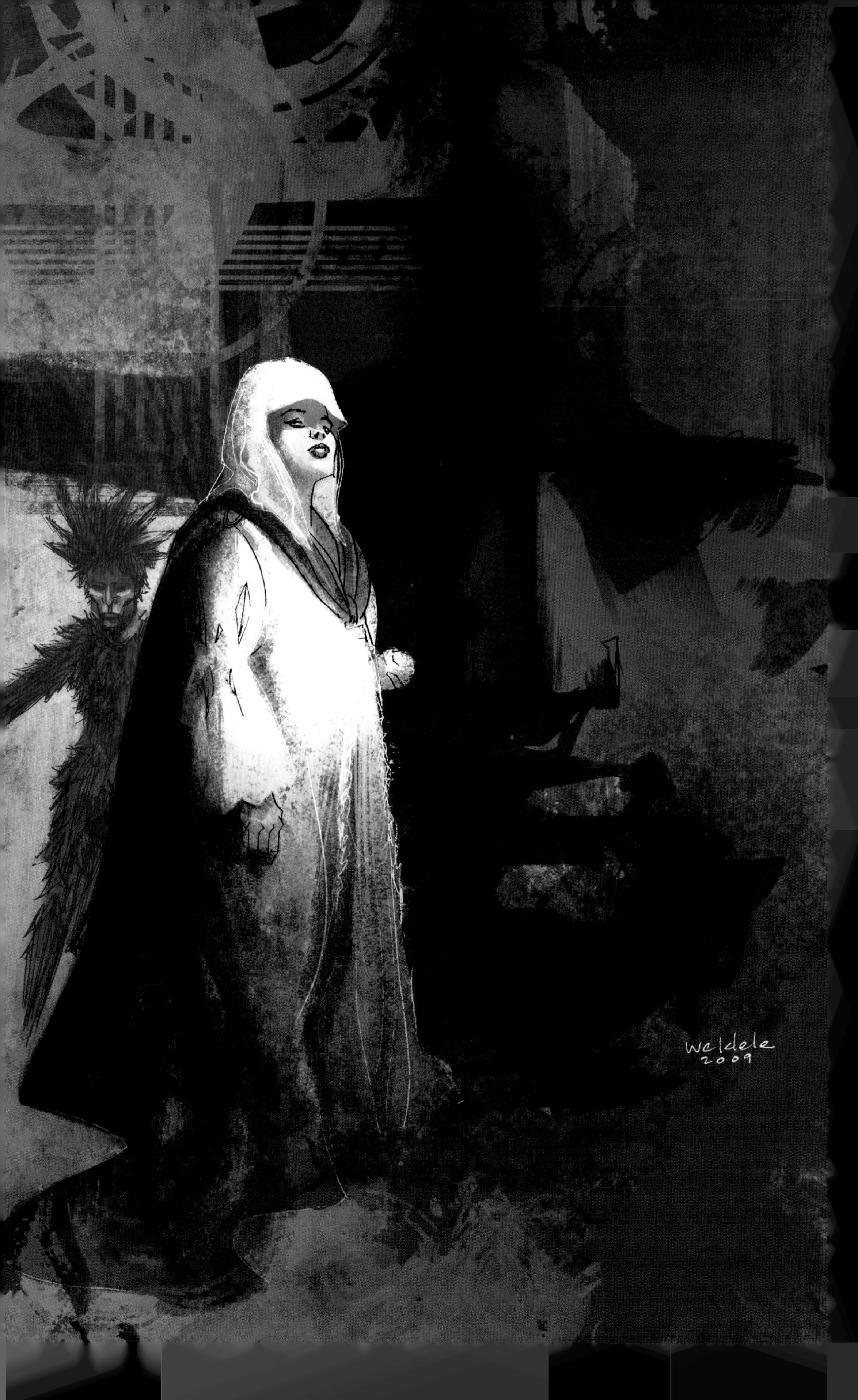
Weldele
2009

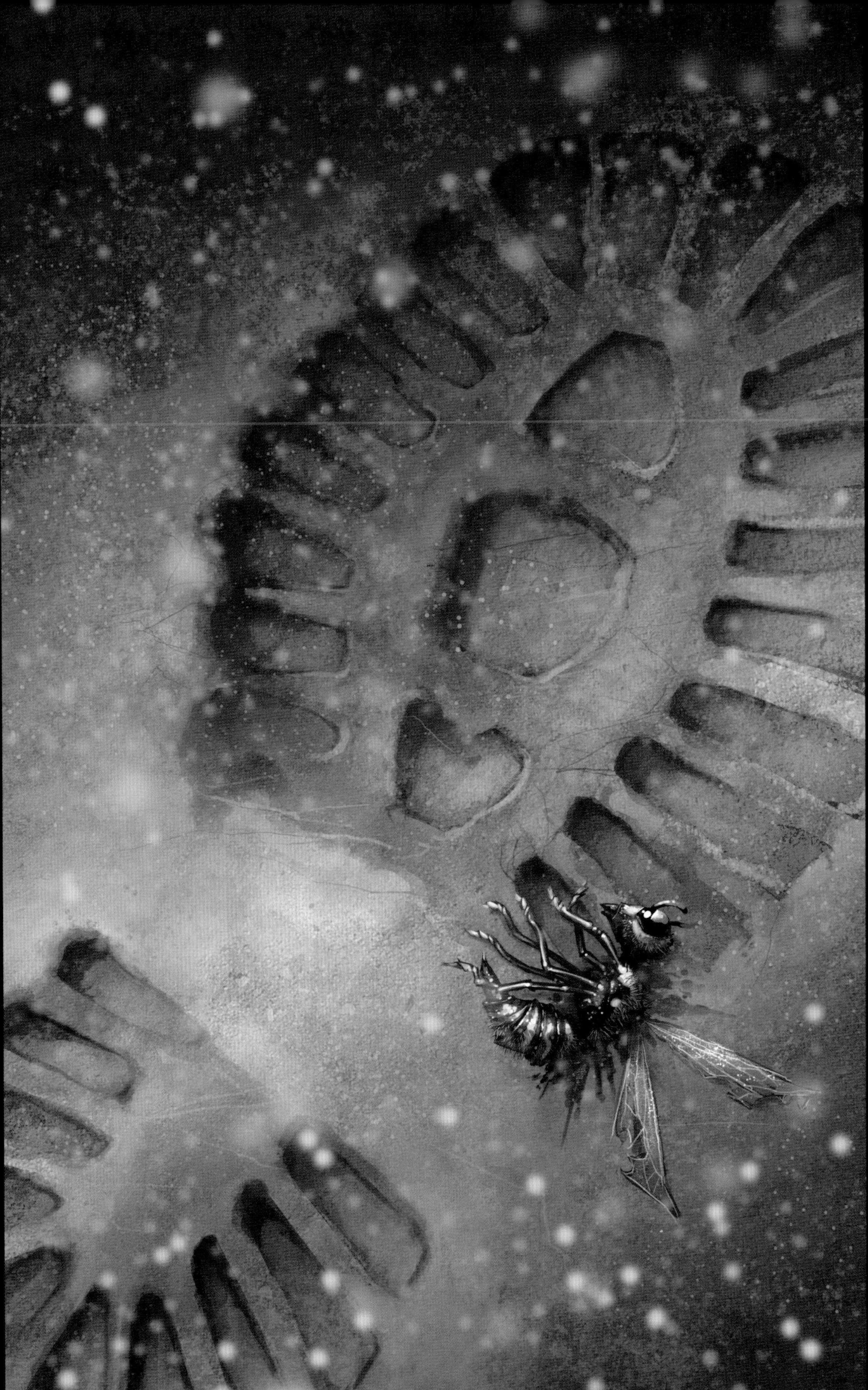

COVER 8B
SCOTT KEATING

IN STORES NOW!

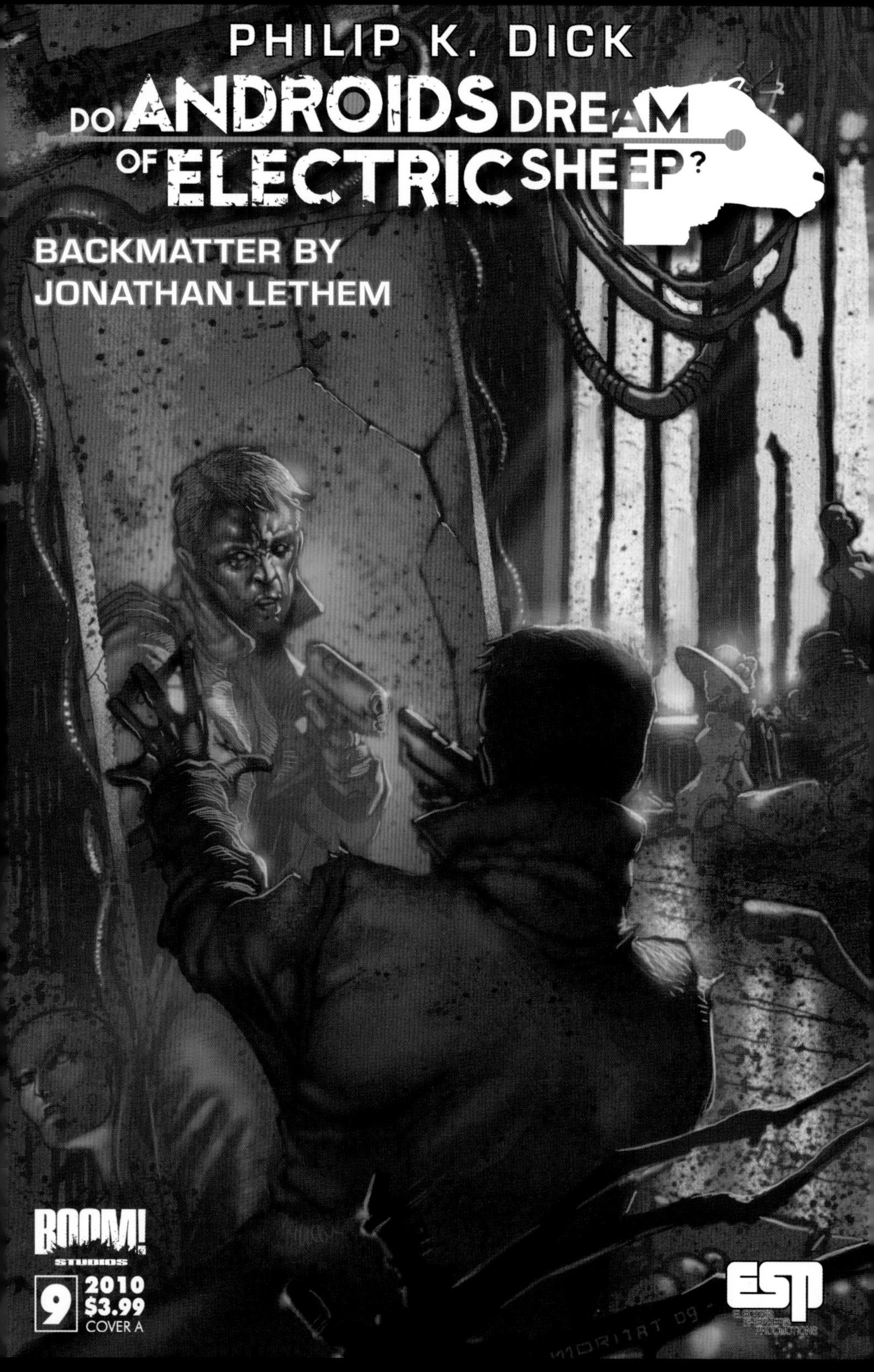
PHILIP K. DICK
DO ANDROIDS DREAM OF ELECTRIC SHEEP?
BACKMATTER BY JONATHAN LETHEM
BOOM! STUDIOS
9
2010
$3.99
COVER A
ESP

DO ANDROIDS DREAM OF ELECTRIC SHEEP? #9

PHILIP K. DICK'S SCIENCE FICTION MASTERPIECE CONTINUES IN THIS NEW, EXCITING ISSUE! WITH THE FIRST OF A FOUR PART BACKMATTER ESSAY BY NEW YORK TIMES BESTSELLING AUTHOR JONATHAN LETHEM!

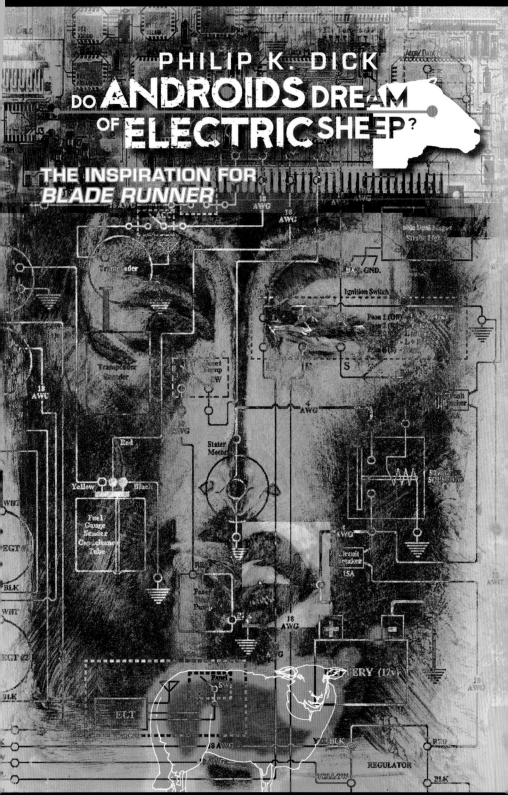

DICKPARKERBL

PHILIP K. DICK

Over his writing career, which spanned three decades, Philip K. Dick wrote and published 36 Science Fiction novels and 120 short stories. The themes that intrigued him in his writing still resonate with readers today, asking difficult philosophical questions such as "What makes us human?" and "What is reality?" Toward the end of his life, he explored deeply personal metaphysical questions about the essence of God.

DO ANDROID

OF ELECTR

Dick's greatest desire was to be recognized as a literary writer, not as a science fiction "hack." Unfortunately, this was not realized during his lifetime. Of twelve realist novels written by Dick, only one—*Confessions of A Crap Artist*—was published before his death.

Some of his most critically acclaimed and award-winning sci-fi titles include: *The Man in the High Castle* (1963 Hugo Award), *A Scanner Darkly* (Grand Prix du Festival at Metz, France 1979), *Ubik* (Time Magazine selection of 100 best English-language novels 1923 - 2006), *Flow My Tears, the Policeman Said* (John W. Campbell Award), *The Three Stigmata of Palmer Eldritch*, and *VALIS*. Dick's work is published in 27 countries and has been translated into 25 languages.

Dick was inducted into the SF Hall of Fame in 2005, and between 2007 and 2009 the Library of America published thirteen of his sci-fi novels, placing Philip K. Dick's name beside William Faulkner and Ernest Hemingway.

DICKPARKERBL

Nine of Dick's novels and short stories have been adapted to film, most notably: *Blade Runner* (1982, based on the novel *Do Androids Dream of Electric Sheep?*), *Total Recall* (1990, based on the short story *We Can Remember it For You Wholesale*), *Minority Report* (2002), and *A Scanner Darkly* (2006).

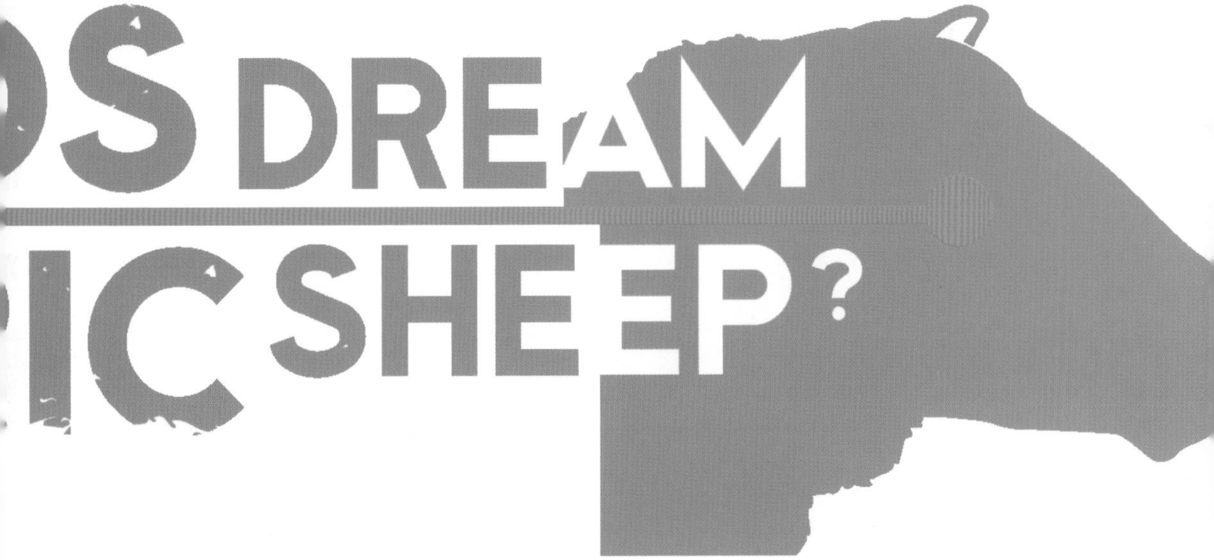
DS DREAM
IC SHEEP?

Dick struggled his entire life with the loss of his twin sister shortly after birth, as well as with depression (for which he was prescribed amphetamines) and numerous other phobias. He later became addicted to amphetamines and used them to fuel his drive to write quickly and sell his work to support his family. He incorporated much of his personal struggles, including depression and drug addiction, into his writing. Seeking female companionship was a constant throughout his adult life; he married five times and had three children.

On March 2, 1982, Philip K. Dick died of heart failure following a stroke in Santa Ana, California.

DICK PARKER BL

TONY PARKER has lent his art beyond the world of Philip K. Dick. In addition to the BOOM! Studios titles *Warhammer 40,000: Fire and Honour*, *Warhammer 40,000: Defenders of Ultramar*, and the exclusive Warhammer Online graphic novel *Warhammer Online: Prelude to War*, Parker has worked on over 125 pen and paper RPG books (including several painted covers). Parker has also offered his artistic hand to Upper Deck for their Marvel Masterpiece cards, *Conan*, and *The Ultimate Spider-man 100 Project* and *The Hulk 100 Project* for the HERO Initiative.

DO ANDROID

OF ELECTR

BLOND is one of the most prolific and talented colorists in the comic book industry today. In addition to *Do Androids Dream of Electric Sheep?*, he has colored Top Cow's *Hunter-Killer*, *Witchblade*, *The Darkness*, Marvel and IDW's *New Avengers/Transformers*, and Marvel's *Ultimate Fantastic Four*.

DICK PARKER BL

RICHARD STARKINGS is the creator of Image Comics' hit series *Elephantmen* and the Eisner Award-winning series *Hip Flask*. Although he lettered *Batman: The Killing Joke* with a pen, Starkings is perhaps best known for his work with the Comicraft Design and Lettering Studio, which he co-founded in 1992.

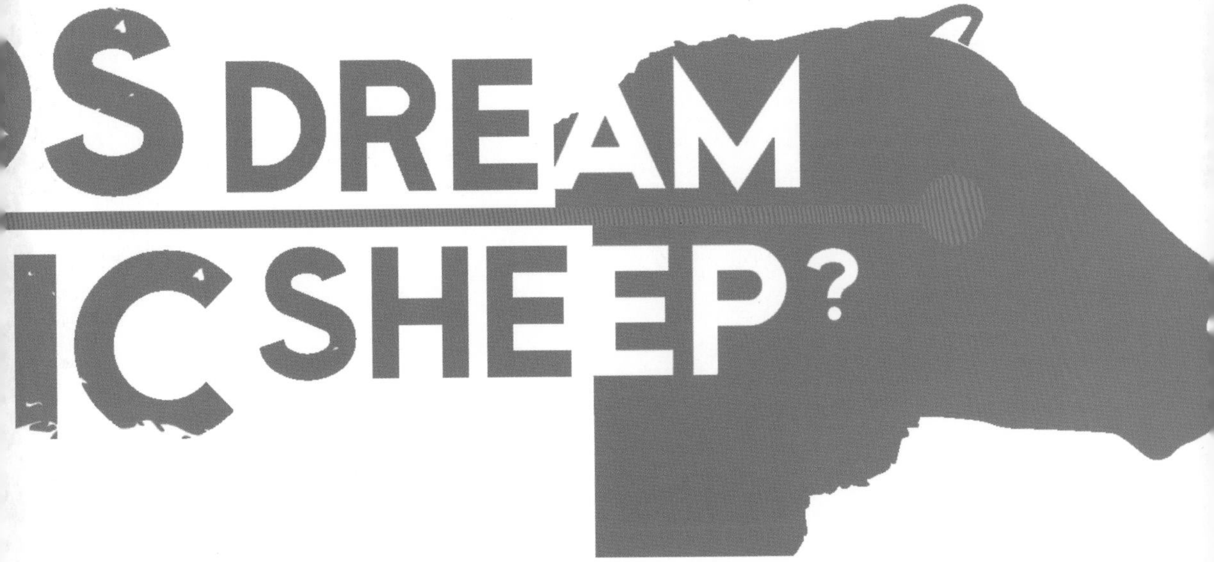
DREAM
SHEEP?

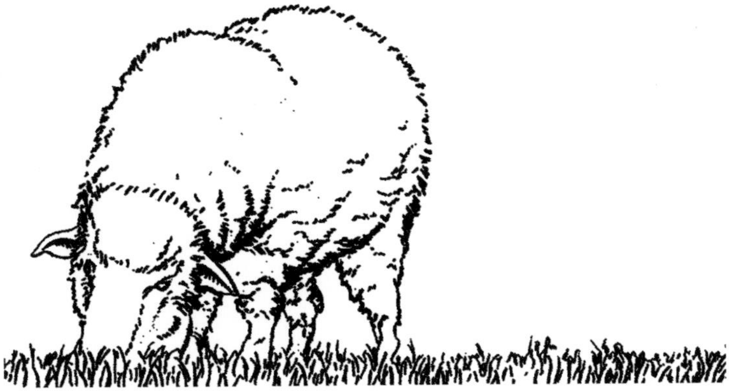

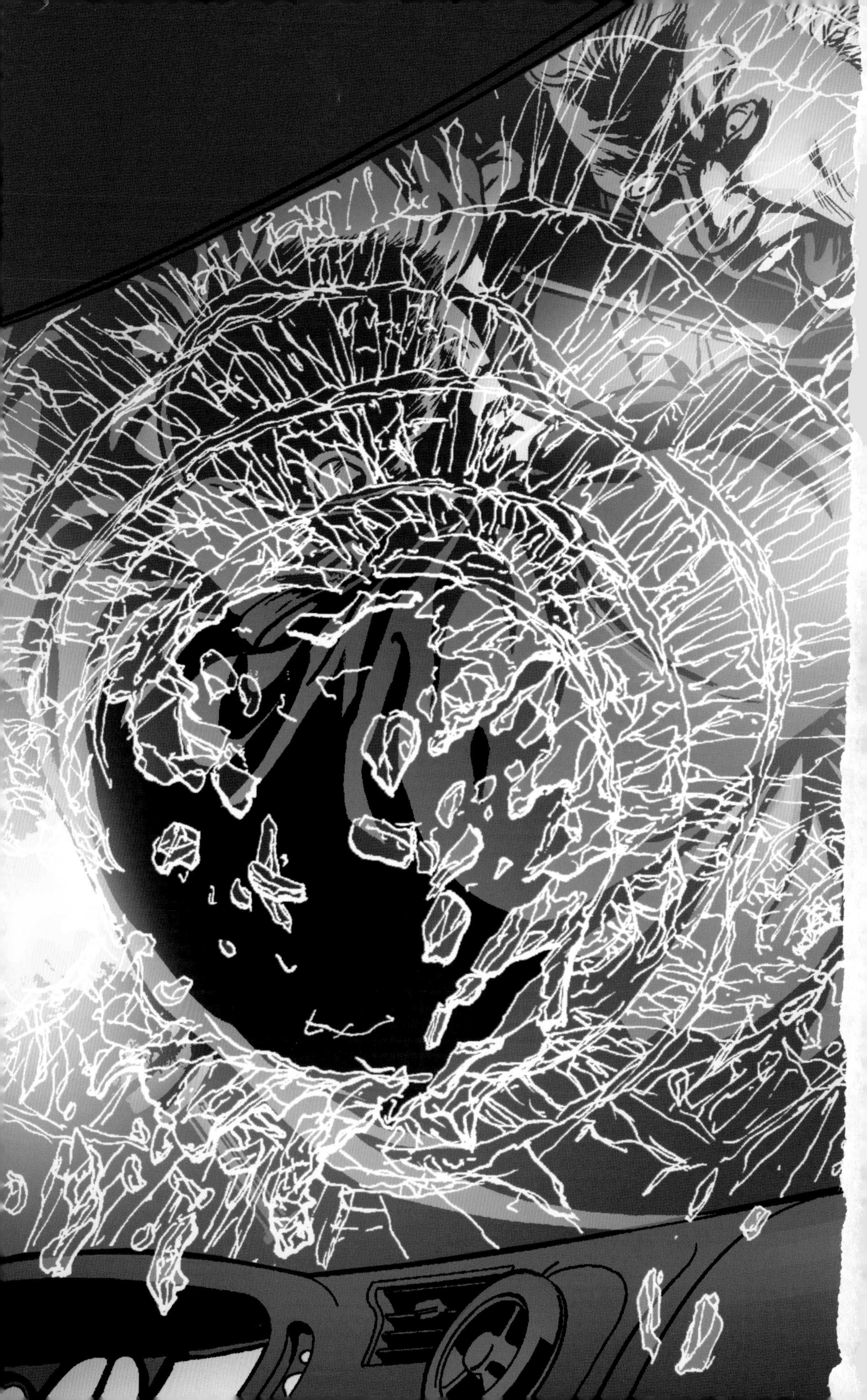

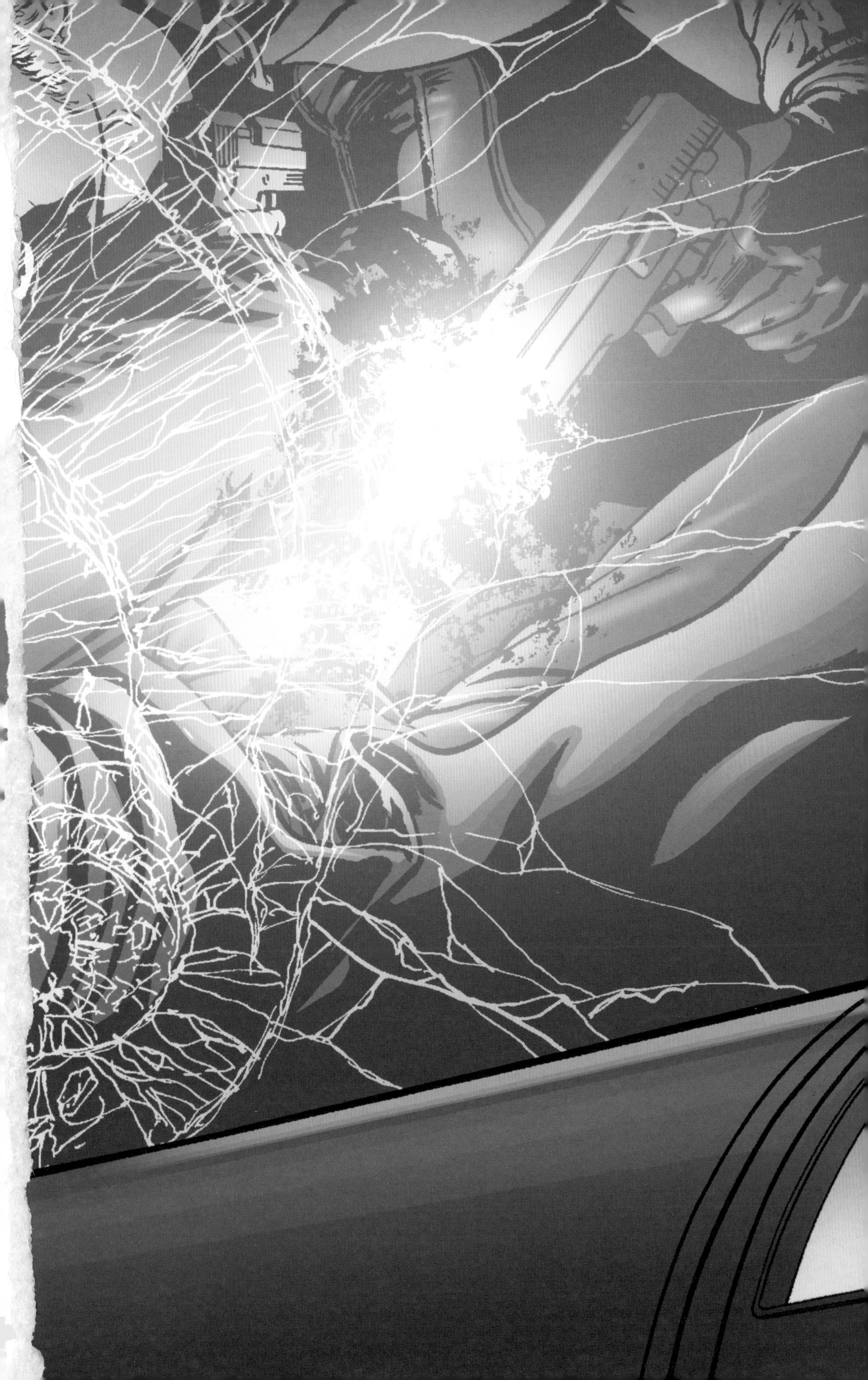

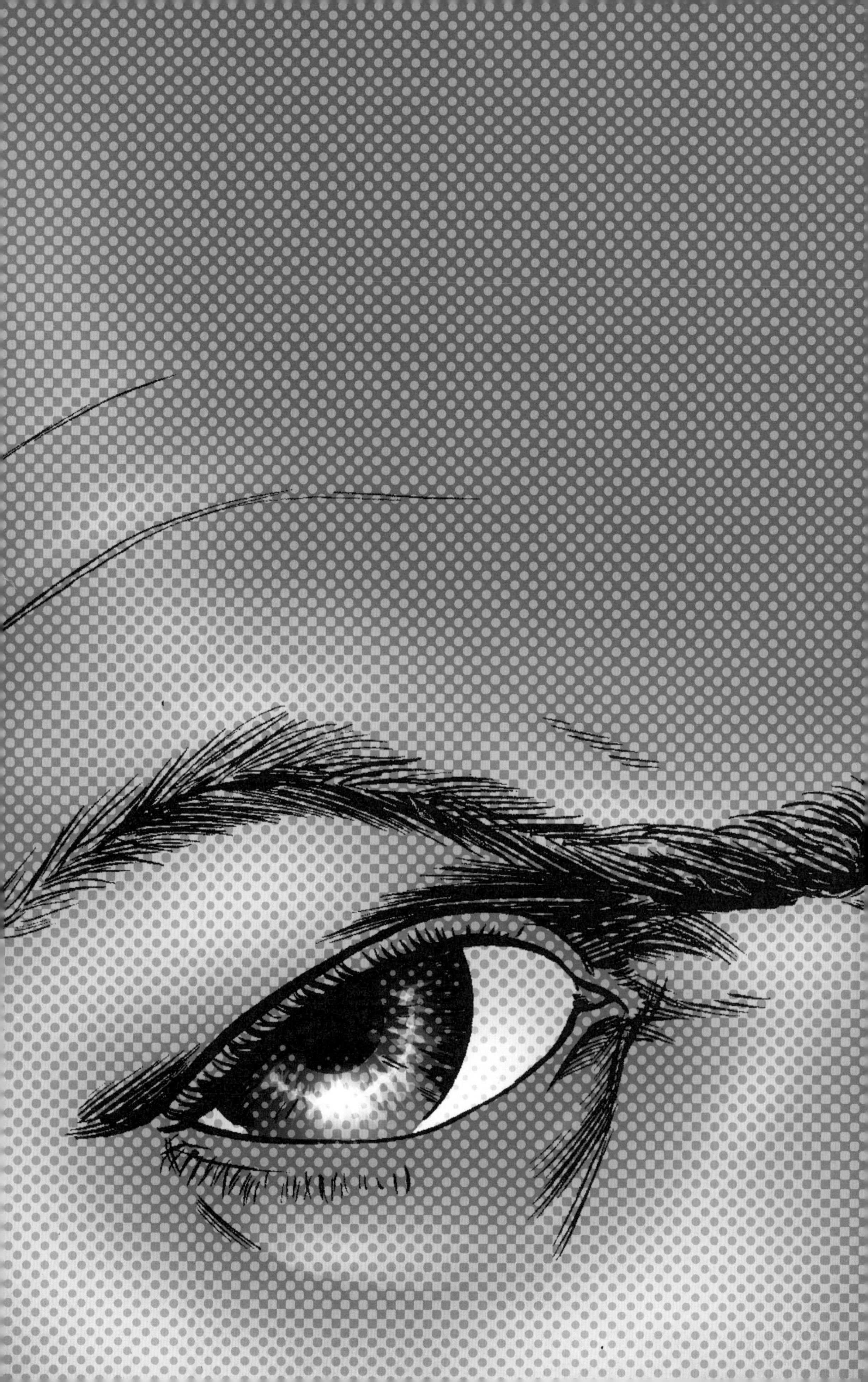